Twayne's United States Authors Series

EDITOR OF THIS VOLUME

Sylvia E. Bowman

Indiana University

Tennessee Williams

Tennessee Williams

TENNESSEE WILLIAMS

By SIGNI FALK

TWAYNE PUBLISHERS
A DIVISION OF G. K. HALL & CO., BOSTON

Tennessee Williams, Revised Edition

Signi Falk

First edition copyright © 1961 by Twayne Publishers, Inc.
Revised edition copyright © 1978 by G. K. Hall & Co.
All Rights Reserved

Published in 1978 by Twayne Publishers
A Division of G. K. Hall & Co.
70 Lincoln Street
Boston, Massachusetts 02111

Printed on permanent/durable acid-free paper
and bound in the United States of America

First Paperback Edition, 1985

Library of Congress Cataloging in Publication Data

Falk, Signi Lenea.
  Tennessee Williams.

  (Twayne's United States authors series; TUSAS 10)
  Bibliography: p. 183–91
  Includes index.
  1. Williams, Tennessee, 1911–
—Criticism and interpretation.
PA3545.I5365Z64   1978   812′.5′4   77–16575
ISBN 0–8057–7202–2
ISBN 0–8057–7445–9 (pbk.)

In memory of my foster parents
Clyde and Jewell Tull

Contents

About the Author

Signi Falk developed her first interest in drama from listening to the shop talk of her foster parents, the late Clyde and Jewell Tull, who directed plays at Cornell College, Iowa, and for several summers led play companies on the Chautauqua circuit. After she received a B.A. from Cornell, she directed plays in secondary schools. While she was an instructor at Mid-Pacific Institute, Honolulu, she also earned a master's degree from the University of Hawaii, where she wrote a thesis entitled "Twisted Personalities from the Plays of Eugene O'Neill."

She received a Ph.D. in English from the University of Chicago, where her thesis, "The Vogue of the Courtesan Plays," 1602-10," focused on Jacobean comedy. She has had articles published in *Modern Drama, College English, Modern Language Notes,* and the *AAUP Bulletin,* and has also written a number of short stories, some of which were published in *The Husk,* a literary quarterly. She has written two books for the Twayne United States Authors Series: *Tennessee Williams* (1961), and *Archibald MacLesih* (1965). She is at present professor of English, *emerita,* Coe College, Cedar Rapids, Iowa.

Preface

The production of *The Glass Menagerie* in early 1945 suddenly lifted Tennessee Williams from poverty and obscurity to affluence and fame. In the years since the middle 1940s he has become one of the most prolific of American writers, pouring out plays, film scripts, stories, articles on the theater, memoirs, and interviews. His name has appeared so frequently that he has become one of the best known members of the present literary world. A controversial figure early in his career, he was caught between the critics who deplored his preoccupation with sex and violence and those who defended his daring to probe into the dark areas of human desire and compulsion. Some critics welcomed him as an original talent; others questioned whether he had not sacrificed this talent for commercial success. Some recognized his compassion for the sensitive caught in a competitive, brutal world, but others thought that he made a fetish of glamorizing the derelict. He has been extravagantly praised and mercilessly censured, often for the wrong reasons.

This study, an updating of the 1961 edition, attempts to present an objective analysis of the drama and the fiction that comprise the considerable literary accomplishment of Tennessee Williams. This work gives attention to his early poems, stories, and short plays: a close record of his personal experience, but also a basis for his later work. Few references are made, however, to the interrelationship of different works, because his echoes and repetitions are so frequent that an exhaustive listing is not possible. This study occasionally refers to the multiple drafts of the same work to suggest Williams' habit of rewriting during the rehearsals of a play, and usually before the play is set in print.

The book retains the format of the 1961 edition which was organized as a series of discussions about certain character types, about the way in which this major figure relates to other characters, and about what that relationship says of the writer's view of the world. Summaries of the plays attempt to elucidate the meaning and to suggest at times elements in the script that work for theatrical effectiveness or the lack of it. This study gives a wide sampling of critical comment, primarily from working journalists who seek to discover the meaning beneath the theatrical display and to separate what is good theater from what is good drama. Since Williams writes for the theater and not the library, these reviews help the reader who first meets the play on the printed page. The original production, as well as its duration, is always noted; but only some of the revivals, an extensive subject in itself, are mentioned.

Many brief quotations from the poems, stories, and plays of Tennessee Williams are incorporated in the narrative which usually follows the sequence of the work being discussed. These brief quotations, representing the playwright most often at his best but sometimes not, are an integral part of many statements. It is customary to locate passages in the text, a practice not followed in this study because of the brevity and frequency of many quotations. To interrupt the thought sequence by locating these quoted fragments by page number or footnote is to risk disrupting the reader's attention. Frequent reference to time and place within the discussion should help the reader locate the quotation if he wishes to do so. The edition used by the writer is always given.

Tennessee Williams is very much a public figure, partly due to his being an actor at heart, partly due to the candor with which he speaks to reporters. Biographical information has been assembled from several sources: prefaces and news articles written by the author; reports from friends and colleagues; interviews with the writer. The intensive personal substance of so much of what he has written, the detailed biographical data that has recently emerged, and his own volatile reaction to critical comment add to the complexity of making a fair evaluation.

The world has changed in the decades since *The Glass Menagerie,* but so have the plays of this most productive playwright and writer of short stories and memoirs. As Williams is still working and producing, the final chapter is yet to be written.

SIGNI LENEA FALK

Coe College

Acknowledgments

Permission has been granted by Random House, Inc. to quote from *The Glass Menagerie,* Copyright 1945 by Tennessee Williams and Edwina I. Williams.

Permission has been granted by Simon and Schuster to quote from *Moise and the World of Reason,* 1975.

Permission has been granted by New Directions Publishing Corporation to quote from the following works by Tennessee Williams:

Five Young American Poets, (Series III). Copyright 1944 by Tennessee Williams.

In the Winter of Cities. Copyright 1944, 1949, 1950, 1952, © 1956, 1964 by Tennessee Williams. Copyright 1946, 1949, 1950, 1951, by New Directions Publishing Corporation.

27 Wagons Full of Cotton. Copyright 1945, 1953 by Tennessee Williams.

One Arm and Other Stories. Copyright 1939, 1945, 1947, 1948 by Tennessee Williams.

I Rise in Flame, Cried the Phoenix. Copyright 1951 by Tennessee Williams.

Battle of Angels. Copyright 1940 by Tennessee Williams.

A Streetcar Named Desire. Copyright 1947 by Tennessee Williams.

Summer and Smoke. Copyright 1948 by Tennessee Williams.

The Eccentricities of a Nightingale. Copyright © 1964 by Tennessee Williams.

You Touched Me! by Tennessee Williams and Donald Windham. Copyright 1939 by *Story Magazine, Inc. Copyright* © 1966 by Tennessee Williams.

The Night of the Iguana. Copyright © 1961 by Two Rivers Enterprises, Inc.

The Rose Tattoo. Copyright 1950, 1951 by Tennessee Williams.

Cat on a Hot Tin Roof. Copyright 1955 by Tennessee Williams.

Baby Doll. Copyright 1945, 1946, 1953, © 1956 by Tennessee Williams.

Camino Real. Copyright 1948, 1953 by Tennessee Williams.

M

Chronology

1911 Thomas Lanier Williams born March 26, Columbus, Mississippi.

1919 Family moved to St. Louis.

1927 Essay, "Can a Good Wife be a Good Sport?" *Smart Set* (April).

1928 Story, "The Vengeance of Nitrocis," *Weird Tales* (August).

1929 University of Missouri, where he won small literary prizes.

1931 Monotonous stretch with shoe company relieved by all-night writing; nervous breakdown and recuperation in Memphis.

1935 July 12: *Cairo, Shanghai, Bombay!,* a farce produced in Memphis.

1936 Washington University, St. Louis; Willard Holland, director of Mummers, a little theater group, produced a one act and two long plays: *Candles in the Sun* and *Fugitive Kind.*

1937 State University of Iowa; awarded Bachelor of Arts degree.

1937 Prefrontal lobotomy performed on sister, Rose.

1938– Became an itinerant writer: Chicago, St. Louis, New
1940 Orleans, California, Mexico.

1939 "The Field of Blue Children," *Story* (summer issue), first work to appear under the name Tennessee Williams.

1939 Group Theater Prize of $100 for one-act plays, *American Blues,* and four long plays submitted: *Candles in the Sun, Fugitive Kind, Not about Nigtingales,* and *Spring Storm.*

1940 Audrey Wood secured Rockefeller fellowship, $1000; Williams entered advanced playwriting seminar, New School, New York; *Battle of Angels* opened in Boston, a fiasco; Williams given $200 to rewrite play.

1940– Thin years; partial renewal of Rockefeller grant; variety of
1942 small jobs.

1943 Audrey Wood secured Metro Goldwyn Mayer (MGM) contract for six months at $250 a week; scripts rejected; Williams wrote *The Glass Menagerie,* a manuscript submitted to and refused by Metro Goldwyn Mayer. Grandmother dies of cancer; Citation from National Institute of Arts and Letters.

1944   American Academy of Arts and Letters Award and $1000; represented in *Five American Poets,* 1944, Third Series; December 26: *The Glass Menagerie* opened in Chicago.

1945   March 31: *The Glass Menagerie* opened in New York for 561 performances; won New York Drama Critics Circle Award on the first ballot; won fourth annual award of Catholic Monthly, *Sign;* won Sidney Howard Memorial Award of $1500 given by the Playwrights Company; Williams retreats to Mexico; March 25: *Stairs to the Roof* produced at Pasadena Playhouse; September 25: *You Touched Me!* opened in New York for 100 performances.

1946   *27 Wagons Full of Cotton and Other Plays.*

1947   December 3: *A Streetcar Named Desire* opened in New York for 855 performances; won for Williams a second New York Drama Critics Circle Award; won Pulitzer Prize; film version, 1951; Ballet of *Streetcar* opened New York, December 8, 1952; Williams' parents separate permanently.

1948   *One Arm and Other Stories,* limited edition; second edition, 1954; October 6: *Summer and Smoke* opened in New York for 100 performances; *American Blues: Five short Plays;* first visit to Rome.

1950   *The Roman Spring of Mrs. Stone.*

1951   February 3: *The Rose Tattoo* opened in New York for 300 performances.

1951   *I Rise in Flame, Cried the Phoenix.* Two limited editions; acting edition, Dramatists Play Service.

1952   Elected to National Institute of Arts and Letters.

1953   March 19: *Camino Real* opened in New York for 60 performances; *27 Wagons Full of Cotton,* augmented third edition.

1954   *Hard Candy,* limited edition; trade edition, 1959.

1955   March 24: *Cat on a Hot Tin Roof* opened in New York for 79 performances; won third New York Drama Critics Circle Award, second Pulitzer Prize; death of grandfather, the Reverend Walter E. Dakin, aged 98.

1956   December 18: *Baby Doll,* film, opened in New York; *Four Plays; In the Winter of Cities* (poems).

1957   Year of psychoanalysis; death of father, C. C. Williams; March 21: *Orpheus Descending* opened in New York for 68 performances; film, *The Fugitive Kind,* 1960.

1958   January 7: *Garden District (Something Unspoken* and *Sud-*

denly Last Summer) opened off-Broadway; *Suddenly Last Summer.*

1959   March 10: *Sweet Bird of Youth* opened in New York for 95 performances; Williams first trip to the Far East; *Garden District.*

1960   *Three Players of a Summer Game* (short stories); November 10: *Period of Adjustment* opened in New York for 132 performances.

1961   December 28: *The Night of the Iguana* opened in New York for 316 performances; film version, 1964.

1963   January 16: *The Milk Train Doesn't Stop Here Any More* opened in New York for 69 performances; film adaptation, *Goforth,* 1967.

1964   *Three Plays of Tennessee Williams; Grand.*

1966   February 22: *Slapstick Tragedy (Mutilated* and *Gnädiges Fräulein)* opened in New York for seven performances; April 20: *Eccentricities of a Nightingale* produced by the Washington (D.C.) Theater Club; also by Goodman Theater (Chicago), February, 1967; *The Knightly Quest and Other Stories.*

1968   March 27: *Seven Descents of Myrtle* opened in New York for 29 performances; film, *Last of the Mobile Hot Shots,* 1970.

1969   January: Williams converted to Roman Catholicism. May 11: *In the Bar of a Tokyo Bar* opened off-Broadway for 29 performances; awards from National Institute of Arts and Letters and from Academy of Arts and Letters.

1972   April 2: *Small Craft Warnings* opened off-Broadway for 200 performances.

1973   March 1: *Out Cry* opened off-Broadway for 13 performances; December 9: First centennial medal of the Cathedral of St. John the Divine.

1974   *Eight Mortal Ladies Possessed.*

1975   June 18: *The Red Devil Battery Sign* opened in Boston; *Moise and the World of Reason;* Williams elected to three-year term on governing council of the Dramatists Guild; *Memoirs.*

1976   May 24: As president of the jury, Cannes Film Festival, Williams deplored violence of films.

1977   May 11: *Vieux Carré* opened in New York for five performances.

CHAPTER 1

The Southern Renaissance and Tennessee Williams

ONE of the most significant phenomena in American culture was the emergence in the middle decades of the twentieth century of a rich and varied literature about and from the South. Writers from this area have distinguished themselves in poetry, fiction, and drama; in journalism of a high order; in the academic fields of criticism and editing; and in a line of textbooks that has changed the pattern of the teaching of literature. Southern writers have exerted an influence on the American literary scene comparable only to that of the great New England writers of the nineteenth century.

Teacher-scholars like Randall Stewart partly explain the Southern Renaissance by saying that the South has been less affected than other areas by the cultural and industrial changes that have tended to break down regional patterns. Other critic-scholars write of the Southern myth as being one undisturbed by modern influences or destroyed by them; but, in either instance, the myth has been a rich source of material for the writer. A kind of regional loyalty to tradition exists; a nostalgia for a pattern of aristocratic, nonurban life that was rich in promises; an awareness of distinctive character, mores, and beliefs peculiar to the Southern areas — and all have provided inexhaustible resources.

A considerable part of this literary flowering began among writers from Kentucky and Tennessee at Vanderbilt University in Nashville with John Crowe Ransom and a group of his students — men like Allen Tate, David Davidson, Merrill Moore, and Robert Penn Warren — and with *The Fugitive,* a little magazine of verse published between 1922 and 1925. In 1930, these fugitives and other Southerners, among them John Gould Fletcher and Stark

Young, published a collection of essays entitled *I'll Take My Stand,* a "manifesto of American Southern agrarianism." They proposed the idea that the South, with its type of old-fashioned social and political reform, might counter the materialism and the cultural barbarism of the North that was threatening to destroy what was best in the Southern tradition.

Some of these writers became the vanguard of the new intellectuals and founders of the relatively recent and exclusive "New Criticism." Their influence was extended through the textbooks of Robert Penn Warren and Cleanth Brooks, and their convictions determined the editorial policy of such influential periodicals as the *Kenyon Review.* The fiction and the poetry of Katherine Anne Porter, Caroline Gordon, Randall Jarrell, and Robert Penn Warren, whose *All the King's Men* (1946) is often regarded as a classic, have added to the stature of this coterie. H. L. Mencken, an energetic apologist in the 1920s for the culture of the Old South, paved the way as editor of *The American Mercury* for other writers who also found industrial America falling short of the American dream of fulfillment.

Two of the most widely read Southern writers stand apart from any group, Thomas Wolfe and William Faulkner. Wolfe (1900–1938) recorded his life in Asheville, North Carolina, in his autobiographical novel, *Look Homeward Angel* (1929). In this and later novels he described a man of gigantic appetite and capacity for experience, a man-child who stood alone, shocked by the vulgarities of ordinary people. In an avalanche of words, pruned by a sympathetic editor, Wolfe wrote of himself and of the South as it touched him.

The greatest figure of the Southern Renaissance is William Faulkner (1897–1962), most of whose life was spent in Oxford, Mississippi. This town and the surrounding country, under the fictional name Yoknapatawpha County, provided material for his many novels and stories, which speak far beyond this limited territory about the tragic condition of modern man. Faulkner's work encompasses a rich and complex overlay of several civilizations that range from the life of the Indian to that of the Negro slave; to the disruption of Southern culture after the Civil War; to the cheap and corrupt materialism of a later industrial society; to the fragmented, external twentieth-century life in which all religious and moral codes have become mechanical rituals. Faulkner was a writer of seemingly inexhaustible imagination and energy, but his work continued to result from his close observation of life and people. On the burning issues of intolerance and segregation he offered neither a specific nor a political solution. In his treatment of Negro and white, in which the black often stands superior to the decadent society of which he is a part, Faulkner places the value where it should be — on the individual.

Among other writers who have contributed to the Southern Renaissance are James Branch Cabell of Virginia, whose *Jergen* (1919) has often been compared to the satires of Rabelais and Swift; another Virginian, Ellen Glassgow, honestly portrayed a decadent society; Erskine Caldwell, in *Tobacco Road* (1932) and in *God's Little Acre* (1933), sensationally described rural Georgians, both white and black; another gifted Georgian, Flannery O'Connor, concerned herself with the deformed and the grotesque; Carson McCullers, best known for *A Member of the Wedding,* wrote of Georgia mill towns and backroad areas in terms of human loneliness; the 1930s brought Margaret Mitchell's successful novel of the Civil War, *Gone with the Wind* (1936); Truman Capote, who epitomized fascination with the morbid and the degenerate, represented "the Southern Gothic gone to seed." Working in a different area, Paul Green, with Frederich Koch and the Carolina Playmakers, produced in the 1920s a number of good regional plays; in the next decade, Lillian Hellman faced midtwentieth-century issues with her tightly plotted, unsentimental dramas; Lillian Smith focused her attention on the black and raised questions about Christianity in practice; two black novelists, Richard Wright and Ralph Ellison, portrayed the ugly vengeance not only of whites but of Negro against Negro; and in a still different way, the works of Eudora Welty and Harper Lee made distinctive contributions to the understanding of the South.

Tennessee Williams, who is part of this rich and varied literary tradition, became a name after the enthusiastic reception of *The Glass Menagerie* in New York City in March 1945. He is akin to the Romantic spirit of Thomas Wolfe, who wrote mostly of himself and his own experience. Like Erskine Caldwell, Williams has veered toward the sensational and off-beat; and, like him, he has also achieved financial success and an international reputation. Like Carson McCullers, he has created his own special world and has an affinity for lost souls and derelicts; like her, he has attempted to wring from old material the quality of myth. In his Introduction to her novel *Reflections in a Golden Eye* (1950),

Williams described the world of the artist and the lunatic whose sense of the dreadful differs from that of conventional society. Williams indicated in this introduction that the "sense of the awful which is the desperate black root of nearly all significant modern art" may be expressed by "diseased and perverted and fantastic creatures." Williams, like Truman Capote, glamorized decay in a kind of specious poetic writing.

Having achieved spectacular success as a young writer, Williams for three decades has tried to create works of comparable merit and appeal. He has known not only success but also the humiliation of failure. His style changes but not his dedication to the writing that he has repeatedly called his reason for living. However his work is judged in later years, Tennessee Williams has had considerable influence on American and international stages.

CHAPTER 2

Search for a Medium

T HE relationship between Tennessee Williams' private life that
has been so extensively exploited by himself, his friends, his
interviewers, and his critics, and his writing with its autobiographical basis seems to be, as he has often admitted, a form of psycho-
therapy. And the most important of his experiences, as related to
his writing, are those of his childhood. Strongly attached to his
mother and his maternal grandparents, and devoted to his sister
Rose, Thomas Lanier Williams, as he was then called, spent a
happy, idyllic childhood in quiet Mississippi towns during those
years when his father worked as a traveling salesman. The children's Negro nurse, Ozzie, told them bedside stories, some of them
frightening; and Tom and Rose created their own. His mother
recalls asking him, a small boy, why he was striking so angrily into
the rocks. "I'm diggin' to de debbil," he answered, possibly
because of the stories Ozzie told.

In early childhood, he was struck with diphtheria, which made
him an invalid for an almost two-year period; this experience
enabled him to indulge in his own fantasies and to glory in feminine
solicitude, but also led to the hypochondria that has followed him
the rest of his life. The strong attachment to his mother, accen-
tuated to an unfortunate degree, paralleled an estrangement from
his father, a boisterous extrovert, partner in an incompatible marriage. When a younger brother, Dakin, was born in 1919, Tom
spent several months with his grandparents in Clarksdale, Mississippi, the "Blue Mountain" of his plays and the symbol of a happy
youth.

When he was eleven, his mother bought him an old typewriter;
he began writing poems and stories, an avenue of escape for a boy
too shy to talk in class. The story "The Resemblance between a
Violin Case and a Coffin" suggests that he began writing seriously
when he discovered his sister had left childhood and was lost to

21

him. By the time he was in high school, he was winning advertising contests; he later wrote amusingly about his literary popularity in school and with women's clubs and poetry groups. He learned that shyness was no handicap in writing, just as he was to learn, when his plays were produced, that he could "level" with an audience more readily than he could talk with a friend. He admits that from the time he was fourteen he was a "dedicated writer" and that from the beginning his own fear and terror of losing what he most loved gave his writing "an atmosphere of hysteria and violence." His first story, "The Vengeance of Nitrocis," a violent piece written when he was sixteen, "set the keynote for most of [his] work that followed."[1]

While attending the University of Missouri, he continued to write as well as to participate in the usual "Joe-college" activities; he achieved modest recognition for his poetry, fiction, and plays until his father, embarrassed about his son's failure in the Reserved Officers Training Corps (ROTC), found him a job as warehouse clerk at the shoe company in St. Louis, work that he hated, but later recognized as valuable experience for a writer. Young Williams relieved the monotony of his days by writing all night, a routine that led to a nervous breakdown, to release from the business world, and to a year's recuperation with his grandparents in Memphis, where his first one-act play was produced. A year or so at Washington University, financed by his grandmother, afforded him acquaintance with Willard Holland, director of the Mummers, an experimental theater in St. Louis, who taught him production techniques and produced some of his plays. He shared ambitions with Clark Mills McBurney, who introduced Williams to the poetry of Hart Crane, Ranier Maria Rilke and the French Symbolists. While McBurney and Williams operated a "literary factory" in the McBurney basement, Williams tried his hand at long plays, parts of which he was to rewrite and use again. He left the university after a series of crises, the worst being the tragic operation on his gentle sister Rose, a prefrontal lobotomy, the most horrible experience of the young writer's life. He completed college at the State University of Iowa, where his attendance at the seminar in playwriting conducted by the late E. C. Mabie and his association with the free spirits working in the university theater advanced his knowledge of writing for the stage.

After graduation, and after being unable to find work, he spent a happy interlude, though a desperately poor one, in the Vieux Carré of New Orleans. For about two years he continued to live a hand-to-mouth existence, while wandering through the West to the Pacific Coast, to Mexico, and back across the country; but he closely observed life around him, and wrote and wrote. Chance recognition from a contest for which he submitted some of his work brought him in contact with important figures in the literary and theatrical world: members of the Group Theater, and the agent Audrey Wood who was to become his mentor and guide in the professional theater.[2] As Williams later admitted, his "longer plays emerged out of earlier one-acters or short stories . . . written years before. I work over them again and again."[3]

I   Five Young American Poets *(1944)*
In the Winter of Cities *(1964)*

Most of Williams' earlier poems, published in *Five Young American Poets* (1944), some of them revised, are incorporated in the later volume, *In the Winter of Cities* (1964). Both the earlier and later verse expresses certain themes and ideas, presents insights into character and experience, and indicates a range of perspective and some of the mannerisms that were to mark the later plays of Williams. In the more serious of two prefaces to the earlier volume, *Five Young American Poets,* Williams says that the poems record "an unattached and nomadic existence of six or eight years duration" before a few plays gave him the fortuitous association with Audrey Wood, Margo Jones, the Theater Guild, and the Rockefeller Foundation. He "took to the road because the alternative [work at the shoe factory] was something too dull to endure."[4]

Some of the poems say that the nature of art is often more truthful than acceptable to conventional society.[5] "The Dangerous Painters" (Manhattan, 1943) touches on the difference between the artist's life and the work elegantly displayed in museums without "the debris of his life." "Morning's in Bourbon Street" (Santa Monica, 1943) speaks of Irene, "her outspoken pictures . . . as brutal as knuckles smashed into grinning faces," but unsold. She is the artist, "the most destructible element in our society" and one "who painted the most powerful canvases" but had to whisper to men through shutters to support her body.[6] "Photograph and Pearls" tells of a son's letter which does not disturb "his elegant mother's dominion of pearls" with news of Paul Gaugin's paintings, "the formalized, purified image of the lust that diseased him."

The unspeakable truth, usually sexual, is often couched in religious terms. In "The Legend" (New Mexico, 1940), the encounter of an aggressive girl and an acquiescing boy is given cosmic significance, and perhaps unintended humor; for their private sexual act is accompanied by a battle of angels, storm, and thunder. The "something unspoken," usually homosexual, in "Across the Space" and in "A Separate Poem," suggests the comparable intensity of religious and sexual passion. "San Sebastiano de Sodoma" is a softly sweet tribute to the "emperor's concubine," the saint loved by Diocletian and martyred when he became a Christian. "Iron is the Winter" speaks of "the demon robot's face" that breaks the frozen silence: "as earth divides, our bodies meet and burn / and in our mouths we take the holy bread."

Williams also wrote about the plight of the lonely fugitive caught in an aggressive, conventional society. "Lament for Moths" (Jacksonville, 1942) is a plea for the delicate ones haunted by "mammoth figures." "Intimations" (St. Louis, 1941) describes the poet — spiritual kin to three historical figures, DuBarry, Jean of Arc, and Savonarola — as enveloped in bandages to ward off abusive blows. The poet in "The Summer Belvedere" (Santa Monica, 1943) wants to remain detached from the world of suffering and hysteria, the dying and the holocaust of war. In "Cried the Fox" (Taos, 1939), dedicated to D. H. Lawrence the poet as a fox, a desperate fugitive, is pursued by the killer pack. There are, however, comic touches in such later poems as "The Road," an amusing piece about a drummer, and "Lonesome Man," a character who does not "want love from the mercantile store." "Beanstalk Country" raises questions about whether the mad, who enter "from space we never entered," have not the advantage over so-called normal men. "Pulse" (Santa Monica, 1943) suggests in a series of images the fragmentary and vivid quality of intuitive experience.

A number of vignettes, early portraits and character studies, illustrate Williams' interest in unconventional people. "The Jockeys of Hialeah" suggests a variety of racetrack figures and their indiscriminate sex. "Carrousel Time," in calliope rhythms, depicts the comic circus freaks; and "Tuesday's Child" humorously speaks of brother Jack and his mistresses. Jests about advancing years in "Gold Tooth Blues" and "Kitchen Door Blues" are broadly comic. A few poems touch on different aspects of old age: "Old Man with Sticks," for whom hatred has outlived passion; "Shadow Boxes," old women, "veteran shadows" of their former selves; "Old Men are Fond" of the "little certainties" that circumscribe their lives. In "Cortege" (Santa Monica, 1943), the unloved wife of a lawyer is buried with commercial display; and the children anticipate "future betrayals."

The happiest poems catch the exquisite world of childhood. In the poem "In Jack-o-Lantern's Weather," an expansion of the earlier "The Marvelous Children," Williams conveys the magic, self-centered state of a child's imagination. He was to say later that this poem describes his feeling, "the obsession that to desire a thing or to love a thing intensely is to place yourself in a vulnerable position" and to lose it.[7] "Recuerdo" gives flashes of the poet's own childhood: his grandmother; Ozzie, the black nurse; his sister; and his own sexual awakening. Three pieces, "Which is My Little Boy," "My Little One," and "Little Horse," carry lighthearted rhythms for children.

These volumes represent experiments in poetic form: some poems are written in loose extended statements; some in mannered lines represent poetry "by typographical courtesy." A number of memorable phrases and sharp images — such as the fragments quoted — anticipate the facility in language that Williams was to develop. Along with effective symbols are the less fortunate, sometimes obscure references, and the posturing of poetry. Dudley Fitts, who reviewed *In the Winter of Cities,* found in the early poems "the weakest elements of his art — the self-consciousness, the pretty playing with symbolic devices and the gadgetry of sentimental color," and "an undisciplined flood of talk."[8] John Woods said of the same volume that the poet "has two qualities, an occult ability to find the poem and an exasperating insistence on burying it in extensions and assumptions and false moves." Woods missed in the poems "that singing tension between formal and conventional rhythms, that music which is the authority of poetry."[9]

II One Arm and Other Stories *(1948)*

The collection, *One Arm and Other Stories,* which was originally published in 1948 in a limited edition of fifteen hundred copies and reprinted in 1954, reflects, like the poems, Williams' wandering years through sordid rooming houses, on city streets, and on the obscure corners where derelicts hide. Some of the stories have the aura of confession. Williams, who has developed a skill in evoking an emotion, indicates his sympathy for the unfortunate and his fascination for the macabre. He also indicates his own system of values as he rejects workers in favor of ne'er-do-wells and seems to prefer the vagrant of both sexes.[10]

"The Field of Blue Children" (1939) tells of the adolescent yearnings of a popular college girl who finds release in writing poems and of a shy, awkward boy, Homer Stallcup, who is in love with her. The boy's poetry is uneven: some lines are oblique and obscure expressions reminiscent of Hart Crane; some are simple and straightforward as in Sara Teasdale. After she reads with more emotion than understanding the collection of poetry that he thrusts into her hands, she impulsively seeks him out one moonlight night. He takes her to the scene of one-poem, an acreage of blue flowers. The lover's tryst is delicately veiled with poetic lines about winds soft as the hushed cry of children at play and about dancing flowers. After the rendezvous, the girl, more practical than poetic, returns the boy's poems; and she marries a steady provider. In her later years, she has a momentary tinge of regret, but settles into contentment. Williams has translated into fiction his youthful attraction to Hazel Kramer, an interest that displeased his father, who succeeded in separating the young people.[11]

"The Important Thing" (1945), an early statement about Puritan repression, describes the diffuse enthusiasms of an unattractive college girl from Hardwood, Kansas, whose natural feelings have been warped by a Calvinist God of Judgment, and the groping curiosity of a college boy who has written a one-act play with involved symbolism. Unsuccessful as lovers, they clasp hands as friends; and neither one is alone.

"Portrait of a Girl in Glass," which has all the essential elements — characters, plot, and setting — of *The Glass Menagerie,* is closely autobiographical. The story describes the restricted lives of an overly solicitous mother, an abnormally diffident daughter, and a son trapped in a monotonous warehouse job and in the frustrating situation at a home from which the father has disappeared. The daughter's room in the dingy, third-floor apartment in St. Louis looks down an area called Death Valley, where a vicious chow tears defenseless kittens to pieces. The drawn shades keep the room in perpetual twilight and mute the shabby furniture and the sentimental picture of Christ, but give a soft, transparent radiance to the hundreds of little glass ornaments on the shelves that Laura loves, washes, and polishes. As she reads, she suffers with Gene Stratton Porter's Freckles; and she revels in records like "Whispering," "Sleepy Time Gal," or "Dardanella," souvenirs that the father left. The brother, like the author, secretly hides in the warehouse lavatory to work out rhyme schemes; but he turns late in the evening to Laura, for she can smoothe his nerves "worn rather thin from trying to ride two horses simultaneously in two opposite directions." As in the play, the mother in the story makes the same disastrous plans for her daughter; the brother leaves home, but his itinerant life is at times haunted by his sister's face.

Stories about derelicts, often sexual deviates, are treated by Williams with sympathy and understanding. The candor of some of the description, seemingly written to elicit certain emotional response, may have increased the sales of the limited edition of *One Arm and Other Stories*. When told in the first person, the stories seem to be as autobiographical as "The Angel in the Alcove," which describes the occupants of a seedy rooming house: a suspicious landlady, a dying artist, and the destitute writer, whose solace is the clay figure reminiscent of his grandmother. One scene suggests an early experience in homosexual love between the writer and the moribund tubercular. "The Poet," a rather arty story that combines disease, alcohol, and creative energy, might confirm for the Philistine the idea that men who write poetry are not safe company for women and children.

"One Arm," the title story of the collection, describes Oliver, a maimed Apollo; a light heavyweight boxing champion, he had lost the center of his being when he had lost his arm. After a New York vagrant initiates him into the underworld practices common to Times Square and the parks, he soon accepts homosexual relationships with the tramps for whom he arouses so extraordinary an excitement. His vagrant career culminates at a drunken party on a broker's yacht off Palm Beach, for he and a girl prostitute have been hired to perform the sex act before a camera and a stud party. The two slowly undress, they go through a series of intimate embraces, but he suddenly revolts and dashes from the scene. Shortly afterwards, he splits open the skull of the sportsman, does not understand his own actions, and flees. Arrested, he fully confesses the killing, is sentenced for murder, and waits for the execution.

These last days, because of the publicity given the trial, bring a deluge of letters from male correspondents who recall the brief hour spent with him as the richest time of their lives. Because his physical beauty and the "charm of the defeated" made him irresist-

ible, Oliver becomes for these men a father confessor who listens
unseen to their disclosures of guilt as if he, like Christ, could
assume all the world's sins and, through his own sacrifice, purify
the sinners. Though first revolted by these uninhibited confessions,
Oliver begins to realize how much he has meant to hundreds of
strangers and also how much he is indebted to them, not in money
but in feelings. An earlier realization of this mutual relationship
might have given Oliver a way toward integration; but, at this late
date, the letters only rouse his self-interest; and, just as strangers'
fingers sought his body, he makes love to himself.

In one scene, a young Lutheran minister looks at the young
Apollo and recalls the childhood dream of a panther that had
awakened and initiated him to Eros. Like the homosexual letter
writers, he is torn between sympathy for the misunderstood and
terror before this innocent-looking criminal. When Apollo rejects
his chaplain's solace but asks him to rub the sweat from his back
and flanks — he calls himself a truly clean whore — the minister
becomes nauseated and has to be carried out. The story, in spite of
rhetorical flourishes, contains not only a subtle analysis of primitive strength and of terrible loneliness, but also a glimpse into the
subculture of the derelict world. These social outcasts contrast
sharply with the concupiscent, rich sportsman and his friends who
are the dubious representatives of law and justice and with the
squeamish, repressed minister who is ignorant of sin and
forgiveness.

"The Yellow Bird" (1947), a successful excursion into humor
and fantasy, relates the moral decline of a Southern girl of contradictory inheritance. The emergence of the twentieth-century Alma
Tutwiler from a shy, mousy girl into a thirty-year-old spinster who
is determined to make up for her lost time indicates that she has the
vigor for a free life that is comparable to that of generations of
sober citizens, true reformers who had attacked sin. For all her
loose living, her face retains the look of bright, fresh innocence. In
time she bears a lusty male child who later returns in the evenings
with fistfuls of gold and jewels. After her death, her bastard erects
a curious monument depicting three sexless figures upon a dolphin:
one carries a crucifix; one, a cornucopia; one, a Grecian lyre. The
name of the yellow bird, Babo, the interlocutor between the first
Goody Tutwiler, the first sexual rebel, and Satan, was traced on the
side of the fish.

"The Night of the Iguana," the short story on which the play is based, is another study of a Southern spinster of contradictory inheritance; for she is the descendant of oversexed degenerates and squeamish old maids. Attempting to foist her charms on two writers, the only other guests at the Acapulco hotel, she becomes more and more indiscreet, until she moves into a room adjoining theirs. Her excuse is an iguana that is tied beneath her window. When she enters his room and the older man tries to rape her, she fiercely resists his advances. And yet she has been freed from "the strangling rope of loneliness" just as the iguana is released. The themes of disease, homosexuality, loneliness, and frustration are spelled out against the earthy laughter of the local Mexicans; and the sexual act is orchestrated with some fancy rhetoric.

Two other stories describe timid little men who are victims of harsh circumstances and their own sensibility. "The Malediction" concerns Lucio, "a panicky little man" who finds shelter with an oversexed lady, companionship with a stray cat, and work in a factory that keeps his hands busy but not his mind. Lucio, seeing God in his own image, says, "God was, like Lucio, a lonely and bewildered man Who felt that something was wrong but could not correct it," Who wanted to hide Himself from the "hostilities of chance." The second story, "Desire and the Black Masseur," is a clever piece of writing in which timid little Anthony Burns, still childlike at thirty, is the nondescript kind of person who has unsuccessfully scuttled from one kind of protection to another. His basic desire, about which the writer is mysterious, has been so overwhelming that it has consumed him. Williams says of the moral dilemma of man, as if he were echoing Strindberg, "For the sins of the world are really only its partialities, the incompletions, and these are what sufferings must atone for." Man conceals this incompleteness through dreams and art, or through violence. Little Anthony Burns surrendered himself to abusive treatment by others to purge himself of his own guilt.

The instrument of atonement is a Negro masseur who strikes Burn's soft belly, turns him over, pounds his shoulders and buttocks, and evokes pleasure and pain. "The little man grew more and more fiercely hot with his first true satisfaction, until all at once a knot came loose in his loins and released a warm flow. So by surprise is man's desire discovered." The manager, alerted by cries of pain, orders the Negro to take away his perverted little beast. The latter part of the story, set in the Lenten season, seems to compare the illicit passion of the black and the little man with the massive atonement where preacher and audience, like crazed animals, are caught up in "the fiery poem of death on the cross." The Negro turns cannibal and, after a twenty-four hour feast, an air of completeness returns. There may be for Williams a deep religious symbolism in the connection between homosexuality, cannibalism, and atonement — and the crucifixion and resurrection.

III   American Blues *(1948)*

The short plays in the collection *American Blues*[12] won for Tennessee Williams a prize and an introduction to the literary agent Audrey Wood; and these works mark the beginning of his dramatic career. *Moony's Kid Don't Cry* dramatizes the marital crisis between a young woodsman who regrets that he gave up his friends and his ailing wife who regrets that she chose marriage instead of the boss's attentions. When the husband accuses his wife of seducing him and is about to leave, the disillusioned wife shoves the sick, month-old baby into his arms; and the young father becomes absorbed with his infant son. This one act is forcefully and honestly written; the dialogue conveys the inarticulate frustrations of a young couple who are living in hopeless poverty.

An even deeper poverty exists, however, in *The Dark Room*. The husband is mentally incompetent; the older sons have left home; the younger are still in school; and the daughter, rejected by her lover because of her religion, hides in the dark room. By promoting a delayed and piecemeal confession, a social worker schooled in the Puritan tradition elicits from the immense Italian mother the news that her daughter's boyfriend, now married, brings food to her dark room. When the social worker announces that the girl will be taken as a delinquent, the mother says that the authorities had better hurry to do so because the girl is very pregnant. Given a tragic situation, Williams handles the verbal conflicts between these two women with considerable humor.

The Long Stay Cut Short or The Unsatisfactory Supper portrays the hopeless position of an old lady who has been used and discarded by all relatives who want to avoid the expense of her last illness and funeral. Old Aunt Rose, a tragic figure described without sentimentality, is aware that she intrudes but she is supported by a childlike religious faith. The story escapes into fantasy and perhaps symbolism as a sudden high wind blows her into her beloved rose bushes.

The Case of the Crushed Petunias (1941), an experiment in comedy, symbolic names, mood music, and perhaps parody, portrays a twenty-six year old prissy miss of Primanproper, Massachusetts, who is won by a young man with big feet who is dedicated to rescuing her from a fate worse than death — virginity. Apparently running away from his wife, Mrs. Dull, he convinces the young lady to reject DEATH UNLIMITED in favor of LIFE INCORPORATED.

Ten Blocks on the Camino Real (1948) makes the same statements as *Camino Real* (1953) about the misadventures of a little man, the defeated one, in an unfriendly world. Written during a period of convalescence, the dramatist gives more than half the play to the amorous adventures of a literary prostitute, to an extensive seduction scene, and to a sentimental lament of two lovers who regret wasting their life on women. The rest of the play is a comment about life on Camino Real, a matter of Starvation, Frustration, Swindling, Brutality, Indifference, and Death. A guitar player as master of ceremonies links the series of symbolic actions. Williams, who resurrects many age-old stage tricks, substitutes abstract ideas for observed images and he indulges in stretches of pseudopoetry, a kind of literary posturing that appears in his later plays. For instance, when the aging courtesan tells of her first night of love, her lines are accompanied by tango music and a choric dance. "That was the night that was talked about in the poem, the one that says that 'The stars threw down their spears and watered heaven with their tears!' "[13]

IV   27 Wagons Full of Cotton *(1945, 1953)*

The collection of short plays in *27 Wagons Full of Cotton* reflect the life Williams knew in the Vieux Carré, New Orleans, before and after the failure of *Battle of Angels* in 1940. These plays, written out of his own experience and observation, have been recognized as some of his best work. Some of the experiments in dramatic technique are successful and some reflect the playwright's penchant for communicating through symbols.[14]

Three of these plays are studies of the prostitute. *This Property Is Condemned* portrays a thirteen-year old delinquent, her doll in her arms; innocent looking in spite of heavy makeup, cheap jewelry, and a bedraggled party dress, she lives off the chance contributions of railroad men or refuse from garbage cans. She tells a

boy how her older sister, the girl friend of a large number of railroad men, died a sordid lonely death — one unlike that of Greta
Garbo as Camille, who was made beautiful with white flowers and
violin music. Ignorant of any life but that of her dead sister, or of
the depths of squalor in which she now lives, this abandoned child
dreams of the kind of suitors her sister had. *Hello from Bertha* portrays a diseased relic from a "good-time house" in the red-light district of East St. Louis. Cared for by strangers, she angrily resists
the transfer from her sordid room to a hospital ward. Too independent to seek help, she sends a message, "Hello from Bertha," to an
old lover. In *The Lady of Larkspur Lotion,* a dyed blonde of forty
who dreams of a rich Brazilian plantation suitor is defended by a
young writer who speaks to the brutal landlady about his 780-page
manuscript and calls himself Anton Pavlovitch Chekhov. When the
blonde, named for a lotion that is "a common treatment for body
vermin," complains of flying cockroaches in her room, the poet
speaks of their need to indulge in fantasy to make their lives endur-
able. These lies "are stuffed in the mouth by the hard-knuckled
hand of need, the cold iron fist of necessity." An early version of a
familiar Williams' situation, the play handles with humor and compassion the plight of social derelicts.

    The Long Goodbye is an early experiment in memory technique.
Through a series of flashbacks and through the dialogue between a
young writer and his Italian friend, the story of the breakup of a
lower middle class family emerges: the father suddenly disappeared; a mother ill with cancer precipitated her own death; a sister exchanged modest accomplishments for glamor and drifted into
prostitution; and a son moves out of the place where he was born.
In this trial flight, Williams anticipates not only his later effective
dialogue but also the self-conscious philosophizing that was to
become so familiar: "You're saying goodbye all the time ...
because that's what life is, just a long, long goodbye!" *Lord
Byron's Love Letter* reveals with bitter humor and irony how a desperately poor forty-year old spinster and her grandmother try to
wheedle money from Mardi Gras tourists, two caricatures from
Milwaukee. The women read excerpts from a romantic girl's diary,
the grandmother in the play, about her meeting Lord Byron and her
implication that her acquaintance with the poet was more than the
touch of his hand. The tourists leave suddenly when the band plays,
ignoring pleas for money.

    In *The Strangest Kind of Romance,* a contrived dramatization of the story "The Malediction," Williams vacillates between character study and social protest. The protagonist, the little man who does not belong in a machinist's world, is compatible with his cat and with the Old Man, a Walt Whitman figure, who shouts his maledictions against the business world: "Devour the flesh of thy brother, drink his blood! Glut your monstrous bellies in corruption!" Apparently more akin to the world of commerce are an oversexed landlady and a boxer who replaces the little man.

Some of the early plays indicate Williams' talent for creating distinctive characters and contrasting them with stereotypes. In *Auto-De-Fe,* in which the action occurs near Bourbon Street, in the Vieux Carré of New Orleans, the setting contrasts with a garrulous mother who lives by the simple household rules of practical hygiene and a neurotic son who is tormented by the corruption — the brutality, the crime, and the decay — that surrounds them. At work, he comes upon a lewd picture of two naked males; overwhelmed by the conscience of all guilty, dirty-minded men, he sets fire to the house and inhabitants as a form of retribution. The mother anticipates Amanda Wingfield; the son, with his problem and sense of guilt, Williams' many treatments of the homosexual. In *Portrait of a Madonna,* Williams sympathetically portrays a sex-obsessed Puritan: an aging Southern belle, delicate and over-refined, she is lost in the world of her own delusions. Since her mother's death, fifteen years before, she has become a recluse, buried in the accumulation of twenty-five to thirty years of debris, cared for by strangers, and supported without her knowledge by church contributions. She imagines that she has finally won the man of her dreams from the Cincinnati girl he married and that she is expecting his child. An old porter, who pities the woman, and an impertinent wise-cracking elevator boy, who sees her as a disgusting old hag, keep her occupied until authorities from the state asylum arrive. When the Doctor and Nurse, performing their duty wearily but efficiently, come to take her away, she believes that she is being arrested on moral charges by the church. The effective picture of repression and guilt anticipates the final scene of *A Streetcar Named Desire.*

The fine old drummer in *The Last of My Solid Gold Watches,* "Mistah Charlie" Cotton, wears fifteen watch chains criss-crossed over his huge expanse of chest and belly; and each chain is attached to a gold watch that represents his achievement as ranking salesman of the year for the Cosmopolitan Shoe Company in St. Louis. This

old warhorse, who has probably received the last of his solid gold
Hamiltons, tries to alert an indifferent, bad-mannered "young
peckerwood" to the old traditions of the South. Not only have
genuine leather and craftsmanship given way to substitutes and
flashy appearance but the old qualities of character — self-reliance,
independence, initiative — have been replaced by ignorance and
lack of respect.

In *27 Wagons Full of Cotton,* Williams presents a dramatic
elaboration of a smoking-car story, one rich in overtones of irony
and sardonic humor. The frequent references to the "good-
neighbor policy" and the allusion to a speech by President Franklin
Delano Roosevelt suggests the germ idea of the anecdote. The play
opens as the sixty-year old Jake Meighan, a grossly heavy and pur-
poseful man, rushes out the door and around the house with a
gallon can of kerosene. His large and simple-minded wife, Flora, is
soon startled by the sound of an explosion. Jake returns almost
immediately and tries to impress upon her that he has not been off
the porch. She has a child's inability to lie. Complaining about her
lost white purse, she stands on the steps "with a slight idiotic
smile" while indoors Jake sings about his loving baby.

At noon of the following day, Jake gloats over destroying the
mill of Silva Vacarro, the superintendent of the once-prosperous
Syndicate Plantation. The old husband brags to Vacarro, one of
Williams' virile Italians, a Roman Catholic and a *persona non
grata* in this Southern town, that he had prevented marital problems by marrying a tremendous baby doll of a woman. He orders
her to keep the Italian happy while he gins out in his own mill the
twenty-seven wagons full of cotton. "Th' good-neighbor policy,
Mr. Vacarro. You do me a good turn an' I'll do you a good one."
At first, Flora's babbling does not interest her guest. Observing the
white purse in her hands, he pontificates about woman's role of
motherhood as her defense against loneliness and a feeling of
emptiness. His suspicions are aroused when she inadvertently
involves Jake in the affair of the burned-out cotton gin. Her confusion confirms his suspicion; and, since he believes that the world
is built on the principle of vengeance, an eye for an eye, an idea
explodes in his head. Very deliberately he flatters the heavy, dull-
witted woman until she almost admits her husband's guilt; and
then, with whip in hand, he drives her into the house. As the sound
of the gin pumps are heard in the distance, a wild cry of despair
comes from inside; a door is slammed; the cry is heard again.

At nine o'clock the same evening, the ravished Flora appears and is highlighted by the ghostly brilliance of a full moon; her hair loose and disheveled, she is naked to the waist except for a torn strap about the breasts. Dark stains on her shoulders and cheeks and a dark trickle of dried blood from her mouth testify to the revenge wrought upon her. Jake, the other brute in this woman's life, brags about how he "drove that pack of niggers like a mule-skinner"; for the blacks have brainless bodies that have to be driven. He is completely deaf to the implications of his wife's report that the little Italian intends to bring another twenty-seven wagons the next day and each day for the rest of the summer. Maddened by her giggling laughter, he spits out his contempt for her size and helplessness; and, smug in his certainty about outsmarting Vacarro, he exits to the toilet. Flora, no longer Baby but Mama, cradles the big white purse and softly croons a lullaby. Williams calls the play a "Mississippi Delta comedy"; the characterizations and details of the scene are sharp and vivid, but the brutal violation of this huge, simpleminded woman is hardly comic.

The Purification, set in the clear, breath-taking country around Taos, New Mexico, is an early poetic drama that reveals, during an informal trial, the story of plunder and genocide; of incest and murder; of retribution and purification. The Judge, who does "not believe in one man judging another," observes that, because a crime has been committed and allowed to go unpunished, not only is rain needed for the land, but truth, as a kind of purification, is needed for man's spirit. The play is patterned on the gradual and dramatic unfolding of ugly truth, a technique as old as *Oedipus Rex.*

The Spanish Father and the Castilian Mother represent the invading Conquistadores who poured their blood on the desert "to make it flower," who took "these golden valleys" from the Indians. The Spanish parents speak circumspectly of their murdered daughter, Elena, who had married the Rancher, the "former repair man," an echo of the D. H. Lawrence type of unsuccessful lover and symbol of death. When the Judge seeks the truth from Rosalio who had an unusual attachment for his sister Elena, he refers to the enigmatic truth of music, or the uncaptured song of a bird torn by a falcon, but then bluntly comments on the effect of the bird song: "Our genitals were too eager!" The Indian woman, Luisa, confirming kitchen gossip, tells how she came upon the naked brother and sister who were doing a kind of "dance" and

about five of her goats that drank of the purest water and died —
crystal water polluted at the source. The dead Elena appears as two
different apparitions: Elena of the Springs, symbol of life, and
Desert Elena, symbol of death. Dressed in a tight, coarse sheath,
her hair wrapped close to her head, she carries a cactus in one hand;
in the other, a wooden grave cross wound with dusty artificial
flowers. Against a slow dance by the chorus, the beat of drums,
and guitar music, the Rancher gives a lyrical account of Elena's
flight, a romantic description of drunken abandon that evades the
whole truth.

As the Judge describes the ominous, smoldering character of the
Rancher, who as a gentle boy withdrew from the world, a little
more of the truth emerges. His youthful self-discipline, closer to
repression than noble reticence, finally gave way to an unfulfilled
blackness that bred "a need for destruction." The Rancher confesses the turbulent state of his own being, his need for a wife, her
rejection, and his violence upon discovering the incestuous lovers.
Rosalio curses him for trying to defile "this quicksilver girl," the
sister whom he has seduced; but, as the vision of Elena of the
Springs, life and love, returns, the guilty Rosalio plunges the knife
into his own breast. As a final gesture of retribution, the Rancher
gratefully accepts the knife from the Mother with the words, "As
one who has suffered over-long from drought," and kills himself.
The air is cleared after this so-called retribution, the guilt exposed
and paid for; the rains begin; and the people rejoice. The theme of
freedom and honor is stated entirely in sexual terms, but left untouched is the ugly greed of the Mother and Father and their generation which left the native people dispossessed of their land. Williams shows his interest in theatrical devices to evoke emotion, in
music and choral movements, and in a mannerism he likes to call
"mystery."

These early plays, like the short stories, reveal an interesting new
talent and justify the enthusiastic support given the playwright. He
had already tried themes and dramatic techniques that were to be
used later. He revealed not only his ability to write skillful, articu-
lated scenes in which the dialogue flows in beautifully phrased
idiom, but also his weakness — an artificial, more contrived style.

V   The Battle of Angels *(1940)*[15]

The Battle of Angels, a "lyrical play about memories and the loneliness of them" and Williams' fifth long play, differs from many of the short plays in that it begins with a thesis, rather than with an observed situation, and that the message is overloaded with multiple characters, rhetoric, and violence. A museum, which displays objects related to the Good Friday tragedy of the previous year, frames the action that occurred in a small sleepy town of the Deep South. The setting contrasts two ways of life: a "mercantile" store, a general merchandise mart selling such things as food, tobacco and shoes, represents the materialistic interests of most local citizens, and its high Gothic windows suggest a church-oriented community. In contrast to the "harsh and drab" reality of this small business is the confectionary establishment at the back, which for the proprietor's wife is a land of dreams and pleasure. [16]

The proprietor, sixty-year old Jabe Torrance, is dying of cancer and is an ugly version of the Southern business man; and Myra his thirty-four year old wife was a one-time Southern belle who took "the next best thing" and is now trapped in a loveless marriage. Gossipy townswomen are shocked during her absence to discover separate bedrooms. Along with their bulky, pin-headed, mill-hand husbands and their giggly teen-age girls, these women communicate the perspective of this small community. In contrast to these satiric grotesques are the originals and eccentrics, one of whom is Vee Talbott, the wife of a racist sheriff. A barren woman and a religious fanatic, she has painted Expressionist portraits of the Apostles to resemble men in the community and is looking for a model for her Jesus portrait.

Two other characters are obvious symbols of freedom. One, the decadent aristocrat, heavy-drinking, sex-obsessed Cassandra Whiteside, suggests rebellious freedom gone berserk. The other is the virile, handsome, twenty-five year old poet-itinerant-lover, Valentine Xavier, a D. H. Lawrence primitive uncorrupted. His symbol of freedom is a snakeskin jacket; his means of communication, his eyes and his hands. Val asks Myra for work because he is lonesome, weary of contact with strangers, and tired of being the fox chased by hounds. He believes that most people are sentenced to "solitary confinement inside their own skins."

The town comes to life with the arrival of this attractive stranger, and the shoe business flourishes. At first Myra is irritated by his "slew foot" pace, by his preoccupation with writing a book about "life," by his sexy approach to the women customers; but his seeming innocence soon charms her into laughter. The relationship

changes rapidly; fearful of touching her, he talks about leaving;
with her plea and the sound of the cotton gin in the background,
they reach each other in "a compulsive embrace" and rush into the
confectionary; later this retreat is redecorated in blue and hung
with Japanese lanterns and dogwood blossoms, apparently to symbolize Williams' idea of resurrection.

The situation with the decadent aristocrat Cassandra is very different. The tension between Sandra and Val, seemingly based on a
kind of mutual understanding, is immediate and violent: she is pro-
vocative; he, antagonistic. After a brief exchange, she wants to take
him dancing, juking, drinking, cohabiting in the graveyard on
Cypress Hill, or "just one word — live!" He re..ses her offer, fixes
her car, and is rudely slapped on the face because he ignored the
"Male at Stud" sign that she had hung on him. In high rhetoric,
she describes the primitive and the aristocrat, both seeking freedom, as outcasts "whose license has been revoked in the civilized
world." She recognizes that Val is better than she, for her blood
has "gone bad from too much interbreeding."

Val's search for philosophical truths seems to have been handicapped early by his sexual attractiveness to women. He confesses to
Myra that, since he had run away from his sharecropper heritage at
fourteen to live like an animal at Witches' Bayou, he had felt something important was going to happen to him. He had soon been distracted from his goal by a naked and lonesome girl to whom he
taught words of love on a bed of cypress and moss. Sexual contentment made him realize that she was just a woman and not the
answer to his big questions. After ten itinerant years on different
jobs, he had settled down in Waco, Texas, where the plain wife of
an oil superintendent had come to his cabin when he was drunk;
and what had happened had been accidental. The trouble had come
when he had tried to leave town and she had screamed bloody rape.
Women, always women, and his wandering hands had obstructed
the fulfillment of his dream.

When the well-groomed and wealthy David Anderson enters the
store and asks for Myra, the audience learns that he had jilted her
for a more acceptable girl, and that he must be the reason she had
transformed the confectionary into an imitation of the Blue Lake
Casino. In contrast to this successful former lover, Myra with her
limited resources is repeatedly generous, particularly to those in
need. Conscientious in her attentions to her sick husband, she tells
Val that Jabe accuses her of wanting him to die.

The impending doom for the lovers, which culminates on Good Friday, is brought to a head in a rush of incidents, some related, some symbolic, and some theatrical. Religious Vee Talbott brings Val her latest picture, which the gossips seize and ridicule — Valentine Xavier as Jesus. Val infuriates the sheriff, who was expecting to get free labor, when he gives the itinerant singer, Negro Loon, ten dollars for his guitar and a job as teacher. The drunken mill hands become enraged by Val, this "red neck peckerwood" with a Northern education, who says bluntly that "the land belongs to the man who works the land!" They insist on knowing his draft number, which Myra hurriedly fakes. Myra, as did the Waco woman earlier, tells Val that she is pregnant and wants to run away with him. When Val refuses and says he rejects being bound to anything, Myra speaks of the barren fig tree that bore fruit one spring and then died. Val watches with "troubled presentiment" as the Conjure Man offers him a token.

Sandra rushes in with the report that the officers have arrested the light-colored Negro chauffeur caught with her on Cypress Hill. She begs Val to leave with her: "We belong to the fugitive kind. We live on motion." Then Williams mixes sex, prophetic hysterics, and cosmic overtones as Sandra crosses to Val, drops her red velvet cape to the floor, lets her white evening gown cling nakedly to her body, and says that, whenever she looks at him, she feels the weight of his body bearing her down. She is not ashamed to admit her passion, the one thing "that seems to stand for anything of importance. . . . They've passed a law against passion . . . we're going to be burned like witches because we know too much." She answers Myra's perplexity by adding, "Damnation! You see my lips have been touched with prophetic fire." She, like her mythical prototype, tries to warn Val that "time is used up," that the "atmosphere is pregnant with disaster." With accompaniment from the elements, she shouts dramatically, "A battle in heaven. A battle of *angels* above us! and *thunder!*"

She kisses Val passionately, Myra "springs at her like a tiger," Sandra faints, and Val carries her upstairs. The sheriff enters with Mrs. Ryan, the Texan; Myra hedges about the whereabouts of Val; the Texas woman sees the Jesus-Val picture and dashes out to look for him in "the sporting house on Front Street." When Jabe's knocking is unattended, he comes down the stairs, an apparition of death; Myra defiantly confesses her joy of life, Val tries to leave, and Jabe shoots Myra; the Waco, Texas, woman, followed by the

drunken mill hands carrying pine torches to use on Val, is momentarily stopped by the Conjure Man, who holds up Val's snakeskin
jacket, the symbol of *"the hard, immaculate, challenge of things
untamed."*
   In the Epilogue, the gossips display the relics from the tragedy:
the Jesus picture, Myra's "ecstasy blue" dress, the phone with the
receiver off the hook, a cashbox with the drawer open, blood stains
on the floor that are repeatedly refurbished, the now dusty confec-
tionery store, the Conjure Man from Blue Mountain, the blow
torch, a replica of the one used on Val. The tourists, like those in
Lord Byron's Love Letter, leave without paying the fee for seeing
the display.
   Williams overlays his "cornpone melodrama" with a generous
accompaniment of theatrical devices, symbols, mood music, and
background noises. As already suggested, the characters are heavily
symbolic. The final scene, dated Good Friday, with the sound of
church bells and the reported sermon on the last words of Christ,
relates this violent Southern yarn to the Christian story. The sexual
overtones, however, predominate: the rooster crows repeatedly; the
volume of the cotton gin changes to suggest emotional tensions;
religious repression of normal sexual relationships is implied; and
an analogy exists between Val's book and Myra's expected baby.
The viciousness of the female gossips, the senseless brutality of
their husbands, the abusive treatment of the blacks, and the blowtorch killing of Val under the cottonwood where lovers customarily
park add to the ugly picture of the community. As the play rises to
its inevitable conclusion, the whole cosmos responds to the little
human story on the Delta; the river rising to the flood stage
threatens to break the levee, and the storm increases with lightning
and thunder.
   In the Preface to *27 Wagons,* Williams describes the theater of
Willard Holland as "Something wild, something exciting, something that you are not used to"; something that delivered a hard
punch to the solar plexus; something that made a difference to
those who came to see the show. This spirit seems to pervade this
early long play, which he rewrote many times; he called a later version *Orpheus Descending* (1955), and the film based on this script
was *The Fugitive Kind* (1958).
   The play opened in Boston on December 30, 1940, where the
audience, already disturbed by the substance, was literally driven
out of the theater by the smoke bombs, which the technicians failed

to control. The playwright wrote his mother that *Battle of Angels,* a "sex play with cosmic overtones," closed because "non-poetic audiences did not quite understand the production, an allegorical play."[17] Williams could not understand the charges of immorality over the Myra-Val relationship, nor over his equating his sex symbol, Valentine Xavier, with Jesus.

The Theatre Guild gave Williams $200 to rewrite *The Battle of Angels.* Dejected by this theatrical experience and depressed by a 4F notice from his draft board and by his fear of heart trouble, he escaped into the first of four operations for a cataract on his left eye. Then for a few desperately poor years after the Boston fiasco he lived in New Orleans and Mexico, places where he was happily at home, and wrote some of the short stories and one-act plays already discussed. Returning to New York because of the false hope that his play was going to be produced again, he supported himself with a series of small jobs, one in a Greenwich nightclub. His meeting with Donald Windham led to the collaboration on *You Touched Me!,* a dramatization of a short story by D. H. Lawrence.

VI I Rise in Flame, Cried the Phoenix *(1941)*

In *I Rise in Flame, Cried the Phoenix,* a drama about the last moments in the life of D. H. Lawrence, Williams presents his mentor seated one late afternoon on his porch above the French Riviera. The tiger's fury is still raging in his emaciated body, and behind him is a large banner of "the Phoenix in a nest of flames." He argues with his German wife, Frieda, "rather like a Valkyrie," who calls him a "sly old fox." Lawrence questions whether he has been waging war with bourgeois ideas of morality, prudery, intellectuality, and other abstract forces in society, or whether he has been fighting the old maid in himself. Appalled by the number of his women admirers, he wonders if he has only created a god for "Alma the nymphomaniac and the virginal Bertha," women who think of him as an "oracle of their messed up libidos." He regrets that he spent his life on books rather than on violent action. Frieda charges that he cannot endure the fact that Jesus Christ suffered "the *original* crucifixion!," for Lawrence wants to die alone, "like a lonely old animal," not surrounded by women.[18]

When Bertha, a small, sprightly English woman who honors Lawrence as God, reports that his London exhibition of paintings was rescued from a group of ladies' club members who tried to slash the picture of Adam and Eve, Lawrence shakes with laughter. He says that he painted life, "fiercely, without shame." The public banned his books and wants to burn his pictures. As the sun goes down, he repeats the metaphor of the harlot of darkness, the aggressive woman trying to seduce the sun, and shouts in triumph, "He'll climb back out of her belly and there will be light. . . . And I am the prophet of it!" In the end there will be "great blinding, universal *light!*" He dies alone, untouched by women.

Williams recognizes, in the foreword, that much of Lawrence's work is "chaotic and distorted by tangent obsessions," but, taken as a whole, "is probably the greatest modern monument to the dark roots of creation." Williams was to incorporate into his own work a number of Lawrence's ideas and symbols, but some critics question whether he had read the novelist correctly. Antagonism to women dominates this one-act play; and this concept, along with other ideas from Lawrence, was reflected in the later work of Williams: the artist as the Christ figure, the search for God, the admiration for the male primitive, the contrast between the rapacious and the defenseless, the importance of physical love, the sexually aggressive and the repressed woman, the celebration of the body, the association of sex and cosmic significance, the conventional opinion such as that of ladies' clubs against truth in art, the truth portrayed with candor, and the grotesques and the deformed as a part of life. Williams used many symbols usually associated with Lawrence, among them the fox and the rooster representing sexual vigor, the tiger in a frail body, and the cannibal image.[19]

VII   You Touched Me! *(1945)*[20]

Written in collaboration with David Windham and suggested by a D. H. Lawrence short story of the same title,[21] the play *You Touched Me!* dramatizes the conflicts between religious proprieties and the rites of Pan. This significant and universal theme about the human need for sympathy and understanding is, however, somewhat overwhelmed by Williams' comic scenes of clashing temperaments, by boisterous melodrama, by romantic sentimentality, by high-flown rhetoric, and by a rash of symbols.

Captain Cornelius Rockley, exponent of freedom and sex, a raucous, bawdy, old soak who traded his ship, the *Polar Star,* for a barrel of rum, carries on a feud of "epic fury" with his bossy tabby-cat sister, Emmie, symbol of frozen virginity. As protection against this self-righteous female, the Captain had adopted years before a "charity boy" called Hadrian, a natural son of Pan and currently a fighter pilot on leave during World War II. The Captain's daughter Mathilda, a dreamy girl who has *"the delicate, almost transparent quality of glass"* and who, like her creator, idolizes Hart Crane and writes poetry, is caught between the compelling force of sterile virginity, her domineering aunt, and life, represented by her father and the young Pan in uniform.[22] Virtue is flanked by the Reverend Guildford Melton, a little man of mincing refinement and limited intellect who seems to be edging toward "spiritual companionship" in marriage with the stiff and proper Emmie. When other action flags, the maid Phoebe, the "nymph," shrieks when she is poked, tickled, and chased by the inebriated Captain.

For years Hadrian has tried to destroy the diffidence that imprisons the timid Matilda, and their romance is as old as the fable of the sleeping beauty. He, another Williams lonely boy, believes, as does the Captain, that warmth and tenderness can be expressed in the fingers' touch. Matilda's awakening begins when she, thinking that she is bidding goodnight to her father, mistakenly strokes the forehead of the young pilot. At the very same moment, Emmie is angrily "gunning" the fox in the chicken coop; and she ineptly shoots "the Stoneyfield rooster," the ribbon winner, and thereby reduces the masculine world. The love scene between Matilda and Hadrian the following morning is marred by adolescent pontifications by the young man — by the author's theories about frontiers of the mind, that "the future is not conceited [*sic*]" but selects "such things as music — poetry — and gentleness," and that "the world is only dangerous when it is locked out." Shortly afterwards, Matilda appears in *"a delicate, filmy, blue-green dress and a pair of feather slippers"* and becomes Williams' heroine in love. When Emmie, always suspicious of the early signs of liquor and sex, locks Matilda in her room, the Captain urges Hadrian to lay siege: "Virginity is mostly the consequence of bad environment an' unfavorable social conditions." In an incredibly naive scene, the manly pilot scratches at the girl's door and whines like Flora, the Pekinese. The lovers' reach for an understanding sends the shy girl walking through a rainy night to brood over her predicament. When she returns in the morning, she is suddenly assertive; she speaks a "damn" or two and rudely asks her suitor, "What's stopping you, you fool?" Their embrace is accompanied by music and tinkling bells and by such precious lines from the pilot as, "Little silver Mathilda, little bells, little bells!"

The pranks and the ribald singing of the Captain nearly wreck the proper romance between forty-year old Emmie, "aggressive sterility," and the timid Reverend Melton; but they finally reach agreement about a celibate life together. The bottle-happy Captain, fearful that he may have risked his own freedom, often repeats his tearful line, "The bird of remorse — has got his beak in my heart."[23]

There are some good comedy scenes, such as the dialogue between Emmie and the Reverend, or the clash between the Captain and Emmie. Two different ways of life are briefly expressed when the Captain talks to his sister about the destructive power of a so-called good woman:

CAPTAIN (*Yelling at her from foot of stairs*): You want to do with my daughter what you did with my wife?
EMMIE: Protect her from you? That's right.
CAPTAIN: Turn her into a lifeless piece of clay!
EMMIE: That's an astounding statement.
CAPTAIN: True! You weaned her from me. Holy, holy, holy! Nothing but helping others in your dear brain. Some people have got that power — of turning life into clay. You're one of that kind, Emmie.
EMMIE: Insane Babblings!
CAPTAIN: But others have got a different kind of power. Their touch turns clay into life. Hadrian's one of that kind. (Act 3, Sc. 1)

This early comedy has aspects that indicate Williams' talent for humor as well as for caricature: for example, the studies of Emmie and the Reverend and the clashes between the stiff woman and her exuberant brother. The dialogue, when not self-consciously poetic or philosophical, reveals an ear for natural speech. The playwright's use of symbols such as the potter's shop for death, or the flute and rooster for life and sex, come straight from Lawrence. Williams was to use again the dramatic ideas and the scenes tried out in this play: Emmie's literary circle and her paper against Shaw appear in *Summer and Smoke;* the Captain's story about the sexy porpoise, in *Cat on a Hot Tin Roof;* and the figure of Hadrian's mother, who is only described, in *Summer and Smoke, Eccentricities of a Nightingale, The Glass Menagerie,* and others.

Joseph Wood Krutch thought that the scenes between hero and heroine were marred by an attempt to give them wider significance:

"There may be some connection between phallic worship and a new league of nations, but it is not to me a very clear one." Shortly after the hero appears, playing a penny flute, "he is in the midst of a passionate speech about the new world order, and to me it does not become quite clear whether society is to be saved through better international understanding or whether, as Lawrence sometimes seemed to think, all we need is more and better copulation."[24]

The lean and wandering years after the failure of *Battle of Angels* were somewhat alleviated for the playwright by his enjoyment of bohemian life in New Orleans and by the encouragement of his grandmother, who sent him love, sympathy, and occasional money from her meager savings. When Audrey Wood secured for her young protégé what was for him a munificent contract, six months with Metro Goldwyn Mayer at $250 a week, Williams learned from the inside something of the film industry. The scripts he wrote on assignment were rejected; but, given time and a living, he turned to the writing of *The Glass Menagerie,* which the film barons considered as commercially impossible.

CHAPTER 3

The Southern Gentlewoman

L IKE D. H. Lawrence, Tennessee Williams, the son of a Puritanical mother and a boisterous father, was strongly attached to his mother during a serious childhood illness, later rebelled against her moral restrictions, and glorified the sensual.[1] Williams' studies of Southern gentlewomen, his most distinctive contribution to the American theater, develop this conflict between the Puritan and the Cavalier that he had first portrayed in his earlier poems, short stories, and plays. Amanda Wingfield and her daughter Laura of *The Glass Menagerie,* Blanche du Bois of *A Streetcar Named Desire,* Alma Winemiller of *Summer and Smoke* and of *Eccentricities of a Nightingale,* and Hannah Jelkes of *The Night of the Iguana* are sympathetic variations of the type.

The conflict between the delicate person and the brutal one appears in the poem, "Lament for Moths," a theme that dominates so much of Williams' work. Another poem, "Beanstalk Country," favorably contrasts the delicate and the slightly mad with the so-called normal. "Intimations" suggests a spinster poet far behind the times (*In the Winter of Cities*). The short story, "A Portrait of a Girl in Glass." (*One Arm*), which is about the girl who retreats into her world of glass ornaments and phonograph records, is translated into Williams' first successful play. "The Resemblance of a Violin Case and a Coffin" (*Hard Candy*) describes the neurotic intensity and the latent sensuousness of a girl emerging into her teens. "The Yellow Bird" (*One Arm),* a comic narrative that contrasts the Puritan-Cavalier tradition, ends in fantasy, as do *Summer and Smoke* and *Eccentricities of a Nightingale.* "The Case of the Crushed Petunias" (*American Blues*) is a comic portrayal of a shy miss who is rescued from the curse of virginity by a clumsy lover. The short story "The Night of the Iguana" (*One Arm*) tells of an oversexed Southern spinster who is released from her "rope of loneliness" by an attempted rape. In the one-act play *Portrait of a*

46

Madonna (*27 Wagons Full of Cotton*), an aging church worker, wracked by her religious teaching and by her sexual dreams, is led away by officers of an asylum. The Southern gentlewomen also represent the culture and the gentility, sometimes rather seedy, that disappeared during the decade of World War I. Though at times eccentric, these females are superior to the domesticated housewives and gossips who correspond to the average and the acceptable women. The male counterpart in this conflict is represented by young men who are sometimes attracted to this frustrated gentlewoman but who are sometimes almost emasculated by a domineering mother. The D. H. Lawrence derivative, the red-blooded symbol of sexual freedom who contrasts to the nondescript intellectual young man, sometimes establishes the conflict that is the essence of the play.

I The Glass Menagerie *(1945)*[2]

In the production notes to the first published edition of *The Glass Menagerie,* Williams expressed the hope that this memory play in seven sharply recreated scenes would anticipate "a new plastic theater" that would replace "the exhausted theater of realistic conventions."[3] Since poetic imagination could transform the concrete into an inner truth, he rejected photographic realism in favor of unconventional techniques. In this same preface, his stage directions call for screen devices to project images and legends, for nostalgic music to enhance emotional overtones, and for shafts of light in different intensities to strengthen the dominant mood of a scene.

Tom Wingfield, an itinerant dreamer like his creator, is trapped not only in a monotonous warehouse job but also by responsibilities to his mother and his sister. Sometimes the narrator who introduces the scene and sometimes the actor in it, Tom sets the play in the 1930s. He describes Americans as going their blind way, dancing, making love, and as being mildly disturbed by labor troubles at the same time that the Spaniards are being methodically slaughtered at Guernica. A lonely soul, Tom is ignored or slightly ridiculed by his fellow workers at the plant where he works until the big Irishman, Jim O'Connor, pays attention to him.

Amanda Wingfield, the mother who is addicted to bromides and fantasies, is a middle-aged Southern belle. Garrulous and at times comic in her obsessions, her view of life is warped by her Puritan strictures; but she lives in delusions about her girlhood conquests. Her husband, present only in a blown-up photograph over the mantle, is described as a telephone man who fell in love with long distance and left his family for good. Deceived as a girl by his smile and uniform, she currently deludes herself about the seventeen gentleman callers who presented themselves one Sunday afternoon, men who later achieved wealth.

Just as willfully, Amanda ignores present reality. Overanxious to have her daughter, Laura, securely married, she refuses to recognize the girl's painful shyness or to admit to her slightly crippled leg. She insists that Laura not refer to herself as a cripple, that she speak only of a "little defect," and that she distract attraction from it by developing charm and vivacity. Amanda has known what can happen to a Southern girl without a home of her own: "I know so well what becomes of unmarried women who aren't prepared to occupy a position. I've seen such pitiful cases in the South — barely tolerated spinsters living upon the grudging patronage of sister's husband or brother's wife! — stuck away in some little mouse-trap of a room — encouraged by one in-law to visit another — little birdlike women without any nest — eating the crust of humility all their life!" (Sc. 2)

Though Amanda is proud of Tom, she is insensitive to his position. She carps at him continually about his eating habits, his smoking, his going to the movies, his late hours, his boredom with the warehouse job, and his need for adventure. When he tries to explain that man is by instinct a fighter, a hunter, and a lover, she is offended by his language. Reflecting her early twentieth-century Puritanism, Amanda believes that Christian adults should be concerned with things of the mind and spirit and leave dirty words like *instinct* for monkeys and pigs. Another argument erupts over a D. H. Lawrence novel that Tom brought home from the library, for she dismisses this writer as insane and offensive.

Exasperated by his mother's everlasting nagging about his running away to the movies, Tom bluntly tells her how much he detests the life he is leading. He is appalled by the idea of spending fifty-five years cooped up in a celotex workroom with fluorescent lights for sixty-five dollars a month; of waking up every morning to her maddening cheerfulness, "Rise and shine, rise and shine"; of returning each day to the warehouse, over and over again, in order to record shoe numbers. He would rather be dead. Tom Wingfield is a poet-dreamer who is something like his creator who also struggled against routine and conformity. Tom's shoe factory job, the poetry writing, the cramped living quarters, and the very close relationship with the sister are all echoes of Williams' own experience.[4]

Laura, the morbidly shy and overly delicate sister, is as fragile as the little glass ornaments and phonograph records that are her escape. Through her timidity, her suffering from the friction between Tom and Amanda, and her retreat into a world of dreams, Laura evokes genuine sympathy; she is the one who must be cared for, loved, and understood. Her charm and delicacy win the audience, just as they have won her brother. Perceptive of others' feelings, Laura senses her mother's need to romanticize her past and so stands as a buffer between the mother and son. For one so sensitive and shy, the clanking brace on her leg is torture. During her final semester in high school, she becomes nervously ill, fails her final examinations, and does not graduate. When her desperate mother spends fifty dollars on a secretarial course, Laura becomes nauseated during the typing speed test. Amanda forces her to join a young people's church group where she might meet some nice boys. Because Laura won't or can't talk, the girl is humiliated.

The mother makes another attempt to provide for her daughter by asking Tom to find a clean-living, nondrinking suitor. When from his limited acquaintance he invites a warehouse friend to dinner, her hopes skyrocket. Tom admits that he has said nothing about Laura and tries to make his mother be a little more realistic:

TOM: Mother you mustn't expect too much from Laura.

AMANDA: What do you mean?

TOM: Laura seems all those things to you and me because she's ours and we love her. We don't even notice she's crippled any more.

AMANDA: Don't say crippled! You know that I never allow that word to be used!

TOM: But face the facts, Mother. She is and — that's not all —

AMANDA: What do you mean, not all?

TOM: Laura is very different from other girls.

AMANDA: I think the difference is all to her advantage.

TOM: Not quite all — in the eyes of others — strangers — she's terribly shy and lives in a world of her own and those things make her seem a little peculiar to people outside the house.

AMANDA: Don't say peculiar.

TOM: Face the facts. She is.

Refusing to listen, Amanda tries with grim feminine energy to

change Laura into a pretty trap; for, on the ill-fated evening when
the girl is so nervously ill that she cannot eat dinner, the determined
mother crudely isolates the young man and her daughter.

Tom describes Jim O'Connor, the gentleman caller, as a high
school hero; he was evidently one of those dynamic extroverts
whose youth, looks, and enthusiasm won him the vote as the boy
graduate most likely to succeed. Time and circumstances have
proven otherwise, but he does work on self-improvement courses in
public speaking and in radio engineering. Jim, the very average
white-collar worker, the not too imaginative American, is, ironi-
cally, the boy whom Laura has secretly loved for years; but her only
association with him has been his several pictures in the high school
annual.

Amanda's planned evening, begun in panic for Laura, becomes
her dream made real for a brief time. It is a beautiful love scene set
to candlelight — of necessity, since the electricity was turned off
because Tom had appropriated the money to buy a merchant sea-
man's membership. When Laura brings out the high school annual
with all its romantic memories, she restores some of the old excitement to the disappointed hero. He brashly analyzes Laura as a victim of an inferiority complex, talks to her as if he were addressing
his public-speaking class in evening school, and is completely
impervious to the reactions of his little one girl, wide-eyed
audience. He says that she has magnified her trouble with the
brace, that she ought to forget it, and that she should think of herself as superior in some way. Jim then talks in big terms about his
own future plans, becomes a little abashed at his own egotism, and
then remembers his evening class lesson about success that comes
from interest in other people.

Laura responds to Jim's encouragement by showing him her precious glass collection. After she picks up her dearest treasure, the
thirteen-year old unicorn, she points to the single horn on his forehead; she admits that he is extinct, but she asserts that she loves him
because he must feel lonesome. This little glass figure is a living
thing to her; she talks about his accepting without complaint his
companions — horses without horns:

LAURA: Hold him over the light, he loves the light! You see how the light
shows through him?
JIM: It sure does shine!
LAURA: I shouldn't be partial, but he is my favorite one.

JIM: What kind of thing is this one supposed to be?
LAURA: Haven't you noticed the single horn on his forehead?
JIM: A unicorn, huh?
LAURA: Mn — hmmmmmmmmm.
JIM: Unicorns, aren't they extinct in the modern world?
LAURA: I know!
JIM: Poor little fellow, he must feel sort of lonesome.
LAURA (*smiling*): Well, if he does he doesn't complain about it. He stays on the shelf with some horses that don't have horns and all of them seem to get along nicely together. (Sc. 7)

Laura is carried away with the conversation, but Jim's attention is soon distracted by the music from across the alley. He gallantly asks Laura to dance; they take a few steps in a clumsy waltz and hit the table. There is a shatter of glass. The unicorn is broken.

LAURA: Now it is just like all the other horses.
JIM: It's lost its —
LAURA: Horn! It doesn't matter. Maybe it's a blessing in disguise.
JIM: You'll never forgive me. I bet it was your favorite pieces of glass.
LAURA: I don't have favorites much. It's no tragedy, Freckles. Glass breaks so easily. No matter how careful you are. (Sc. 7)

Jim is won by Laura's unique charm, but he is even more impressed with his own power. Like the clumsy stumble-bum who broke the unicorn, and seemingly unaware of what has happened to the girl, he talks about making her proud and not shy. He kisses her and then realizes his mistake; for, seeing her bright, dazed look, he dimly senses her love for him. After he pops a mint into his mouth, he bluntly explains that another girl has strings on him. Unaware that he is destroying all the self-confidence that he might have built up in the girl, he talks of the power of love that has made a man of him. The playwright says of his heroine that the holy candles have been snuffed out, that her face has *"a look of almost infinite desolation."* Laura gently places the broken unicorn that has lost its unique quality and any resemblance to her in the hand of the big Irishman and closes his fingers around her favorite ornament. He seems unaware that he has broken not only her unicorn but also her heart.

When Amanda discovers the awful conclusion to her planned evening, she brutally accuses Tom of allowing them to make fools of themselves and of recklessly spending their slim resources; she has completely forgotten that Tom had tried to reason with her. When he leaves abruptly to escape to the movies, Amanda, left alone, comforts her wounded Laura; and her reassurances are strong enough to bring a smile to the girl's face. The tragic dignity of this brief scene, when Amanda's speech cannot be heard, recalls her earlier observation about Southern gentlewomen without a home of their own.

Tom, fired for writing poetry on the boss's time, leaves his home, as did his father, to find escape. He cannot succeed, for he finds in every city there is a reminder of his sister: "Oh, Laura, Laura, I tried to leave you behind me, but I am more faithful than I intended to be! I reach for a cigarette, I cross the street, I run into the movies or a bar, I buy a drink. I speak to the nearest stranger — anything that can blow your candles out! (*Laura bends over the candles.*) — for now the world is lit by lightning! Blow out your candles, Laura — and so goodbye — *(She blows the candles out.)*" (Sc. 7)

The Glass Menagerie came into the American theater like a fresh spring wind. An original play that was about a part of the country not then well known, and that was cast and directed by the best talents, it became an exciting experience for many theatergoers. Despite Williams' distaste for the photographic, his play presents a good blend of imagination and realism; but it has overtones that are more complex than immediately apparent. One critic referred to the "unforgettable fragrance and glow" that Laurette Taylor gave to Amanda, "a poignantly pathetic figure" who evokes compassion, never scorn.[5] Every actress who later played this complex role gave it a slightly different dimension, some emphasizing the humor, others the pathos.[6]

Stark Young, who came from the same locality as Tennessee Williams, found all the language and motifs "free and true," and he believed the Southern speech of Amanda to be "the echo of great literature, or [to indicate] at least a respect for it." He said, "No role could be more realistically written," with variety and the "almost unconscious freedom, perhaps, of true realism." He felt, however, that since both son and father were born wanderers and adventurers, their parallels should have been heightened.[7] Many comments about the original production suggest a too close attention to the theatrical effects called for by the playwright.[8]

Later critics, who compared the original production with the revivals, agreed that time had not weakened the play "in spite of the sentimental patina.'' Writing about the twentieth-anniversary revival of this play, critics agreed that, although the play might be called a dream, it contained more information about its people than had Arthur Miller's Willy Loman in *Death of a Salesman.* One wrote that Williams' play "transforms autobiography into lucid, objective art,'' and that beneath the honest portrayal lies an awareness that there are "no solutions, nor exits from necessity.''[9] Another referred to the "play's lyricism ... which ennobled the writer's bitter recollection of his youth.''[10] Another, commenting about the best of Williams in the "lightning flashes of things instantly recognized,'' calls attention to the scene when Tom, maddened by his mother's carping, screams at her about his wild life — all fiction.[11]

Close to the third anniversary of the Chicago opening of *The Glass Menagerie* and shortly before the New York opening of *A Streetcar Named Desire,* Williams wrote an essay, "On a Streetcar Named Success,'' in which he commented on the shock of fame. The reception of the earlier play terminated one part of his life and began a very different one: from oblivion and from scratching for a living to "sudden prominence''; from a precarious tenancy in rented rooms to a suite in a first-class hotel with room service; from casual dress to expensive clothes. Success descended like a gloom; he was to recall "an ominous let down of spirit followed me like my shadow.'' He found that "success brings leeches'' and makes a person a "public Somebody,'' a fiction created by mirrors. His own "well of cynicism'' frightened him; he suspected praise as flattery; he hated to respond to the repeated enthusiasm over *Menagerie.*[12] After three months of this kind of "popularity,'' he retreated to the hospital for an eye operation; then he went to St. Louis, where he met William Inge, an aspiring playwright; and he sojourned in Chapala, Mexico, where he wrote *The Poker Night,* which was later incorporated into *A Streetcar Named Desire.* As he was to admit later, "once ... [one] fully apprehend[s] the vacuity of a life without struggle,'' one recognizes that luxury, not poverty, is "the wolf at the door.'' He joined William James in calling success the "bitch goddess.''[13]

II   A Streetcar Named Desire *(1947)*[14]

As an epigraph to *A Streetcar Named Desire,* Williams cited the quatrain of Hart Crane that begins, "And so I entered the broken world / To trace the visionary company of love." These lines might have prefaced the "broken world" of several unhappy love affairs, from Amanda and Laura in *The Glass Menagerie* to Alma Winemiller of *Summer and Smoke,* as well as that of the heroine in this play. The Southern gentlewoman in *Streetcar,* Blanche Du Bois, is a refined, hypersensitive, and decadent aristocrat who is pitted against her brother-in-law, Stanley Kowalski, who is the epitome of the pleasure that an animal enjoys in his body. This primitive laborer is married to Blanche's sister Stella who loves him in spite of their different inheritance and who is undisturbed by the vulgarities of their friends and neighbors. The arrival of the older sister threatens their happy marital arrangement, but the increasing conflict between the mentally unbalanced visitor and the animalistic young husband precipitates her insanity.

The action occurs in a modest flat in the Vieux Carré section of New Orleans that is poor but has "a raffish charm." The easy mingling of white and black in the area is expressed by the "Blue Piano" music that emerges periodically. Throughout the play, street vendors and other participants in street life either highlight the emotional drama erupting in the flat or fill in the background.[15]

Just before Blanche enters, delicate as a moth and dressed in white, as if she were about to take cocktails in the garden, Stan yells at Stella, heaves a package of bloody meat at her, and leaves to go bowling. On her way to her sister's residence, Blanche repeats the directions given her: she is to take the streetcar named Desire, transfer to one named Cemetaria, and to get off after a six-block ride at Elysian Fields — names with symbolic overtones. Having seen the flat, she soon fortifies herself against the shock of her sister's quarers by surreptitiously drinking Stan's whiskey. When she meets her quiet sister, she criticizes her lifestyle, reports that the plantation, "Belle Rêve," has been lost after the deaths of many older relatives, and hysterically complains of her own hardships while Stella was "in bed with her Polack." Her feverish talk, her attention to her figure and to the showy clothes she brought, and her frequent returns to the whiskey that she later says she never touches give an early clue to her state of mind.

Stanley exemplifies the primitive hero, such as Mellors in *Lady Chatterly's Lover* by D. H. Lawrence, a type that Williams had already tentatively portrayed both in Hadrian in *You Touched Me!* and, to a degree, in Val Xavier in *Battle of Angels.* Williams' glorification of the male — Stanley — appears in his description of this paragon: *"Since earliest manhood the center of his life has been pleasure with women, the giving and taking of it, not with weak indulgence, dependently, but with the power and pride of a richly feathered male bird among hens."* In addition to this *"satisfying center"* are *"his heartiness with men, his appreciation of rough humor, his love of good drink and food and games, his car, his radio, everything ... that bears his emblem of the gaudy seed bearer."* (Sc. 1)

The first clash between Blanche and Stan occurs when he learns about the loss of the plantation, which he has dreamt of owning and which he thinks she has squandered. He yanks out of the trunk, which dominates the kitchen, her garish clothing and her costume jewelry, which he thinks are expensive. When he takes up a sheaf of papers, poems by a dead husband, she tells Stan that his touch contaminates them. Vague about the loss of the plantation, she tells about spendthrift grandfathers, uncles, father, and brothers who over the years mortgaged the land to pay for their "epic-fornications." Although Blanche flits from one subject or one feeling to another, she always returns to her own delusions about herself; but her crude and sexy byplay rouses Stan's suspicions about her own virtue. It is he who tells about Stella's expected child, joyful news to Blanche.

The next clash occurs when Stella and Blanche return about two-thirty in the morning and interrupt the men's poker game. Inspired by a Van Gogh picture of a billiard parlor, the dramatist calls for the raw colors from childhood's spectrum and gives vivid characterizations of Stan and his poker-playing pals in a dialogue with an idiom that rings true. Some of the ambiguity in the play arises from the author's glowing admiration of the capacity of Stan and his friends for unlimited physical pleasure; and, on the other hand, he evinces a sympathy and admiration for Blanche, who has been caught up in an incredible history of adultery and slow death of older relatives; and who has lived through a considerable sexual history of her own, a story that she sometimes glazes over with deceit and lies.

Blanche singles out Mitch as the one seemingly respectable player who can satisfy her needs. His ingenuousness recalls Williams' other gentleman caller, Jim O'Connor, of *The Glass Menagerie.* Mitch talks of heavy perspiration and of his fight against getting soft in the belly, but he has a code of honor and a diffidence about women that make him a little awed before the seemingly aristo-

cratic Blanche. At this first meeting she stops him on his way to
"The Little Boy's Room" and speaks pathetically of her great sor-
row, of her need to cover up the ugly truth — she asks him to cover
a naked light bulb with a Chinese paper lantern — and of the
esthetic problems of an English teacher who works with "bobby
soxers and drug-store Romeos."

When Blanche turns on the radio to encourage Mitch to dance,
Stan in a drunken fury seizes the radio and hurls it out the window.
He brutally strikes his wife, who tries to send the men home; in the
brawl that follows, the women escape. When he realizes that his
wife has left, Stan throws back his head and howls her name. When
she returns quietly, tears in her eyes, they rush together like moan-
ing animals. He falls to his knees and presses his face against her
delicately rounded belly. When she tenderly raises him to her, he
lifts her into his arms and carries her into the dark flat. The sight of
this connubial bliss, following so closely upon the scene of drunken
brutality, momentarily stuns Blanche, but she soon focuses on
Mitch, the one unattached man who might offer kindness.

The following morning Stella is serene and happy, and the tran-
quility on her face is likened to that of the narcotic inner peace
reflected on the images of Eastern idols. After she explains to
Blanche that the row wasn't serious, she assures her sister that she
is not in a situation from which she desires to escape. Blanche,
blinded by her delusions, babbles about telephoning an old beau,
Shep Huntleigh, a rich oil man and married, to plead for an escape.
She tries to impress upon Stella the depths to which she has sunk in
her marriage; and, unaware that Stan is nearby, she describes him
as subhuman — as an ape, as a survivor of the stone age who bears
raw meat home to his mate, as a throwback after thousands of
years of civilization. She pleads with her sister not to return to the
brutes. When Stan enters, Stella embraces him fiercely; and the
music of the "Blue Piano" reaches a crescendo with trumpet and
drums.

Stan avenges these continuing insults as he begins to confront
Blanche with veiled questions about a man named Shaw, the hotel
"Flamingo," and the town of Laurel. He has obviously struck a
sensitive subject, for Blanche later explains herself to her sister in
halftruths. She says that soft people have to seek the favor of hard
ones, have to play a seductive role, have to resort to magic — to
pay for a night's lodging. She has been running from one shelter to
another while trying to escape the storm. She has depended on

men's lovemaking to give her a sense of existence. To Stella, whose approach to sex is frank and simple, this talk is morbid. Blanche senses that her welcome is wearing thin and that her last refuge lies in marrying Mitch. She who flirted so obviously with Stan, who exhibited herself before the poker players, who called a strange young man collecting for papers a young Arabian prince and kissed him softly on the mouth, this nymphomaniac plays prim and coy with Mitch. Then a chance remark from him about loneliness elicits her confession about her early marriage.

The boy Allen whom she had married, though not effeminate looking, had had something different about him, a tenderness, an unmasculine softness, and a nervousness. Struggling in quicksands, he had turned to her for help and she slipped down with him. Then she had found her husband with an older man, the situation unmistakable. She remembers having said to him, "I saw! I know! You disgust me." Allen had then shot himself. As Blanche pours out this half-crazed confession, the polka music and the locomotive whistle suggest her psychological state. As Mitch takes her in his arms, she says, "Sometimes — there's God — so quickly."

On a September afternoon, Stan returns armed with revenge against the sister-in-law who had called him an ape. He reports to Stella that Blanche is not a modest white lily but a liar; that she was so famous at the Flamingo Hotel that she had had to turn in her room key; that she had been fired from her teaching job because she had seduced a seventeen-year old boy. He also tells Stella that he has reported his findings to Mitch, his wartime buddy and best friend, and that he has bought for Blanche a return ticket to Laurel. Stella, who refuses to believe these reports, remembers the older sister she had known as a child. During Stan's and Stella's recital, Blanche indulges in a hot bath to quiet her nerves; she occasionally sings a saccharine ballad; or she asks Stella for another towel to dry her hair. When she finally leaves the bathroom, she senses a crisis.

At the birthday party that evening, at which Mitch does not appear, Blanche tries to entertain. When Stella calls Stan a pig for his table manners, he reminds her that he had pulled her down from the columns and that she had liked it. Stella, suddenly aware that her baby is arriving, asks Stan to take her to the hospital. Later that evening, an unshaven Mitch faces Blanche with the lies she has given him. Her deteriorating mental condition conveyed by the polka music, she spills out the hideous story of her degradation: her intimacies with strangers after her poet-husband's death, her affair with the seventeen-year old boy, and her dismissal from her teaching job. She needs Mitch as a refuge from the world, from the endless familiarity she has had with the dying.

Then she adds another chapter. On Saturday nights soldiers from an army camp not far from the plantation would return drunk from town, stagger across her lawn, call her name, and she would answer their calls. Later the paddy wagon collected the boys and returned them to the camp. During the later part of Blanche's account, a Mexican woman calls her wares, *"Flores para los muertos, flores —— flores ——"* It is against the old woman's mournful cries that Blanche insists that she never lied in her heart. Her legacy has been death, all the hideous, ugly manifestations of the dying that she faced alone. The opposite of death, she says, is desire. Mitch, perhaps angry over the way he has been deluded, approaches to take what he has "been missing all summer." When she asks him to marry her, he says she is "not clean enough" to take home to his mother. When he moves closer and she screams "Fire," he suddenly leaves.

Stan returns from the hospital to find a very much confused Blanche decked out in a crumpled, white satin evening dress and shabby silver slippers, a rhinestone tiara on her head. In her drunken exhilaration, she talks of a Caribbean cruise with her one-time sweetheart, now a millionaire; and she haughtily refers to Stan and Mitch as swine. Angered by her superiority and pretensions, Stan flatly tells her that her talk is all lies, conceit, and tricks; tells her to look at herself in her rag-picker outfit, the queen who has been swilling his liquor. The rest of the scene is fever pitched. Like a cornered animal, Blanche makes desperate calls to Western Union. Her state of mind is pictorially suggested by the lurid reflections, grotesque and menacing shadows, that appear on the walls; the mood is intensified by the off-stage noises that symbolize inhuman jungle cries. Through the transparent back wall, the audience can see a portrayal of the struggle between a prostitute and a drunk, a scene interrupted by a policeman's whistle.

When Stan emerges from the bedroom dressed in his silk wedding pyjamas, he grins at her deliberately and corners her. She tries to get away. In the background, the "Blue Piano" begins pianissimo and increases to the roar of an approaching locomotive. Stan moves stealthily toward her. Frantically she breaks a bottle and threatens to twist the broken end in his face. He springs toward her, snatches her wrist. Then come the beautifully loaded lines: "Tiger — tiger! Drop the bottletop! Drop it! We've had this date with each other from the beginning! (*She moans. The bottle-top falls. She sinks to her knees. He picks up her inert figure and carries her to the bed. The hot trumpet and drums from the Four Deuces sound loudly.*)"

In the final scene, which occurs weeks later, Blanche, now obviously deranged, appears dressed as if she were going to dinner with Shep Huntleigh. She immediately recognizes that the doctor is not the man from Dallas; but, when he speaks softly to her and smiles, he is another suitor; she is won. The lurid reflections fade, the unhuman voices grow quiet. Clinging to his arm, she leaves quietly: "Whoever you are — I have always depended on the kindness of strangers."[16] Broken by her excursion into the Vieux Carré and by its realities, she escapes completely into her own world, and does so like an aristocrat.

When Williams submitted the script of *Streetcar* to Audrey Wood in February 1947, she worked quickly with Irene M. Selznick, the producer; and, in consultation with the playwright, they chose the director and actors, tried out the play in Boston in November of that year, and opened in New York on December 3, 1947, for one of the longest runs in theatrical history, 855 performances. The play made Tennessee Williams an international figure, it won him two major awards, and it became big business. It is said to have grossed three million dollars; the motion picture rights led to a film that made over five million and won three awards. Because of this play Williams was a name not only in the theater world but in the academic one in the decades following as students and teachers studied and analyzed his work.[17]

When first produced, *A Streetcar Named Desire* aroused excitement not only for its dramatic effectiveness but for its frank presentation of sex. An extreme reaction was expressed by George Jean Nathan, who wrote that Williams realistically dramatizes "sexual abnormality, harlotry, perversion, seduction, and lunacy," and made a "theatrical shocker" without distilling "any elevation and purge."[18] The play became a battleground for American critics, but the London production developed into a major controversy over moral issues.[19] Though not produced in Moscow, the Russian press expressed the opinion that the play was one "to stupify men and turn them into beasts."[20]

The controversy over immorality undoubtedly increased the

response at the box office, but it also obscured the significant themes in the play. Jessica Tandy, the original Blanche, faced an audience that laughed over the language or sexy talk. Marlon Brando as Stanley made it difficult for later actors to create their own interpretation. As Harold Clurman wrote of the original production. "The characters and the scenes are written with a firm grip on their naturalistic truth" but elements in the acting "make for a certain ambiguity and confusion." For instance, he felt that Marlon Brando's Stanley, whose "mentality provides the soil for fascism," triumphs "with the collusion of the audience, which is no longer on the side of the angels."[21]

The production itself was elaborate and made use of sophisticated theatrical techniques to heighten both meaning and mood. Most audiences were unaware of the complexity of light and sound effects coordinated backstage, or of scenes like the pantomime offstage that were so crucial to the Blanche-Stanley conflict. The playwright's careful attention to these theatrical devices to heighten the mood and his creation of double scenes to add to the complex emotional development of the play indicate how vividly he imagined the production.[22] His plays have often been called scenarios for imaginative directors, actresses, and actors. By way of contrast to Williams, George Bernard Shaw seems to have prepared his editions with the reader in mind, for he filled in a scene as a novelist would. *Streetcar* was the beginning of the Williams-Kazan team that was to dominate Broadway for a decade. The notebooks of this distinguished director, Elia Kazan, prepared for the production, indicate his care in trying to understand the characters and situations, as well as the possibilities of translating them to the stage.[23]

Most critics recognized that a major American dramatist had come into his own. Brooks Atkinson found the play "almost unbearably tragic." The audience, he reported, came way "profoundly moved.... For they have been sitting all evening in the presence of truth, and that is a rare and wonderful experience." He said of Blanche, "Since she is created on the stage as a distinct individual, experiences identical to hers can never be repeated. She and the play that is woven about her are unique."[24] Joseph Wood Krutch stated that, in spite of the sensational quality of the story, "The author's perceptions remain subtle and delicate and he is amazingly aware of nuances even in situations where nuance might seem inevitably obliterated by violence." He believed that Williams' stories "enable him to communicate emotions which have a special, personal significance."[25]

When *Streetcar* was revived in several American cities twenty-five years later, it was obvious that time had not faded its original impact. Walter Kerr considered the play "the finest single work yet created for the American theater ... a stunningly constructed account of Stanley's gradual — and for him, difficult — exposure of Blanche's pretense."[26] Clive Barnes commented on the humor in the contrast between Blanche's ladylike pretensions and the "deliberate, beer-swilling antics of an unsure Stan." He said that "Williams' language is musical even at its most colloquial" and that the structure of his play is "almost too perfect in its symmetry."[27] Stephen Farber wrote that "Kazan's interpretation clarified Williams' own ambivalence"; that, although Stanley's mockery of Blanche is insensitive, it is "a savagely honest response to her hypocrisy and her thread-bare illusions."[28] To Harold Clurman, the play was "an American parable," a drama "of sensibility crushed by a brutishness so common" that the audience mistakes Stan for the hero. He recalled that Williams had once said, with reference to the play, that "if we were not vigilant our country would be taken over by gorillas"[29] — a variation of his earlier assertion about the apes inheriting the earth.

Foster Hirsch called *Streetcar* the culmination of Williams' early period in which he dramatized "the complex pattern of antagonism and attraction between the puritan and the cavalier," but presented the antagonists as equals. He says Williams, the moralist, as in *Cat,* punishes Blanche; for "betrayal of the defenseless homosexual is the supreme sin."[30] Since Williams thought that he was about to die when he wrote *Streetcar,* the play was to be his swan song that "said everything [he] had to say." On his way of writing, he told one interviewer, "I *see* somebody.... I saw Blanche sitting in a chair with the moonlight coming through a window onto her." The first title was "Blanche's Chair in the Moon," and Williams wrote one scene in December 1944. He felt so intensely about *Streetcar* that it terrified him; he could not work on it, so he put it away; then, when he returned to it in 1947 after *Summer and Smoke,* "it wrote itself, just like that."[31]

Having written two fine plays, both of which were to be revived over and over again; having earned the respect and admiration of top-flight critics for creating a new kind of theater; and having made money for himself and profits for many in the entertainment business, Tennessee Williams in his thirties faced a terrible challenge — to continue the standard he had set for himself and to meet the expectations of the public.

III   Summer and Smoke *(1947)*[32]

After the success of *The Glass Menagerie,* Williams reworked *Summer and Smoke,* originally titled *A Chart of Anatomy.* His earlier short story, "The Yellow Bird," a possible source, spoofs at conventional sexual inhibitions and concludes in comic fantasy. Although the play gives serious treatment of the Puritan-Cavalier conflict, Williams divides the issue by developing in two parallel lines the separate stories about the two main characters: Alma Winemiller and Dr. John Buchanan, Jr. As in the story, the play concludes in fantasy.[33]

Williams mounts his "tone poem" in a setting of broken walls and interiors reminiscent of a Chirico painting, a foreground set against a wide expanse of sky. Two symbolic pieces underscore the theme: in the public square, a stone angel that represents Eternity has wings lifted and hands cupped as for a drinking fountain; in the doctor's office, an anatomy chart represents the physical side of man. These are the outward symbols of the Southern gentlewoman, Alma Winemiller, daughter of an Episcopal minister, and of her neighbor, the virile young doctor, John Buchanan, Jr. The play belongs to the years before 1916 and is set in the sleepy Mississippi town of Glorious Hill.[34]

Alma, an adult at ten, has a spiritual quality and an "extraordinary delicacy"; but her fussy concern about John Jr.'s runny nose and dirty face and her constant attention irritate him. When John gives her a quick kiss, yanks her hair ribbon, and runs away, Alma, alone and hurt, crouches at the fountain. A decade or so later, Alma's attention is still so focused on young John that her affectations, her hysterical laugh, her strained singing have earned her the ridiculous title of "nightingale of the Delta." Burdened by a mother, spoiled as a child, later irresponsible and perversely childish as a woman, one who never assumed the duties of maintaining the rectory, Alma appears older than her years. John is "a Promethean figure," a brilliant contrast to the "stagnant society" of which he is a part; he is not yet marked by the dissipations that relieve "his demonic unrest"; and he is distinguished by the radiance of "an epic hero." To his aged father, there is no room in the medical profession for a waster, drunkard, and lecher; and, of the five hundred babies that the father had brought into the world, he regrets that he gave himself "the rottenest one of the lot."[35]

At the first reunion of the young couple on a July Fourth evening, John throws a firecracker at Alma and sets off her hysteria. She recites the details about his brilliant medical school record and about his isolating the epidemic fever germ at Lyon, but she soon turns to her own nervous condition. When John tells her that she swallows air, as hysterical women often do, and that her *doppelganger* is badly irritated, he means that another self within is in conflict. He tells her that he had watched an imitation of her at a party, of her singing with exaggerated gestures and facial expressions, and that he had heard about her "putting on airs" and her "fancy way of talking." Alma, hurt by this "unprovoked malice," speaks of her cross at home and of her need, as a minister's daughter, to be selective in her company. During this conversation, two girls pass by whom Alma identifies. Rosa Gonzales, dressed in "outrageous finery," is the daughter of the Mexican who runs the gambling casino at Moon Lake.[36] The other, Nellie Ewell, is Alma's sixteen-year old voice pupil to whom John lent a medical dictionary. The daughter of a merry widow who meets trains to attract traveling salesmen, Nellie is consequently ostracized from society.

Alma, who watches John's house night and day, tries every ruse in her limited repertoire to win the attentions of the young doctor. Her attempt to interest him in the literary club of pseudointellectuals who bore him ends in his abrupt departure. At two o'clock the morning after the club's meeting, Alma bursts into his office and interrupts Rosa, who is helping John bandage his arm injured in a brawl with her. He tells Alma that he had abruptly left the literary session because he likes only meetings between two people; and, as if he were trying to widen her horizons, he talks of "the four-dimensional continuum we're caught in" and of the distance from the earth of "the Magellanic clouds." When he applies the stethoscope to the reluctant spinster's breast, he hears, according to his creator, that "Miss Alma is lonesome." Alma reminds him of his promise of a ride; and, though he wonders if it would be worth trying, he promises to call for her on Sunday at eight. After she leaves the scene, John takes Rosa roughly in his arms. She is standing by the anatomy chart.

The Sunday evening date reveals the desert stretches between the young doctor and the minister's daughter. Alma is distressed over their being at a disreputable casino "where anything goes." John orders wine and a performance of "Yellow Dog Blues," takes from Alma the pills that he had given her, because he fears she might become a dope fiend, and voices his distaste for the medical profession that is "walled in by sickness and misery and death." After a slight argument about indulging the senses, Alma likens "the secret, the principle back of existence" to a Gothic cathedral where everything reaches up — "the everlasting struggle and aspiration for more than our human limits have placed in our reach." She then turns to her own wistful personal complaint about herself. John says that she has a great deal more excitement under the surface than most women, kisses her, but calls her Miss Alma because he cannot forget that she's a preacher's daughter. When she asks what he wants in the woman he marries, he answers that "intimate relations" have more to do with "connubial felicity" than mutual respect. When she is offended by this "coupling of beasts," he answers that some day he is going to ask her to place the soul — Alma being Spanish for soul — on his office anatomy chart. She leaves abruptly, deeply hurt, calling him no gentleman.

The second part of the play is called Winter. John and Alma, the "white-blooded spinster," continue the argument over the spiritual and physical life. He gives her an anatomy lecture that is illustrated by the office chart: "This upper story's the brain which is hungry for something called truth and doesn't get much but keeps on feeling hungry! This middle's the belly which is hungry for food. This part down here is the sex which is hungry for love because it is sometimes lonesome. I've fed all three, as much of all three as I could or as much as I wanted — You've fed none — nothing" — perhaps "watery subsistence" for the belly, but only "hand-me-down notions! — attitudes! — poses!" for love and truth. He confesses that he could not have taken her that night at the casino: "I'm more afraid of your soul than you're afraid of my body. You'd have been as safe as the angel of the fountain — because I wouldn't feel *decent* enough to touch you...." (Sc. 8)

The other side of John's personality is revealed in a scene with Rosa. Dressed in the usual white linen, his face marked by satiety and confusion, John wonders if anyone else could have degenerated so fast in one summer. He orders the exhausted Rosa, whom he is about to marry, to continue dancing, though handicapped by the office furniture and the anatomy chart. He cynically asks why her father wants him, whose gambling losses have been considerable, for a son-in-law. In an account recited to accordion music, she tells him that she had lived in a one-room house with a dirt floor, along with four other people, three geese, and a game cock; she has memories of hearing her pop's lovemaking. Rosa Gonzales sees in the young doctor the chance to rise from the life she had known as a child. Her drunken father enters at this point, waves his gun and refuses to leave. John retreats to Alma in the rectory, and he buries his face in her lap — a scene reminiscent of the stone Pieta. Across the street, meanwhile, Dr. Buchanan, called home by Alma at the request of busy-body Mrs. Bassett, angrily tells the drunken Gonzales, "Get your — swine out of — my house," and repeatedly strikes him with his cane. The drunken Mexican fires his revolver.

After the murder of his father, John stamps out the fever at Lyon, covers himself with glory, and prepares to marry Nellie Ewell, not out of love but out of the desire to have "settled with life on fairly acceptable terms." Alma in her desperate need tells him that the girl who once said "No," exists no longer. When she kisses him, he is embarrassed. He tells her that she has won the argument about the chart, that he has come around to her way of thinking. Each one was trying to find in the other person something he needed, but neither one quite knew what it was. In a symbolic gesture, he strikes a match and says that what he had once thought was Puritanical ice he now believes was flame: "I still don't understand it, but I know it was there, just as I know that your eyes and your voice are the two most beautiful things I've ever known — and also the warmest, although they don't seem to be set in your body at all. . . ."

Alma recognizes that her body does not exist for him, that the tables have turned with a vengeance, and that she is now like his former self. She laughs. "I came here to tell you that being a gentleman doesn't seem so important to me any more, but you're telling me I've got to remain a lady. (*She laughs rather violently.*) The tables have turned with a vengeance."[37] In the final scene, Alma waits at the stone fountain for a traveling salesman, the first, apparently, of her bedroom adventures. Alma, who spoke about man's reaching for the stars, seems to have become akin to Rosa Gonzales. This curious twist of fantasy lacks, however, the humor of the story "The Yellow Bird."

Williams has adapted to a Delta community the tragicomic situation and tone common to Anton Chekhov, whose plays are so frequently concerned with the strange tricks of love. Williams implies that beneath the spinsterish behavior, Alma is basically a nymphomaniac. Among the minor characters who help explain her predicament are her mother, senile and mean; her father, the Reverend Winemiller, harried by this childish wife; Roger Doremus, Alma's effeminate and pseudointellectual suitor; Mrs. Bassett, the nosey, right-thinking neighbor; Nellie, the giggling teenager and Alma's voice pupil.

John Buchanan, the young doctor, first appears like an epic hero, lives through many degrading experiences, but emerges at the end of the play as a tempered idealist. The progression is melodramatic: bored with his father's profession, John becomes the drunken frequenter of the Gonzales' night spot and lover of the daughter Rosa; Alma, a "meddlesome Mattie," upset by his attenitons to the Mexican girl and by the community gossip, recalls the elder Dr. Buchanan from an emergency mission in the next county; the drunken Gonzales, flourishing his pistol, walks into the doctor's office and interrupts a rendezvous between his daughter and the young doctor; abject over his deplorable situation — though still dressed in white linen — John flees to Alma and falls on his knees before her; the old doctor, in answer to the urgent call, returns, enters his office, sees the drunken Gonzales, orders him to leave, and is shot; John, awakened by the murder of his father, becomes resigned to the medical profession; he finishes in glory the work begun by the old doctor; he realizes the serious import of Alma's philosophical lecture about man's spiritual possibilities; but he marries the giggling teenager, Nellie, not Alma.

To Harold Clurman, who observed that "the naturalistic details of portraiture in 'Streetcar' are authentic" because they begin with the "intuitive rather than analytic," the "conscious exposition of theme" in *Summer and Smoke* obscured "the specific sense of his people."[38] Joseph Wood Krutch described the play as "more like a fable or allegory" and the characters as "a bit more suggestive of the protagonists in some old morality play."[39] Williams thought that Alma was his most fully developed character and identified with her: "You see, Alma went through the same thing that I went through — from puritanical shackles to, well, complete profligacy." He defined profligacy as "liberation from taboos. I don't make any kind of sex dirty except sadism."[40] Because of this personal identification, he was so crushed over the critical attacks on *Summer and Smoke* that he wrote an angry letter that denounced critics who did not allow a dramatist to develop.[41]

IV   The Eccentricities of a Nightingale *(1948)*[42]

To Williams, *The Eccentricities of a Nightingale* is a "radically different" version of *Summer and Smoke;* it is "less conventional and melodramatic," but its locale and its characters are the same. He wrote the play in Rome during the summer; he took it to London in the fall with the hope that the new version would be used, but he found that the original was already in rehearsal.[43] This second version does not attempt to resolve the problem of the two main characters but concentrates on the minister's daughter. The doctor's son is not the flamboyant Promethean figure with a penchant for gambling, showy Mexican girls, or giggling teenagers; he is the sensitive and attractive young man with a sense of humor to whom the frustrated nightingale might be attracted. To John, Miss Alma is sometimes appealing; she is different from the Baltimore debutantes whom he found conventional and smug.

The situation in the rectory helps explain the nervous, hysterical, and at times voluble excitement of Alma Winemiller. The reverend, her father, speaks of her mother as one who has "a vicious impulse to destroy," and recalls that a week after their marriage "a cold and secretly spiteful look" came into her eyes as if he had inflicted upon her an unmentionable injury. Alma wistfully observes that women who could bring a *"transcendental tenderness"* to marriage do not marry but teach school or give singing lessons. Both father and daughter refer to the mother as the cross they have to bear; both humor her to keep her quiet or out of the way when callers are expected; and both are humiliated by her spite in public.

New to this version is the mother of John Buchanan, Jr., a "stout dowager," proud and oversolicitous of her offspring, unable to realize that her one chick has grown. She warns her son that in every small Southern town there is a pathetic figure like the minister's daughter and that he must not become involved with her. Hawk-eyed, she interrupts them whenever they are together.

The repressive effect of religion, or its concern for proprieties, is suggested by the strictures that the Reverend Winemiller imposes upon his daughter. When Alma speaks bitterly of the seemingly soft and sweet dowager with "mineral water" in her veins who stalks her son lest he should meet a girl "without money," he rebukes her for wild talk. When she speaks of her many church duties, of her singing at every occasion except for the "conception of infants," her father is shocked. He talks about the imitations given of her at a party, and tries to warn her about her "slightly peculiar" mannerisms and her high-flown phrases that "gild the lily." He urges her to give up her literary club, the little "collection of misfits" who are of no social advantage to her. He says that her gentleman caller, Roger Doremus, with his "little excitements of a sparrow" is peculiar. He disapproves of her taking a sack of crumbs to the square, feeding and talking to the birds. Eccentrics are not happy, he says. Alma, deeply hurt, her fingers "frozen," cannot open the box of amytal tablets, cannot breathe. Her father says this kind of hysteria was the beginning of her mother's condition. But he orders her to keep that same mother out of sight when company is expected.

Alma's destiny is somewhat foreshadowed by the piecemeal story of Aunt Albertine, a notoriety that the rectory had never outlived. She had run away with Mr. Schwarzkopf, the proprietor of the Musée Mechanique, which had as a main attraction a boa constrictor. Aunt Albertine was never seen again; but according to the legend, both were burned to death in the museum, the fire reportedly set by Mr. Schwarzkopf; the woman was found clutching a button off her paramour's coat. Alma says she wants more out of life than a button.

The second play includes from the first version the reunion of the young people at the July Fourth celebration and also scenes at the rectory: one when the father expresses money worries, one with Roger showing pictures of his mother's trip, one of the literary club, and an additional one in which mother Buchanan as Mrs. Santa, her son "Little John" in tow, spreads cheer. Also repeated are Alma's desperate visit to the doctor at two in the morning, and the scene at the fountain immediately after the movie. In this last scene she asks if he knows about a little room with a fireplace. John answers that there have always been these rooms with "sad little tokens" of previous occupants, a sprinkle of powder, a hairpin, withered rose petals, an empty bottle of cheap whiskey in the waste basket. He tells of his own youthful and tentative experience with an anonymous young lady and his precipitant exit. When Alma insists that he take her there, he warns, "You know that it might turn out badly."

The scene in the hotel room between the eager spinster and the unwilling escort is effectively dramatized in symbols. Alma finds some of the expected tokens. They try to take the chill off the room by lighting the fire, but the damp paper and wood do not respond.

Alma tears the plume from her hat — her Cavalier's plume — because "something has to be sacrificed to the fire." John is shocked. He tells her sadly that nothing will revive the fire, that sometimes things say to people what they "find too painful or too embarrassing to say." Alma, desperately twisting her rings, answers, "How gently a failure can happen!" She has to be honest, not having beauty, nor grace, nor desirability. When John says that her honesty is the plume in her hat and that she must wear it proudly, she replaces it, listens to the honky-tonk music below stairs, and says that she may get to know the place a great deal better. She is not ashamed of this New Year's Eve because both of them have been honest. John turns out the light; and, as the fire flickers briefly, he kisses her. When she asks where the fire came from, he answers, "No one has ever been able to answer that question!"

The epilogue is the same as that in *Summer and Smoke* but more credibly anticipated because of the strictures imposed on Alma.

Eccentricities of a Nightingale, written in 1948, revised in 1964, and published in a volume with *Summer and Smoke,* represents Tennessee Williams at his best. Though produced in regional theaters, it did not achieve national attention until the June 1976 Public Broadcasting System presentation of a production by the San Diego Old Globe Theater on the Theater in America series.

V   The Night of the Iguana *(1961)*[44]

The Night of the Iguana, Williams' dramatization of the story by the same title, deepens the character of the spinster and relates her strength to two men — her aged grandfather and a defrocked minister — who are dependent upon her. In *Iguana,* written thirteen years after *Eccentricities,* Williams presents in Hannah Jelkes another deceptively frail heroine who resembles Laura and Blanche, but who is an older woman who has learned to accept what she cannot change, no matter how desperate her situation. Her own predicament and that of her grandfather and the minister, her reaction to the deepening crises, and her attempts to alleviate the suffering afford substance for great drama. Unfortunately, Williams placed a crowd of obnoxious German tourists, sympathetic to the Nazi cause, in the same Acapulco hotel, perhaps to suggest the early 1940s; however, their clumsy and melodramatic antics detract from the central concern of the play.

In *The Night of the Iguana,* which is set in a seedy bohemian hotel on a lush tropical hilltop overlooking the Puerto Barrio in Mexico on one summer afternoon and evening in 1940, Williams presents, but modifies, two other types common to a number of his plays: a sexually aggressive older woman and a born loser past his youth. The proprietor of Costa Verde Hotel, Mrs.Maxine Faulk, a stout and "rapaciously lusty" recent widow in her midforties, has adopted the attractive twenty-year old Pedro as her "casual lover." With a voice like a barking seal, Mrs. Faulk welcomes the Reverend Lawrence Shannon, a former guest who tries to induce his busload of women — eleven teachers and a teen-age, oversexed songbird from a Baptist Female College in Texas — to check in at the mountain hotel. As a guide on probation for Blake Tours, he has reached the nadir of the profession.

Two other guests, the ninety-seven year "young" poet, Nonno, and his granddaughter, Hannah Jelkes, who has wheeled him up the steep and steamy road, are, like Shannon, *"financially* dehydrated."* Hannah, whose keen insight into character has given her portraits distinction, tries to support both of them by selling her paintings to the hotel guests. Nonno is about to finish a poem that he has been writing for twenty years. Mutual sensibilities attract Hannah and Shannon, but the lusty widow resents the intrusion of a rival.

Part of Shannon's tour problem has been Charlotte, "the teenage Medea," who forced herself upon him and afterwards was coerced to her knees to join him in prayer. Miss Fellowes, the aggressive leader, charges Shannon with rape and vows to have him fired. When Charlotte again invades his privacy to demand that he marry her, he tries to argue that "two unstable conditions" should not be united, that he loves *"nobody,"* that he does not have a dime left in his "nervous bank account."[45]

Shortly after his session with the teen-ager, Shannon appears *"like a survivor of a plane crash"* with several pieces of his clerical garb in his hands. He is followed shortly afterwards by Hannah in her artist costume, and the two of them are like *"actors in a play which is about to fold on the road."* As he displays a petulant burst of temper, she begins to sketch him and quietly to ask questions of this minister "accused of being defrocked and lying about it." Hannah, who observes that he is a very difficult subject to paint, recalls that Siquieros depicted Hart Crane with his eyes closed because there was "too much suffering in them." Shannon confesses in self-mockery how he was tempted by a young and pretty Sunday-school teacher, how kneeling to pray led to unreligious intimacies, and how he later struck her, calling her "a damned little tramp."

Scandal erupted when she faked suicide; looking "over all those smug, disapproving, accusing faces" in his congregation, he discarded his apologetic sermon. He refused to praise Western theologies that "accuse God of being a cruel, senile delinquent" who punishes His own creatures because of His own mistakes. The wealthy parishioners of this suburban church allowed Shannon to recuperate "in a nice little private asylum." He wants to return "and preach the gospel of God as Lightning and Thunder ... and also stray dogs vivisected ... and oblivious majesty" that watched the destruction and corruption of a people by the conquerors who brought the inquisition along with the cross. Hannah quietly suggests that he would probably find in that congregation a few old faces seeking something "still to believe in"; that he would throw away his angry sermon; that he would talk about "the still waters."

Hannah's strength is suggested as she prepares to sell her paintings to the Germans who are jubilant about the bombing of London and as she patiently and sweetly cares for her grandfather who can hardly see or hear and whose loud-voiced inquiries continually embarrass her. Nonno, having taken a bad fall in his room, feels certain that he is "going to finish it here," but whether he refers to his life or to his poem is ambiguous. Later, on the patio, he expects to receive a tip for the poem he recites, but the Germans abandon him for the liquor cart. When Nonno loudly asks about the "take," Hannah temporizes; and then Shannon, saying that a poem never earns its just "pecuniary rewards," places a "crumpled Mexican bill" in the old man's hand.

The alternatives for Shannon, the one-time minister, if he is fired by Blake Tours, are to "go back to the Church or take a long swim to China." He had expected to "shake the spook" at this Mexican lodge, but he did not know that the padrona had become a widow, "a sort of bright widow spider." The continual antagonism between Shannon and Mrs. Faulk erupts most noisily when he thrusts the liquor cart into her belly, and she returns it; the two grin as *"fiercely as gladiators in mortal combat,"* an exhibition that delights the shrieking Germans. It is Hannah who quietly intercedes and tells the angry widow that Shannon is trying hard not to drink. She laughs at the widow's implications that she, "a New England

spinster ... pushing forty,'' has designs on Shannon; and, in spite
of the impending storm, she vows to take her grandfather down the
hill. She recognizes not only that the perverse nature of people
makes them torture one another but also that a strain of decency
occasionally makes them want to help others as they can. As the
thunder and storm break on the hilltop, the Germans enjoy ''the
white convulsions of light'' as if it were an operatic climax; but
Shannon, calling on God to strike him dead, holds his hands into
the rain *"as if he were reaching for something outside and beyond
himself."*

In the third act, the forces conspiring to destroy Shannon
coalesce. When Maxine repeats the unsavory details of his early life
that had been related to her in confidence by her late husband, she
tells about the charges of statutory rape that would prevent his
return to the church. She proposes a questionable business arrangement, since both have reached a point where they must ''settle for
something that works.'' Shannon is also cornered when Hank, the
driver, and Jake Latta, a dubious figure assigned by Blake Tours to
take over Shannon's party, forcefully take the bus key and ignore
his requests for ''severance pay.'' Shannon in a frenzy runs down to
the bus; a noisy offstage hullabaloo of female shrieks and squeals
culminates in the report that he has urinated on the luggage. In the
general uproar that follows, the ladies rush off on the bus; the confused Shannon returns and *"with an animal outcry begins to pull at
the chain suspending the gold cross about his neck."* Hannah pre-
vents his attempt to ''swim out to China,'' but she watches in distress as the Mexican boys tie him down in the hammock. The cal-
culating widow reports that Shannon suffers a mental breakdown
regularly; that twice she has had to care for him and pay for his
medical care; and that she will again, if the ''knockout injection'' is
ineffective, have to place him in the Casa de Locos. The Germans
crowd around his captive figure as if he were ''a funny animal in a
zoo.''

Hannah talks to Shannon about his histrionic martyrdom, his
apparent enjoyment over suffering the world's guilt in a ''voluptuous kind of crucifixion.'' As she prepares a sedative for him,
poppyseed tea, he calls her ''an emancipated *Puritan,*'' a ''thin
standing up Buddha,'' who, like all women, wants to ''see a man in
a tied-up situation.'' As she hears her grandfather reciting lines, she
anticipates a difficult night for all three of them, but she rejects
Shannon's suggestion that she place hemlock in Nonno's drink as

"childishly cruel." The padrona, jealous of Hannah's ministrations for Shannon, tries to prevent her further help but is called away by the beer-guzzling Germans.

Hannah tells Shannon that his problem is not liquor but the age-old problem, "the need to believe in something or someone." Her own discovery is people's need for communication that breaks down barriers, a "little understanding exchanged," a "wanting to help each other through nights like this." She knows because she has been through the "subterranean travels," the journeys that tormented people must follow through the *"unlighted* sides of their natures." She did not become unbalanced because her work was an "occupational therapy." She learned to study human faces intently and to "catch something" in a moment before the shutters closed. As she sketched Shannon's face, she was reminded of the old and penniless in the House of Aging in Shanghai; they had been abandoned with small gifts by their families, but they had a beautiful look in their eyes, "clear as the stars on the Southern Cross." She tells how she and her grandfather have built a home — not a house, but a "thing that two people have between them." Shannon, though he has amused himself with the girls, has "always traveled alone" except for his spook. On the promise that she will tell him about her love life, he drinks a bitter sedative. Saying that there are "worse things than chastity," she tells of two pathetic experiences; one of these that he calls a "dirty little episode" is for her an insight into the possible depths of loneliness: "Nothing human disgusts me unless it's unkind, violent." When he asks whether they could not "just *travel* together," she answers that the morning would reveal that idea to be impractical. He recognizes that he may have to accede to Hannah's Oriental moral to "accept whatever situation you cannot improve" — and, in his case, he has to accept the "unconsolable widow."

During the later part of the evening, the struggle of the iguana, tied under the porch by the Mexican boys who anticipate good eating, has increasingly disturbed Hannah. In a dramatic aria Shannon reviews his life: his exposing tour ladies to the most loathesome poverty in nameless countries, his seducing one or several, but his first ravaging them with the horrors of the tropical country they were visiting. As he senses the weakening of his own mind, he envisions his inevitable dependence upon the padrona for the rest of his life. He cannot decide whether wishing for her early death is cruelty or pity. At Hannah's request, he takes a machete to free the

lizard because God does not do it. With the release of the iguana,
Nonno's voice declaims his completed poem in exultation. Hannah
successfully records it, tears streaming from her eyes: "Thank you
for writing such a lovely poem." When Maxine entices Shannon to
a drink and a moonlight swim, she again mouths her proposition
about pleasing both male and female clients — for profit. Hannah
stands alone, desolate; she is aware that her grandfather has passed
on; and she is wishing for a quiet place to stay.

Fedder thinks that Williams has dramatized the Lawrence "situation of a momentary communion of a depraved fox and an uninhibited moth." He places this "medieval saint" among the delicate
Southern women — Alma, Laura, Blanche — and calls Hannah the
strongest of Williams' spiritual figures.[46] Nancy Tischler believes
that the short story recounts the time that Williams spent in Acapulco, Mexico, when he was obsessed with the idea that he was
doomed with cancer; this compulsive dread, so evident in the for-
ties, also colors this play. In early summer 1946, Williams decided
to die in Nantucket, where he and Carson McCullers wrote at the
opposite ends of the table, she on *A Member of the Wedding,* he on
Streetcar.[47] Margaret Leighton, who played Hannah in the New
York production, said that the character, like Williams, "has a
spine of steel" and cannot be shocked.[48] Deborah Kerr, who played
Hannah in the film version, suggests the autobiographical aspects
in Hannah who almost had to prostitute herself to sell her painting
to people whom she hated.[49]

At times Williams seems to have written himself into Shannon,
the rebellious Puritan whose sense of guilt was developed early by a
stern mother and whose idea of God was not that of a kindly old
patriarch but of a destructive force in nature. At other times Williams seems to speak through Hannah who in her work and
acquaintance with the Orient has learned that the deepest religion
lies not only in the perception of another's suffering and in a
willingness to ease his pain but also in the peace that comes with the
acceptance of the inevitable. According to Williams, the Nazis
represent the Stanley Kowalskis, brute force; and the three
Blanches in this play are the minister, the spinster, and her grandfather, all three of whom are learning "how to live with dignity
after despair." To Williams, the moments of violence are "integral
to the meaning"; they are not presented for shock value. He calls
the iguana "a caught thing" which "stands for the human situation," not any particular character.[50] He also asserted that *Iguana*

was an attempt to write a play that would express the idea in "gunfire dialogue" of "how to live beyond despair and still live."[51]

Harold Clurman, who observes that confession and self-castigation are common to Puritan Romantics, thinks that *Iguana* "does give us an idea of how Williams sees and judges himself." Shannon cannot renounce preaching, he shows his clients "the foul byways of man's experience," and he indulges in his promiscuous fornication with minors.[52] Howard Taubman wrote that *Iguana* "marks a turning point [that] reaches the playwright's attitude toward life," for Williams moves away from "raging pessimism" to a kind of "tragic wisdom." No other of Williams' characters has "the heart breaking dignity and courage of Hannah Jelkes."[53] Richard Gilman thought that the play represents the best and worst of Williams as an amalgam of hard, expert realism and of "sloppy lyricism." He found the first act tedious and without direction, or Williams at his worst; the second, with its "long central anecdote," rested securely on a base of true feeling and dramatic rightness and was Williams at his best; and the last, with its sense of painful destiny, was "almost enough to compensate for ... that ephemeral debased theater" that Williams continues to offer.[54] Many critics remarked about the old Williams magic — the ability to evoke a mood and to lighten bleak stretches with flashes of humor — but many were bothered by the obsessive preoccupation with sex, or "the hairline that divides realism from pornography," or by the way that he has "spoken on stage the generally unspeakable."[55]

Considering what Williams accomplished when he rewrote *Summer and Smoke* into *Eccentricities of a Nightingale,* he could achieve a distinguished play if he discarded the extraneous elements and the melodrama in the present version of *The Night of the Iguana* and concentrated on the central image. The makings are there. Hannah Jelkes, the gentle Southern gentlewoman with a New England accent, an Oriental insight, and the courage to stand alone, is a memorable figure.

CHAPTER 4

Southern Wenches

A NOTHER group of plays concerns a type of Southern woman
— one not blighted by the outmoded proprieties of a Victorian
culture or by the bridling restrictions of a Southern Puritanism.
Each of these women seems to know instinctively that sex is the
only valid expression of life and, without having read Freud,
understands that the opposite of passion is death. Among them are
Stella Du Bois, sister of Blanche in *Streetcar* who escaped the many
dyings at Belle Rêve to marry Stanley Kowalski. Nellie Ewell in
Summer and Smoke, daughter of a good-time mother and herself a
"natural" adolescent of the same type, is paired off with Dr. John
Buchanan. In the same play, Rosa Gonzales, a Williams original
and the romantically garish daughter of the casino operator, satisfies the young doctor before he becomes "spiritual." Myra Torrance, in *Battle of Angels,* rejected by her rich suitor and tied to a
materialist dying of cancer, returns to "life" when she takes as her
lover the young vagabond, Val Xavier.

The most uninhibited of the sisterhood, except for Alma Tutwiler in the short story "The Yellow Bird," is Serafina delle Rose of
The Rose Tattoo, and her daughter, Rosa, of the same inclinations.
Maggie the Cat in *Cat on a Hot Tin Roof* is a sexually attractive
woman mated to an indifferent husband. Baby Doll Meighan of the
film play, *Baby Doll,* who is more comic than her original in *27
Wagons Full of Cotton,* presents an amusing version of the willing
but untutored wench about to be "awakened." Williams' portrayal
of these uninhibited women reveals in varying degrees his talent for
comedy; and, written between 1947 and 1956, the plays also show
his interest in creating roles for particular actresses.

I   The Rose Tattoo *(1951)*[1]

The love story in *The Rose Tattoo* is that of Serafina delle Rose, a plump and volatile woman whose uninhibited lyrics on the matrimonial bed leave no doubt that physical love is more spiritual than religion; and her teenage daughter seems to have the same conviction. The play is set in a Sicilian village on the Gulf Coast between New Orleans and Mobile; and, to highlight the mood of this domestic comedy on sex, Williams uses a number of off-stage devices, characters, and sounds: the voices and cries of children, a bleating goat, the cackle and cry of birds and fowl; gossiping neighbors; and two eccentric figures, Assunta, pedlar of aphrodisiacs, and Strega the witch, the evil omen.

Serafina, whose husband Rosario needed none of Assunta's drugs, disregards the pedlar's warning that she will soon wear a black veil; and she fails to recognize her husband's mistress, the blonde Estelle Hohengarten, who orders, as an anniversary present, a rose silk shirt made for a man "wild like a gypsy," and then steals Rosario's picture. But, when the priest a short time later leads a group of black-shawled women toward her house, Serafina knows that her husband is dead. The deeply religious widow, against the wishes of the church, orders her husband's body to be cremated and the ashes placed on the mantel near the vigil light. Pregnant, she also loses her baby boy.

Three years later, she appears like a slattern; she is dressed in a pink slip and her hair is frowsy. Nevertheless, she holds her daughter Rosa under strict discipline. In a fit of moral indignation — because the girl met a sailor at a school dance — she has locked her daughter in the house, hidden her clothes, allowed her to walk around naked — a great stimulant to neighborhood gossip. Rosa, called for by a spinsterish teacher who praises her schoolwork, is finally allowed to attend graduation exercises in her new white dress. Assunta tries to calm the comically desolate Serafina when she is hurt by Rosa's parting remark, "Mama, you look disgusting!"[2]

After a sudden reversal of her decision not to attend graduation exercises, Serafina wrestles madly with her corset and her clothes. She is delayed by Flora and Bessie, described as two female clowns, who are on their way to the American Legion Convention.[3] Their talk about men evokes the widow's contempt for American sexual relationships: "They make life without glory. Instead of the heart they got the deep-freeze in the house. The men, they don't feel no glory, not in the house with them women; they go to the bars, fight in the bars, get drunk, get fat, put horns on the women because the women won't give them the love with its glory. To me the big bed was beautiful like a religion. Now I lie in it with dreams, with memories only!'' The two grotesques jeer at the widow for being a "female ostrich" and imply that her husband was not faithful. Struck senseless, she calls them liars and attacks them with a broom. Alone, she turns to the Madonna image, *"Oh, Lady! Give me a sign!"* (Sc. 5)

When Rosa returns home with Jack, the brother of a girl in the graduating class and a decent boy, Serafina suspects any sailor with a ring in his ear, his memento for having crossed the equator. He is caught between the girl's aggressive advances, and the widow's probing questions and her demands that he respect the innocence of the girl. When the heavily chaperoned young people leave for the picnic, Serafina, suspecting a fate for her daughter worse than death, turns again to the Madonna and asks for a sign. A series of scenes that coincide with the school picnic introduces to the widow a twenty-five year old truck driver with the body of her Rosario but with the face of a clown and with kewpie-doll ears. The emotional widow with strong notions of morality and the clumsy newcomer, Alvaro Mangiacavallo, or Alvaro Eat-a-Horse, gradually edge toward intimacy like two grown children. The scenes are like a parody of the moving love scenes that Williams had already created, and they illustrate a favorite proposition — that physical love is life's supreme gift.

Alvaro enters in a fury to accost the salesman who pushed him off the road and who is a seedy representative of the business world; this cheap pedlar offers the widow a gadget that blows up in her face. This salesman, whose entrance was marked by satiric music, calls the Italian names like "macaroni" and "greaseball," threatens to have him fired, knees him in the groin, and leaves him bawling with pain. The widow soon joins the cry in sympathy. He tells her his sad story of three dependents, an old-maid sister, a feeble-minded grandmother, and "one lush of a pop," all of whom play parchesi all day but also play the numbers. As Serafina and Alvaro grow warm and voluble over a bottle of wine, she talks about her late husband and about the rose that appeared on her breast when she conceived. He tells his dream of meeting an older, sensible lady with a "well-furnished house and a profitable little business of some kind" who will give him "love and affection — in a world that is lonely — and cold!" She becomes testy about expenses when he calls his boss long distance — to learn that he has been fired. When she gives him the rose shirt never claimed, he says it is too good for "the grandson of a villiage idiot."

During this first courtship scene, a goat breaks loose; and it undoubtedly symbolizes the increasing compulsion in the relationship. Alvaro joins the chase; a little boy beats two tin lids together; the wild cries of children mingle with the goat's bleating; and Serafina, like an animal in heat, standing halfway between the shutters and the Madonna, furiously imitates the bleating goat, her face distorted with desire. As the truck driver is about to leave, she tells him, if there is a light in the window, he can return for his jacket, which she will mend. If the shutters are closed, Rosa is home; a mother must set a good example for daughter.

The middle-aged lovers make careful preparations for the rendezvous. A very tightly dressed Serafina waits for Alvaro, as she had earlier waited for Rosario; but, uncomfortably restricted, she is almost caught shedding her corset. Alvaro, shaved and scented by the "ideal barber" and dressed in the suit bought for his wedding four years previously (when he was rejected because the diamond was a zircon), enters with a box of four-year old chocolates. He is proud of the newly acquired rose tattoo on his breast. In his clumsy role as suitor, he inadvertently drops an unmistakable disc in celophane on the floor; and Serafina orders him to go to the Square Roof, the local brothel. He pursues his lady, says his sister wants nephews and nieces, and makes a chance remark about Estelle at the establishment that rouses in the widow the old urge for revenge. With a knife sticking out of her purse, she is about to leave when a telephone call, the answering voice apparently audible to the upper balcony, confirms the rumors that Rosario was not faithful. Angrily, the widow hurls the sacred urn to the floor and scatters Rosario's ashes; she tells Alvaro to leave by the front door, to say loud goodbyes to fool the neighbors, and to return by the back door. Alvaro returns as directed; and the two retreat to the sofa for intimate conversation.

About daybreak, Rosa returns from the school picnic with her sailor boy and pleads with him to seduce her. Jack must fight not only his own urgency and her insistence, but he must keep his promise to Rosa's mother. When Rosa pleads that "it could just happen once" but, if delayed, never, the crow of a rooster echoes agreement. As they face each other sadly, she insists that, even as young as they are, they can "understand how it works out." The first love would be something to remember, be so much better than

the times that come afterward. Against this scene is played the one
in the house with Serafina's long sighs and a long-drawn cry,
"Ohhh — Rosario." To Rosa, unaware of developments when she
was at the high school picnic, her mother is dreaming about her
father and is making love in her sleep; and she asks curtly, "Is that
what she wants me to do, just — *dream* about it?"

Early the next morning, when a drunken, frowsy Alvaro discovers Rosa sleeping on the couch, he murmurs, "Che bella!" —
and the sound is echoed by the "baaa" of the goat outside. Alvaro
drains the Spumanti, leaps on top of the girl, and wakens her. Her
screams alert her disheveled mother, who yells at Alvaro as if he
were an intruder and who orders him from the house. Her comic
pretense does not fool her daughter; indeed, her voluble and sheep-
ish explanations evoke the girl's sharp rebuke: "The only thing
worse than a liar is a liar that's also a hypocrite!" The play ends
with Serafina's discovery of a rose on her breast and with the
happy, pregnant woman being rejoined by her lover, who sneaks
back into the house. Suitcase in hand, Rosa, no longer restrained,
supposedly joins her own lover.

In the preface, "The Timeless World of a Play," Williams elaborates upon the generally accepted idea that art in any form captures
and makes significant an action, an emotion, or a mood "in a
world *outside* of time." He pleads for greater understanding and
for a recognition of the intensity of our own feelings. He indicates
his sensitivity to negative criticism about his work when he concludes by comparing the "world not ravaged by time," the performance of a play, with the nervousness of the dramatist who is waiting for the opening night's reviews and who learns at three in the
morning about his disgrace.[4] George Jean Nathan objected to this
"pseudo-learned treatise" which "seeks to justify his alley-cat stuff
and indeed make it a cosmic epic."[5]

The play reveals Williams' genuine talent for folk comedy which
resulted from his experience in Italy and from his affection for the
Sicilians. The world of the play is robust and healthy, and even the
clerics become part of the joke. One critic suggested that this was a
comic version of *Orpheus Descending;* others disliked the excessive
use of symbols, particularly roses; one discovered several variations
of the phallic symbol.[6] Walter Kerr rightly deplored the conclusion
to *The Rose Tattoo:* it "winds up by junking a character complexity
that has fascinated us all evening in favor of a simple sexual gesture, a gesture that is totally inadequate to the needs of the play."

He finds the first two acts exhilarating and the second act the author's funniest; but the third indicates that the audience knows Serafina better than her creator whose sentimentality about sex leads him into curious locutions about "getting them colored lights going." Even so, Kerr prefers two good acts to the "dead heads" that populate tidier plays.[7]

Henry Hewes thought the 1966 revival more effective than the original because the affectations so dear to the playwright had been minimized. He pointed out what a director can do with a script when he reported that Milton Katselas "emphasizes the grotesquerie" so that the audience laughed at "the ridiculousness of the events" at the same time that it recognized the involvement of the characters. Everything seemed comically ironic: the priest is shocked by finding that primitive people "find God in each other"; Serafina's lust stands beside the symbols of purity; and, simultaneously with her being "restored," she berates the Madonna. Hewes calls this situation a "hilariously earthy" comedy.[8]

II Cat on a Hot Tin Roof *(1955)*[9]

Cat on a Hot Tin Roof was derived by Williams from his short story, "Three Players of a Summer Game," which in turn recalls the weak husband–strong wife motif of *Women in Love* by D. H. Lawrence. Williams' story portrays the deterioration of a young aristocrat because of some mysterious disgust, his brief attraction to a Southern widow, and his passive return to a dominating wife. The play, set in the mansion of a Southern plantation, assembles the immediate family to celebrate the sixty-fifth birthday of Big Daddy, who is not only very ill but also very wealthy and intestate. This study of family rivalries and tensions is dramatized in a series of arguments, some of which lead to the exposure of the delusion or of the lie that has sustained one of them.

The action, concentrated during the birthday evening, takes place in the bedroom of Brick, the younger son, and his wife, Margaret. Two pieces of furniture dominate the room: the big double bed and a monstrous television-radio-liquor cabinet. The tension between the young husband and wife is immediately apparent in his indifferent answers to her voluble account of the birthday dinner — her sharp description of the older son Gooper; of Mae, his wife; of their five "no-neck monsters" (another is on the way) — and in her repeated jibe that they themselves have no children. She is sure that the Goopers plan to control the estate after Big Daddy has died and that they will send Brick to Rainbow Hill, a sanitarium for alcoholics.

Brick, on crutches from a broken ankle sustained when trying to jump a hurdle at two o'clock that morning, combines laconic answers with trips to the liquor cabinet. His wife's certainty that Big Daddy finds her sexually attractive, her acid account of the children's performances at the table, and her comments about Mae's social pretensions are cut short when she catches in the mirror Brick's expression of contempt. She freezes, admits that she has become hard, but reveals her hurt when she says, "Living with someone you love can be lonelier — than living entirely *alone*."[10] She wonders what has happened between them; he, who had been so wonderful a lover, now has "that detached quality" of a player indifferent to win or loss, who wears "the charm of the defeated."

When she mentions Skipper, Brick's football buddy, she touches a forbidden subject; but she adds that ignoring a sore spot only makes it fester and grow malignant. Brick gets another drink. They are momentarily interrupted by Big Mama, who is jubilant about the good medical report given Big Daddy and who grills Margaret about not having children, about whether she makes Brick happy in bed, and about why he drinks. She places the blame entirely on the young wife. Maggie admires Big Daddy; she loves her indifferent husband; but, having known poverty as a child, she also fears age without money. She will not leave Brick, nor will she take a lover; she is determined to beat the Goopers at their own game; she wonders about the victory of a "cat on a hot tin roof."

Though Brick threatens to strike Maggie if she again mentions Skipper, she finishes the story. She confesses that she and Skipper made love, and that each one was dreaming of making love with Brick. She tries to assure her husband that she understands his homosexual relationship, one beautiful in Greek legends but unmentionable in their own time. With Skipper dead, life must continue, even though "the *dream* of life" has ended. When Brick accuses her of considering his true friendship to have been dirty, she insists that only Skipper harbored something "not perfectly pure," that, when she asked him to stop loving her husband, or to admit his love openly, he struck her on the mouth. She believes the truth destroyed Skipper, for he had turned after that conversation to drugs and liquor. When Brick tries to hit her, she says that she may not be moral but that she is honest, that Skipper is dead, and

that Maggie the cat is very much alive. The scene closes when one
of the Goopers' children runs into the room and accuses her of jeal-
ousy because she can not have babies.

In the second act, Big Daddy tries, as he had tried before, to have
a real talk with his son Brick. When the dinner guests assemble in
the bedroom, the Reverend Tooker talks about expensive memorial
gifts in his church; Mae, in exaggerated Southern dialect discusses
her obnoxious offspring; fat Big Mama, laden with flashy jewels
worth half a million, is given to "inelegant horseplay" and loud
laughter; Margaret and Mae spitefully carp at each other. When
Big Daddy is angered by Big Mama, he accuses her of trying to
assume control of his estate because she thought he was dying of
cancer. He recalls his boyhood: how he quit school at ten; how he
worked "like a nigger" in the fields; how he rose to be overseer of
the Straw and Ochello plantation; and how, after these homosexuals died, he increased the holdings over and over, all by
himself. When Big Mama pleads that, in spite of the abuse and the
humiliation she has endured these years, she has loved him, he says
to himself, *"Wouldn't it be funny if that was true. . . . "*

Finally alone, the older man wonders why Maggie, who has a
better figure, has the same look as Mae. The son answers that each,
hoping "to knock off" a bigger piece of the estate, is scratching out
the other's eyes. Big Daddy says he is going to move Gooper and
Mae into another room so that they will not be snooping and
reporting that Brick sleeps on the sofa. He wants to know why his
son has quit broadcasting, but he soon launches into a discussion of
Big Mama's wild buying on a Cook's Tour, and of his own ten million in cash and blue chips in addition to the "twenty-eight thousand acres of the richest land this side of the valley Nile!" But,
despite his wealth, a man "can't buy his life" when it is finished.
He speaks about the starvation he saw on his trip to Africa, about
the money he gave howling children as "you'd scatter feed corn for
chickens," about the prostitution in North Africa, and about a
child barely able to walk who had toddled over and had tried to
unbutton his trousers. He observes that man, even at the point of
dying, is a beast without pity. The indifferent Brick, making another trip toward Echo Springs, his whiskey, says that this is only
another father-son talk that gets nowhere. Big Daddy, reprieved
from death, looks forward to enough pleasure with women to make
up for his forty years of distaste for Big Mama. Since Brick only
wants the oblivion that will bring peace, he is puzzled that his

father is not ready to die.

Big Daddy vows to straighten out his son, an alcoholic; and he asks repeatedly why he drinks, why he throws his life away. Brick, who says he drinks out of disgust, then admits as an after thought that he does so because of mendacity, which is to his father only a five-dollar word for lies and liars. The older man guffaws, recalling the liars and lies he has had to live with — Big Mama; Gooper, Mae, and their five "screechers"; clubs, lodges, and the like. He does not want to leave the estate to the Gooper lot, whom he hates, but he doubts that he should subsidize his son's bottle. As Brick is about to leave, his father says "something was left not spoken, something avoided" because they have not been honest with each other. When Brick says that he turned to drink because time outran him and because he could no longer broadcast games, his father says that his son is using language that is "ninety-proof bull" and that he is not accepting his son's views.

Big Daddy touches a sore spot when he recalls that Brick started drinking when Skipper died, that Gooper and Mae had suggested that there was something not exactly normal about the relationship. Brick grows violent over the innuendo that he is "a queer," that he and Skipper had committed sodomy, even though Big Daddy tries to explain his own considerable experience and sympathy. Brick recounts the general disgust "about things like that" and the cruelty leveled against those suspected. He insists that he and Skipper had a clean and rare friendship until Maggie suspected a dirty relationship. When Big Daddy again asks why Skipper cracked up, Brick announces that they are really into the talk and that it is too late to stop. Brick relates how Maggie had said the friends had gone into pro-football because they were afraid to grow up; how she had insisted on the marriage and had joined them on the road; how she had managed their celebrations even in defeat; how she had all the time been a jealous intruder in a close friendship. She destroyed Skipper, he says, by implanting "the dirty, false idea" and by proving him to be a failure when in bed with her. After that he "broke in two like a rotten stick." Big Daddy, not satisfied with "that half-ass story," tells Brick that he is only passing the buck; that the disgust Brick feels over mendacity is only disgust with himself because he had dug a grave for his friend and had kicked him into it. When Big Daddy accuses his son of not being able to face the truth, Brick asks in spiteful revenge, *"How about these birthday congratulations, those many many happy returns of the day when ev'rybody but you knows there won't be any!''*

Big Daddy, stunned by this retort and demanding a repetition, hears his son casually tell him to leave the place to the Gooper clan. When his father realizes that he has been given a false report, that he is, in truth, dying of cancer, Brick says, "Mendacity is the system we live in. Liquor is one way out an' death is the other." He does not understand Big Daddy's distress because Brick can not understand why anyone cares whether he lives or dies. The two men, he thinks, have been friends because they were "telling each other the truth." As the scene closes, Big Daddy, in a howling rage, damns all lying sons of bitches.

In the third act, which brings to a climax the rivalry for the estate, all the adult members of the dinner party are assembled except for Big Daddy. Brick stands aside, still waiting for the numbing click. The family doctor has been delegated to tell Big Mama the awful news about Big Daddy's cancer; and, when the truth begins to sink in, she calls for Brick, "her only son." In this family crisis, the preacher slinks away; and the doctor, leaving the morphine soon to be needed, also leaves. The rivalry between Margaret and Mae intensifies. Big Mama pleads with Maggie to help them curb Brick's drinking; Mae and Gooper react violently to the implied threat against their share in the estate; Maggie rises to the defense of her husband against the charges of the older brother; and Gooper, having endured a lifelong resentment against the favored Brick, says he has always been treated as "barely good enough to spit on."

Gooper, reminding the family that he is a corporation lawyer and not merely a football player, takes from his brief case his plan, a sort of dummy trusteeship, to take care of the estate. After Big Mama orders him to put away his papers before she tears them up, she pleads for family unity, and asks Brick for a grandson. When Margaret shocks the assembled gathering with the announcement that she's with child, Big Mama rushes out to tell Big Daddy; but his long-drawn-out cry of agony and rage indicates that she will soon have to use the hated needle. When Mae calls Maggie a liar, she is taken away by Gooper, and long cries of agony are heard again. The scene closes with Maggie hiding Brick's liquor and promising its return when he makes her lie come true. She calls him one of those "weak, beautiful people" who need someone to take hold of them "gently, with love." As the curtain slowly falls, she says, "I *do* love you, Brick, I *do!*" Brick, as did his father to his mother earlier in the evening, answers with *"charming sadness";* and, according to his creator, says, "Wouldn't it be funny if that was true?"⁹

Elia Kazan, the director, had a number of reservations about the third act: he felt that Big Daddy was too important a character not to reappear; that Brick should indicate some change after his father's exposé; and that Margaret should be made a more sympathetic character. Williams, who had fallen in love with his own Maggie, could agree to that suggestion; but he did not want Big Daddy to overshadow Brick.¹² "I didn't want Big Daddy to reappear in Act Three and I felt that the moral paralysis of Brick was a root thing to his tragedy."¹³

There are only minor changes in the Broadway version of Act III.¹⁴ When asked why Big Daddy shouted "liars," Brick answers that he did not lie to his father but only to himself and that perhaps he should be taken to an asylum for alcoholics. Gooper and Mae become more despicable in their squabbling over the estate. When the interruptions of the Gooper monsters are increased, "rhubarb" is substituted for drama. Big Daddy enters to tell an old story about a female elephant in heat with an excited male nearby, a story enhanced by his own enjoyment in telling it. Maggie announces her pregnancy as a birthday present to Big Daddy. When the row over that lie breaks out, Brick rises to her defense and expresses admiration for her; and the only positive stand he takes in the play is defense of a lie. Her last speech is an even more romantic eulogy to what she — or Williams — calls "beautiful weakness."

In Maggie and in Big Daddy, and to a degree in Big Mama, Tennessee Williams has added distinctive characters to the American theater; but all the "mystery" does not quite explain the young wife's admiration for Brick. His glorified weakness makes him a passive observer of the power struggle; but, when, in childish spite, he tells his father that he is doomed, his truth telling is hardly noble. Whether Williams was protecting himself against the guardians of public taste in his murky handling of homosexuality, or whether he was tempting public interest, he was writing about a personal problem.

Brooks Atkinson observed that "the drama is thoroughly subjective on the part of Mr. Williams; it is also subjective on the part of the characters."¹⁵ The perceptive reviewer in *Time* commented about the revelations that spill out during the family scenes, — about much talk but no settlement on the central issues, and about whether the play concerns marriage, family, or a man. "And if it means to be a complex of all three, it needs sharper form, greater unity, a sense of something far more deeply interfused." There are too many "theatrical trap doors ... too much explodes, too little uncoils; much more is highlighted than truly plumbed."[10] Marya Mannes, a voice of sanity about a sometimes unhealthy theater, said of the theatrical magic in *Cat:* "It is a shock treatment, administered by an artist of great talent and painful sensibility who illumines fragments but never the whole. He illumines, if you will, that present sickness, which *is* fragmentary."[17]

The question whether or not Brick is homosexual was much discussed. Walter Kerr wrote about the playwright's reluctance to let the play "blurt out its promised secret." In the "fiery scene of open confession ... the truth still dodges around verbal corners" and "refuses to meet us on firm, clear terms."[18] In an interview, Williams suggested that Brick was definitely not homosexual but that he might have tendencies not quite normal.[19] About the 1974 revival, the astute Harold Clurman felt that *Cat* remains centrally ambiguous because Williams still clouded the issue of homosexuality. Brick, rather than Maggie or Big Daddy, evades the subject out of disgust; and his evasion and his social hypocrisy damage the play.[20] Robert Hatch quietly voiced an old-fashioned complaint about a disagreeable evening spent with corpses: "Sex and death and money preoccupy Williams' characters; in the face of death, the sex is regulated to get money." He was unable to care what happened: "Let them die, let them breed, let them grow fat on the wealth — it is none of my business and I don't have to watch."[21]

Although Catharine Hughes called *Cat* one of Williams' "most highly theatrical plays," it was not to be so highly esteemed as when first produced. She thought too many things were still kept in the air at one time: Big Daddy's late discovery of how much he dislikes his wife; Brick's guilt-ridden refusal to admit the basis of his friendship with Skipper; Maggie's motives, whether craving for wealth or for Brick.[22] Brenden Gill, who called the revival "a rousing melodrama" in the nineteenth century tradition (one that roars "in the glory of Southern fustian"), commented on the irony of Maggie: she seems to champion good manners and good breeding, but she wants to be accepted by a coarse, grasping family that lacks the proper social background.[23]

To Stanley Kauffmann *Cat* lies in the mainstream of Williams' plays with its familiar themes about the continuity of the past and the changes in American values. He shrewdly observed that the focus of the play is not Brick's problem but Maggie's struggle. Unfortunately, she is shunted into the background for most of the second and third acts; but she should be in the forefront of the conflict. Other critics agreed with Kauffmann that Maggie represents a healthy new element, one with more fibre than Stella and one with a greater sense of reality than Rosa Gonzales. Kauffmann feels that the homosexual theme — both in the plantation begun by two men and in Brick's secret — dates the play because by the 1970s that theme is common to theater.[24]

Theoretically, *Cat* should be a museum piece two decades after it roused so much controversy, but its revivals continue.[25] Homosexuality has become not only a civil liberty but such a dead subject for the theater that the elephant story that had to be deleted from the revised third act in 1955 received an enormous laugh at a 1973 revival.[26] Williams told Rip Torn, the understudy for Brick and the husband of Geraldine Page, that *Cat* dramatized his own relationship with his father and that the dirty joke was the bond between Brick and Big Daddy.[27] Williams himself does not have "that detached quality" he gave to Brick, who is indifferent to either a win or a loss. When Audrey Wood and her husband, Mr. Liebling, left the performance of *Cat* by a side door, the unpredictable playwright fumed, "Rats! Rats! Leaving a sinking ship."[28] And again, when someone praised *Cat,* which won two major awards, Williams blurted, "The hell with the prizes. I wrote *Cat* for the money."[29]

III   Baby Doll *(1956)*[30]

For the film script of *Baby Doll,* Tennessee Williams himself adapted his two one-act plays, *27 Wagons Full of Cotton* and *The Long Stay Cut Short,* or *The Unsatisfactory Supper,* both of which portray whites in Mississippi. The heavy, rather stupid Baby Doll becomes in the film a curvaceous blond who is stronger in sex appeal than in intellect, one enlightened by a fourth-grade education. Archie Lee Meighan, her husband, like his predecessors in the plays, is a heavy-drinking, not too bright, older man who hates Negroes and "Wops." Shiftless in his work habits, he lives precariously on credit and installment buying; and he would like to banish to the poor house Auntie Rose Comfort, the eighty-year old lady who has outstayed her welcome with all her relatives. Silva

Vacarro, a foreigner in hostile territory, has for a year run a successful cotton mill. Contributing to the local scene are a number of caricatures: an old-line politician, a marshall hardly on the side of the law, and a mob of local drunks who enjoy seeing the Syndicate mill destroyed by flames.

After a few brief scenes that illustrate the low-mindedness of Southern businessmen and officers of the law and which imply that Archie set Vacarro's mill on fire, the script turns to its real business: the sex play between Baby Doll, who has locked her husband out of her room because she is not ready for marriage, and the virile Italian. In one of the longest scenes of the film, Williams writes a variation on his old seduction routine but does so without the brutality so obvious in *27 Wagons.* In *Baby Doll,* the injured Vacarro practices with considerable humor the good-neighbor policy — or, as he calls it, tit for tat — on the susceptible, willing wife. He works up expectation on the girl's part and curiosity on the part of the audience. Williams resorts again to the comic pursuit of the female by the male, the old "rhubarb"; when the situation wears thin and the dialogue drags, Vacarro chases Baby Doll into the attic amid the rotten floor boards and falling plaster. Out of this "action" comes the revelation of the pursuer's honorable intentions: he is not after Baby Doll's virtue but her husband's dishonor, or proof that he was the arsonist. Having retreated to the far corner of the attic to protect her virtue, she signs a statement incriminating her husband; Vacarro had pinned the paper to the end of a twelve-foot pole and pointed it toward her. He looks at her signature *"and throws back his head in a sudden wild laugh."* When she follows him out of the attic and learns that he is about to leave, she asks, "Was *that* all you wanted. . .?"[31]

The two, alone for most of the day, have found a kind of compatibility. The adventure seems to have been a major experience for Baby Doll; she suddenly grows up, becomes articulate, and is sexually awakened by the Italian. In the wild, melodramatic denouement, the sweaty husband, drunk and hysterical, shoots Auntie Rose and is taken off by the police; and the "shy children," natural mates, are free to go off to celebrate Baby Doll's readiness for marriage.

The sexual theme predominates, but the farcical treatment is broader than that in *The Rose Tattoo.* Adapting the hard-hitting one-act plays to a more conservative medium, the film, Williams has compensated for the strictures imposed by making innuendos in some of the lines and by creating preposterous situations. At times the script approaches the broad folk humor of the *commedia dell' arte;* at other times, there are satiric jibes at man's beastliness; at others, unexpected philosophical comments.

Meighan, a grotesque of a Southern business man, is brutal in his treatment of his wife and in his attempt to get rid of his old aunt; he is mean in his charge to Vacarro to "pay special" to have his cotton ginned and in his treatment of Negro help. This old husband, denied his marital "rights," counts the hours until his wife is "ready for marriage"; and his urgency is obvious. Wolf whistles from the laborers whenever his curvacious wife appears add to his helpless frenzy. Baby Doll is not the bruised and ravished victim of the earlier version, but a healthy young animal able to distinguish a friend from an enemy. It is she who reports her husband.

The Vacarro character, more complex than in the short play, is the abused foreigner cheated of his property and determined to see justice done. As one of Williams' Latin lovers, he is soft spoken and well practiced in the arts of seduction, is something of a philosopher, and is sympathetic to the underdog when he invites the ancient Rose to be his cook when Archie orders her out of the house. Baby Doll thinks their house has ghosts, but Silva is concerned about "evil spirits that haunt the human heart and take possession of it." To him, spirits like violence, malevolence, treachery, and destruction spread from one human heart to another like fire. He recalls the faces of the men who looked down on him after he was dragged from the flames — grinning faces.

There are a number of amusing situations and lines. Baby Doll will be ready for love when the furniture is returned. Archie, sent on a fool's errand for a machine part, is denied credit at a Memphis store; and, when he returns, he finds the mill in operation because Vacarro's man replaced the faulty part. When Vacarro lies curled up in the crib, Baby Doll is on her knees before him. When Archie, frustrated and cornered but not yet aware of it, boasts about his "respected position" and accuses Vacarro of seducing his wife, Silva, "not revengeful," admits to a "certain attraction" and recalls a nap taken upstairs, the girl's lullaby, and the cool touch of her fingers, a Williams' cliché from *You Touched Me!*

The film was shot at Benoit, Mississippi, and Elia Kazan, who directed, used many of the townspeople as actors; the softened ending seems to have been his work. The opening in New York precipitated a censorship fight when the National League of Decency

(Roman Catholic) objected: "The subject matter of this film is morally repellent both in theme and treatment. It dwells almost without variation or relief upon carnal suggestiveness in action, dialogue, and costuming."[32] Elia Kazan said that he was trying to catch his feeling about the South: "Not the way things should be, not the way they will some day be, but the way they appeared to me there and then. I wasn't trying to be moral or immoral, only truthful."[33] Williams was apparently mystified that the critics should call the film "one of the most unhealthy and amoral pictures ever made in America." He thought it a funny story.[34]

Gerald Weales, who recognizes the unusual talent for comedy in America's most publicized playwright, called Archie Lee one of Williams' "grand grotesques," a comic figure as horrifying as he is funny; and he suggests that he is the kind of character that the playwright should develop further as a "valid reaction to the world as he sees it."[35]

CHAPTER 5

The Desperate Heroes

T HE freedom of an "unattached and nomadic existence" stimulated the imagination of Tennessee Williams from the beginning, for his protagonist who lives uncommitted to the mores of conventional America stands alone above the average, money-mad, sex-starved, and unhappy jobholder. He walks by himself, a lonely misfit in an artificial society; and he is usually the victim of stereotyped figures who represent Business, the Law, the Church, or Goodness that masquerades as gossiping housewives and their addlepated husbands. This loner often asks the "big questions," is something of a poet, is usually described as "good looking" or "very good looking," and is gifted with a highly charged sexual magnetism. He may be the Defeated, the Derelict, the Lonely Misfit, the Outsider, the Rejected, or the Lonesome One — if he sleeps alone. He is usually "trapped by circumstance" to live in an industrialized society or in a small-town hell where mediocrity and bigotry destroy any sign of originality and humanity.

The type appeared frequently in the short stories and one-act plays. Homer Stallcup, the shy awkward poet in "The Field of Blue Children" (*One Arm*), is rejected in favor of a steady provider. The diffident college boy in "The Important Thing" (*One Arm*) fortifies himself with a quart of wine before he approaches his girl. Itinerants and sensitive men are key figures in "The Angel in the Alcove," "The Poet," and the "baby-faced killer" in "One Arm" (all three stories in *One Arm*). The discarded mill hand in "The Malediction" (*One Arm*) and in the dramatized version, *The Strangest Kind of Romance (27 Wagons)* or timid little Anthony Burns, who is methodically devoured by the black masseur, both belong to the group. Joe, the young writer in *The Long Goodbye (27 Wagons)*; the ardent speechmaker in *The Lady of Larkspur Lotion (27 Wagons)*; and the Northern woodsman of *Moony's Kid Don't Cry (American Blues)* also represent the rebellion against

92

time cards and shiny pants.

These romantic and itinerant primitives may derive from Williams' admiration of D. H. Lawrence or from some facet of his own character. Although Rosalio in *The Purification (27 Wagons)* is an early experimental creation of this type, Val Xavier of *Battle of Angels,* the first full-dress characterization, is an important figure for those interested in the personal story of Tennessee Williams. He reappears, older and more cynical, in the many times revised version, *Orpheus Descending,* and in the renamed film version, *Fugitive Kind.* All of these heroes, in spite of their independent way of life during the search for the "big answer," retain a kind of purity because of their art. Among others are Tom Wingfield in *The Glass Menagerie;* the poet-dreamer-escapist Kilroy of the short play *Ten Blocks on Camino Real (American Blues),* who reappears in *Camino Real;* Brick Pollitt of the short story "Three Players of a Summer Game" (*Hard Candy*) and the same character in *Cat.* The desperate husbands in *Period of Adjustment* grow restive on a routine job, but one of them does about a passionate wife.

All of these men who bear "the charm of the defeated" are contrasted to the radiant primitives like Hadrian, the charity boy in *You Touched Me!;* Stanley Kowalski in *A Streetcar Named Desire;* Alvaro Eat-a-Horse of *The Rose Tattoo;* or the young medic, John Buchanan, of *Summer and Smoke.* The itinerant-poet type, who is a failure in a materialistic world, is always suffused with the playwright's sympathy and at times, created with his sentimentality.

I   Camino Real *(1953)*[1]

When Tennessee Williams reworked the short play *Ten Blocks* into *Camino Real,* he deepened the symbolic meaning of his main character, Kilroy, whom he made two years older; and he also attempted to give universal significance to the experiences of this lonely misfit trapped in a Surrealistic world of decadence. He widened the suggested area of the plaza; developed a "Terra Incognita" out of the rather indefinite "Way Out"; and extended the action to the apron of the stage, to the balconies, and to the aisles of the theater. He made of the longer version a play within a play, for his incorrigible Don Quixote, the lonely Romantic, is seeking a soulmate.

Williams' prefatory quotation from Dante's *Inferno,* Canto I "In the middle of the journey of our life I came to myself in a dark wood where the straight way was lost,'' implies that Camino Real is his own version of hell. He has imitated Dante by using historical and literary figures as symbols, but he has replaced the Italian's vivid imagery describing man's sins and his rich allegorical meanings with light and sound effects, with fever-pitched scenes, or with noisy action.

Camino Real is a kind of grand avenue that has deteriorated; a desolate world, it is meant to symbolize the worst in a contemporary society in which the power of money destroys human qualities like sincerity, love, or kindness. The rich, who suffer from fatigue and boredom, furtively ask questions, as if they were fingering pornographic postcards. A poor man asking for a drink is shot by the guards. Death, symbolized by busy and giggling Street-cleaners, is treated with indifference or cynicism. There is no compassion on Camino Real; the word "brother" is forbidden, and wild birds have been tamed and put into cages.

The plaza of Camino Real, "the royal way," or "the way of life," seems to suggest any romantically decadent seaport from Tangier to Shanghai. The luxury side on the left is represented by an elegant hotel, Siete Mares; and its proprietor Gutman is a caricature of a businessman. This symbol of money and brutality views people as thieves, prostitutes, mendicants, and deadbeats; and he considers the use of the word *Hermano* a signal for riot. With the help of his stooges, he annihilates any sign of independence as an intolerable spirit of anarchy. The Skid Row on the right is represented by the Gypsy's stall, the Loan Shark's establishment, and a fleabag hotel known as "Ritz Men Only." Typical of the operators on this side are A. Ratt; Gypsy, a madame; her daughter Esmeralda; the son and brother Abdullah, and Loan Shark. At the back of the plaza, a flight of stairs mounts an ancient wall to "Terra Incognita," a wasteland between the town and the snow-capped mountains in the distance. In the center of the stage is a dry fountain.

What happens in this modern inferno is supposed to be the dream of that arch-Romantic, Don Quixote, who wears a piece of faded blue ribbon to remind himself of distances gone and of those yet to go, of the green country, and of the spirit in his heart that responds to such words as "truth," "valor," and "devoir," terms weighted by the author's capital letters and exclamation points. When Sancho deserts him, Quixote, sensing the loneliness of the plaza, speaks the line that Williams calls a key to the play: "When so many are lonely as seem to be lonely, it would be inexcusably selfish to be lonely alone."[2] When Quixote lies down to sleep and to dream, he expects to derive new meanings or to recall old ones from the pageant that he envisions.

Gutman announces each one of the sixteen short scenes and thus manipulates the changes, as does the stage manager in Thornton Wilder's *Our Town*. A number of minor characters, abused by the henchmen or swept up by the Streetcleaners, suggest the prevailing and dismal way of life on this plaza. Those characters whose stories are more elaborately related are either historical or literary figures or Kilroy, the synthetic, ubiquitous American. One minor figure is Baron de Charlus, an old fop and homosexual masochist from Proust's *Remembrance of Things Past* who is trailed by Lobo, an exotically beautiful young man. Admitting that he wants to be followed, he says that he escapes the sordid world through homosexuality. Shortly afterwards he is strangled, not for his "sins" but for his lack of money.

One Romantic, Lord Byron, the strongest exponent of freedom, bears some relation to Williams himself. Speaking directly to the audience about listening to the "pure stringed instrument" of his heart, Byron says that at one time he had done just that — before "vulgar plaudits" deadened his hearing. To what degree he is speaking for the playwright is not clear; but Byron does admit, as if for both of them, that fame and fortune alleviated the frightening loneliness of the poet's lot. As if blaming the public for the kind of writing he did during this lush period, Byron-Williams says, *"There is a passion for declivity in this world."* He then describes with shocking particularity the burning of Shelley's corpse: the bursting of the skull, the splitting open of the body, and Trelawney's snatching the heart, a curiously morbid description inserted for shock effect. This brave Romantic has the courage to launch into the unknown in search of "the old pure music." He urges others, *"Make voyages! Attempt them! —* there's nothing else...."

Another Romantic, Jacques Casanova, who is described as a tall, courtly gentleman in his middle years, is denied entrance at the Siete Mares because of his many unpaid bills. In spite of his poverty and the pressures upon him to conform, he retains his pride. He would rather give his snuff box to a beggar than accept the Loan Shark's measly pledge. He is devoted to Marguerite Gautier (the heroine of Dumas' *La Dame aux Camelias*,)[3] who is a drug addict and an escapee from a sanitarium, but is still a beautiful woman in spite of her advancing years. She used to be paid for the pleasure she gave, but she must now pay for the "love" that hopefully will retard her aging. When the plane, Fugitavo, arrives unannounced, Marguerite desperately tries to leave, quarrels with Jacques, who has withheld the necessary papers, but in the tumultuous scramble is left behind. Both enviously watch as Byron departs. She is touched that Jacques remains devoted in spite of her abuse and neglect; he answers that she had taught him that a part of love is tenderness. She says that love is only becoming used to one another — "a pair of hawks caught in the same cage." For all their mutual injuries, they cling together "for some dim-communal comfort." Even though he tries to assure her that she must believe that violets can break the rocks, she tosses her "cobochon sapphire" to a young lover with the hope that he will make her forget that she missed the plane, Fugitavo.

In a noisy scene, Jacques is crowned King of Cuckolds and is befriended by the other Romantic, Kilroy; but Marguerite is stripped of her finery and most of her clothes by the youth she had tempted. Gutman, refusing to accept any more promises about remittances or to listen to Jacques' plea, which the playwright feels is particularly significant — "Careful, I have — fragile — mementoes..."⁵ — pitches the lover's portmanteau over the balcony. A. Ratt immediately offers the cuckolded lover a bed at "Ritz Men Only." As the play closes, Marguerite pays the bills Jacques has accumulated, and they are rejoined as mournful lovers. Their action is indicative of the power of kindness.

The parallel to the poet, Dante, in Williams' inferno is Kilroy, the twenty-seven year old vagrant and all-American GI, who wears around his neck a pair of boxing gloves and, as a memento of better years, a belt with the word *Champ* studded with rubies and emeralds. This self-pitying itinerant complains of his troubles at length: tropical fever on a ship without medical care; forced retirement from the prize ring because of a bad heart that is described "as big as the head of a baby"; forced renunciation of liquor, tobacco, and sex; and a loving wife afraid of a big, hard kiss. Kilroy becomes an easy mark for the roughnecks on Camino Real. He is robbed; he makes friends with a fellow sufferer, Jacques Casanova; and he is forced into a clown outfit, the grotesque symbol of man's loss of dignity: a red wig, a bulbous nose that can be lighted, horn-rimmed glasses, and a big footprint on the seat of his pants. His resistance to the forces of order that label him as "queer" is expressed in a noisy "rhubarb" of a chase over the stage, up and down the theater aisles and balcony, and to the stage.

A seduction scene, part comedy and part sensationalism, may have been written by Williams with an eye to the box office. Kilroy's escape from Camino Real is thwarted by the cunning bawd, Gypsy, who offers him her daughter Esmeralda, whose virginity is restored with each full moon. A temptress reclining on a divan like the *femme fatale* of the silent movies, Esmeralda wears a veil over her face, a girdle below her navel, and green snakes over her breasts. Kilroy, made dizzy by this glittering daughter of Eve, asks, in Tennessee Williams' capital-letter excitement, if her specialty is tea leaves. Mama the Gypsy orders Nursie, a male attendant, to "clock him" and sets out for street adventures of her own. At first the silent and "innocent" siren does not talk, but Esmeralda later stuns her suitor with some heady comments about the stabilization of the monetary system, the class struggle, and Mumbo Jumbo, her term for God. Kilroy prefers a more intimate kind of conversation. When Nursie pointedly warns the lovers that only fifteen minutes remain, the fun begins, fun and so-called poetic dialogue.

This courtship scene, part of the "fertility rites," is a composite of the precious and the "corny," the silly and the sentimental, the caustic and the humorous. This symbolic bedroom scene between a mercenary doll and a disillusioned American GI elicits from Kilroy the observation that love is no better than the four-letter words that youngsters scribble on fences when they run away from school. He talks about being gentle and sincere, a word repeated *ad nauseam;* and he admits that this particular love game was not worth the gloves he had pawned for it. The young prostitute-philosopher-sentimentalist answers, as if she had somehow inherited the guilt of the decadent Calvinists, that lovers feel as if they had degraded themselves and that their regret is larger "than a heart can hold."

The fertility rites scene is followed almost immediately by the death scene, like the symbolic streetcars Desire and Cemetaria in Williams' play, *Streetcar.* Kilroy, pestered by the Streetcleaners, seeks help from Gutman as a nude Eva appears briefly on the balcony. Relevance, or stage trick? But the all-American Kilroy, a man of courage, taunts the messengers of death with verbal hysterics set in capital letters and exclamation points; and, with old-time boxer parries, he faces the inevitable. In a double scene that follows, La Madrecita, who holds the body of Kilroy across her knees, speaks obituary praises at the same time that the medical students perform a postmortem on him, "an unidentified vagrant." The Pieta begs that the audience remember Kilroy when he was at the peak of his career, this boy who speaks in a soft Southern voice, and not when he was frightened and defeated. She says of his admirers, in a somewhat involved metaphor, an image that Williams had used previously for his broken Apollo: "He stood as a planet among the moons of their longing." She makes an appeal to all failures and to all the deformed creatures to pray for one of their own, the one with an oversized heart. Then, in an incredible bit of fantasy, La Madrecita effects Kilroy's resurrection with a touch of flowers.

He wakens, watches the medic remove a gold sphere, and hears them talk about "pathological lesions." He grabs his precious golden heart and sets out on another noisy "rhubarb" chase, accompanied by all the racket the stage technicians could provide. Then comes another surprise: Esmeralda, the philosophical prostitute, embraces in an extended burst of rhetoric all the failures and disillusioned. Her plea for legends and lost causes is one of the fullest and most romantic prayers that Tennessee Williams has made for the defeated and the outcasts.

Kilroy, thinking he has found another true woman in Esmeralda, is soon disillusioned and discarded. Taking the advice of the old knight of dreams, Don Quixote, "Don't! Pity! Your! Self!" — typographical dramatics again — Kilroy walks off "mugging" to the audience, leering about his new friend, the Romantic Good Samaritan. The play closes on a strongly optimistic note when the old knight, watching Marguerite's kindness to Cassanova, delivers the symbolic line: *"The violets in the mountains have broken the rocks!"* As he speaks, the fountain begins spurting water, another last minute suggestion of hope.

Camino Real grew out of Williams' theory about the world, one he formulated when he was quite ill. He substituted not only types for characters, but symbolic scenes for action that would normally grow from character; and he filled the setting with all kinds of noisy stage effects, again "something wild." Concerned that he might not be understood, he frequently overstated his jaded view of the world. As in the early poems, Williams was unable to delete a foggy image or a philosophical phrase that was closer to posturing than to thought. A sampling of critical comments indicates that the reviewers had observed the ugliness of the world with better perspective than did the playwright; they also knew enough about the popular culture to be able to identify elements that were reflected in the play.

Although a number of critics found the play obscure, Brooks Atkinson asserted that there was "no mistaking Mr. Williams' meaning. His world is going out with neither a bang nor a whimper but with a leer and a grimace of disgust. There is no health in it. The Camino Real is a jail-yard of vice."[5] And Harold Clurman noted that, "Far from being obscure, the play reiterates its intention and meaning at every point. In fact, it is too nakedly clear to be a sound work of art." He thought this immature work more appropriate for a small theater where it could be judged for what it was, "a fallible minor work of a young artist of important talent."[6]

In fact, Walter Kerr call the play Williams' "most decisive failure." He thought he had adopted the tools of a philosopher-critic who resorted to symbols and rejected the techniques of imagery that tell an audience "how things look, feel, smell, and actually are." He thought the scene of the Madrecita and the body of Kilroy was badly written.[7] The reviewer in *Time* wrote that Williams, who always preaches "the creed of the high romantic," is "like an eternal child who wants it all, and when he cannot have it all, his heart breaks."[8] Harold Clurman, watching the revival, could accept the "sophomoric counterfeits" and the Romanticism of the "hippies," but not the language. He thought that a line like "We are all of us guinea pigs in the laboratory of God" merely reeked of "flat sentimentality." He recognized certain comic sheet elements, such as the pimp mother, her daughter, their "accompanying shill," and to a degree Kilroy; but he also felt that the play was infused with "the sticky air of corruption," as if the writer were trying to glamorize the lower depths.[9]

Williams, who wrote the play at a time of illness and despair, thought of *Camino Real* as his conception of our world and our time. He thought of the characters as "mostly archtypes of certain basic attitudes" and with certain given mutations. In addition to the "philosophical import," he wanted to give the audience his "own sense of something wild and unrestricted," something like the transforming images of a dream," an idea that sounds like a reflection of the old days with the Mummers.[10] During rehearsals, he and Elia Kazan, the director, cut many lines. Because he loved the play so much, Williams was deeply hurt over the negative reaction of the audience; in fact, some even stamped out of the theater and demanded a refund.[11] After the gloomy opening night, his

angry reception of the Kazans and the Steinbecks, who stopped by
to see him, became a part of the legend about Williams' explosive
temper.[12]

In the afterword printed with the play, Williams attacks the
critics, who seem to prefer "thinking playwrights" rather than
those like himself who merely feel.[13] He has made a number of
explanations about the play: that, written at a time of depression, it
served as a "spiritual purgation"; that he identified himself as one
of the fugitive kind when he gave the play a Mexican locale with
touches from Casablanca, Fez, and Tangier. When the play was
revived, in January 1970, he described the play as portraying the
dilemma of the individual caught in a fascist state, but also as his
own — the difficulties a Romantic faces "in a predominantly
cynical world."[14]

II Orpheus Descending *(1957)*[15]

Tennessee Williams says that *Orpheus Descending,* his revision
of *Battle of Angels* after fifteen years of theatrical experience,
remains the "tale of a wild-spirited boy" who happens into a conventional Southern community and "creates the commotion of a
fox in a chicken coop." In the play, an "emotional record of his
youth," questions that are raised by the itinerant and the three
women (the four main protagonists) are asked repeatedly but are
never answered; there are only "expedient adaptations."[16]

Williams has played many variations on the theme of the poet in
an unfriendly world. In the last three stanzas of the poem
"Orpheus Descending," the writer says to this mythological figure,
as if speaking to himself, that he must learn that some things that
are by their nature incomplete — an idea basic to the story "Desire
and the Black Masseur" — are to be sought for and abandoned;
that it is the nature of things that those who reach for the heights
are destined to fall; that he, fugitive and ashamed, must crawl
within himself, for he is not the stars but the residue of victims torn
by the avenging furies.[17]

In the play, Orpheus is Val (Valentine) Xavier, the poet-itinerant-
lover-savior who descends into the hell of this small Southern town
to rescue Lady (Myra of the old play but changed to an Italian)
from Pluto, or Jabe Torrance, the cancer-doomed, flint-hearted
husband. The inhabitants of this hell are a motley assortment of
commonplace townspeople: frowsy women, silly and malicious

gossips who seem to gloat over the sufferings of others; and their husbands, pot-bellied old boys, remnants of the Mystic Crew, a kind of Ku Klux Klan that keeps foreigners like "wops" and also "niggers" in their places. In contrast to these ultraconventional and vicious townspeople is a ghoulish primitive, the Conjure Man with his bird bones and his blood-curdling Choctaw cry, who seems to be a symbol of pure freedom and death. Also apart from the conventional members of this ordinary community are three women of very different heritage, and each one is involved with the itinerant, Val.

Williams has sharpened the focus of the new play by bringing the forces of evil in more direct conflict with the kindlier and more sensitive elements and by allowing the clash of these opposites to underscore his theme. He seems to have written himself even more into the main character and to have expressed his ideas about the social order in the three women and in the three grotesques who make up a majority of the community.

Val Xavier, now a man of thirty, is a soft-spoken Southerner whose trademark of freedom is still the snakeskin jacket; and he carries a guitar that is covered with the names of famous singers. The guitar is a phallic symbol according to some critics; to others, a symbol of Val's art and purity. As in *Battle of Angels,* Val courts disaster when he seeks to exchange his itinerant freedom for a job in the mercantile store and when he becomes involved with Lady, the love-starved wife. He talks of two kinds of people, the buyers and the bought; but he also mentions one other — "the kind that's never been branded." He describes an unusual symbol of freedom, a bird without legs that has to keep afloat on its wings but, because of that, is protected from the hawks who can't see him when he flies against the sun. The realization that they are two lonely people — loneliness being the quality that Williams associates with sensitivity — brings Val and the wife together. He speaks for them all, the lonely ones: "Nobody ever gets to know *no body!* We're all of us sentenced to solitary confinement inside our own skins, for life!"[18] Lady believes that love is the answer, but Val knows from experience that love has deluded many people.

Lady was "bought" by Jabe Torrance, elderly proprietor of the mercantile store, after she was discarded by Carol's brother, David Cutrere, for a wealthy and socially acceptable girl. Lady's father, "a Wop from the old country," prospered during the bootlegging era and built an orchard and a casino on Moon Lake, a favorite

haunt for young couples who liked "that Dago red wine." When he
sold liquor to "niggers," the Mystic crew went into action and set
fire to the place; "the Wop," the only fighter against the flames,
was burned alive in his attempt to save his property. As the play
opens, Jabe, dying of cancer, returns from the hospital; and Lady
answers his peremptory orders as she has for years.

Since Lady is also a businesswoman, the romance between this
older wife and the thirty-year old lover erupts in a few ugly scenes.
When he takes money from the cashbox, gambles successfully, and
returns what he "borrowed," she accuses him of theft; and their
recriminations are vicious. He calls her an aging, unsatisfied
woman who hired a stranger as clerk by day and, without paying
extra, as a stud at night. Having beaten a "black-jack dealer five
times straight," Val on his profits is about to leave. Lady strikes
him with her fists and in capital-letter excitement cries out, "NO,
NO, DON'T GO ... I NEED YOU!!! TO LIVE ... TO GO ON
LIVING." Her cry of passion, heightened by appropriate mood
music, sends him back to the little alcove where she had established
sleeping arrangements for him. Behind the curtain, his guitar in his
hands, he whispers a song so tenderly that she is won into the little
room. He looks from his guitar to her — the old phallic guitar — as
the stage darkens.

The second woman, Carol Cutrere (Sandra Whiteside of the old
play), an older poor little rich girl, is so exotic in her theatrical
makeup that she may be, as one critic observed, "a Vieux Carré
beatnik." A religious fanatic and reformer, she had made speeches
in earlier years, had written protest letters about the brutal treatment of Negroes, and had spent her inheritance to build clinics.
Then, dressed in burlap, she had walked barefoot to ask the
governor to free a Negro taken with a white whore. Arrested for
vagrancy, she has ever since made that her way of life. Frustrated in
humanitarian ventures, she seems to have turned to sex with a terrible compulsion. She propositions Val, who says that "shacking
up" with strangers is for youngsters; but the two exchange confi-
dences, mostly about sex, with an air *"of two lonely children."* She
seems to be in communication with the Conjure Man, for she can
evoke his blood-curdling Choctaw cry.

The third woman, Vee Talbott, a religious fanatic and the wife of
the ignorant and brutal sheriff, paints pictures according to the
"visions" she experiences in moments of frenzy.[19] Typifying
Williams' idea of the poetic spirit, she works at high tension, stops

briefly for coffee, returns to work while she still has "a clear vision," and "finishes a picture in a ten-hour stretch." She admits that she has accomplished something when she has finished, even though she may feel "burned out." Speaking of painting a Church of the Resurrection with a red steeple, she just "*felt* that way"; she paints as she feels and not as things are because "appearances are misleading." Museums have asked for more of her paintings, but she cannot paint on order, just as she can not live without visions. Val understands this creative force; but their communication rouses the vengeance of her husband, the sheriff.

Jabe, alerted by this local officer of the law that a young man is in his store, clumps down the stairs like a symbol of death and demands an explanation. On this Saturday night before Easter, the confectionary, redecorated to resemble the old Moon Lake casino, is scheduled to open; the tinny mechanical sound of the calliope, hired to attract customers, is heard repeatedly during this scene. When Jabe recalls the mistake her father had made, he admits, apparently for the first time, that he was the leader of the gang that burned out the little retreat built by the "Wop," along with all his vines and the owner himself. After Jabe repeats the confession, which stuns Lady, the nurse with difficulty returns the bleeding invalid to his room.

Vee Talbott, who has painted the apostles with faces of men in the community, tells Val about her last vision, the "TWO HUGE BLAZING EYES OF JESUS CHRIST RISEN!" Val Xavier is her image of Christ. These kindred spirits are likened to "*two children who have found life's meaning.*" At the moment that she falls to her knees and throws her arms around Val, the sheriff enters, accuses him of putting hands on his wife, and other "red necks" join him with their accusing questions. The sheriff, saying he wants no violence, orders Val to leave before sunrise if he values his life.

His departure is fatally arrested by his "looking back." Lady, dressed and groomed for the opening of the confectionary, gives peremptory orders to Val about the new establishment; she speaks of her revenge against the dying Jabe who destroyed her unborn child by David Cutrere, her own life, and that of her father. Val, torn between "*a natural sensibility of heart*" and what life taught him years before in Witches' Bayou, is about to leave with his baggage, guitar, and snakeskin jacket. He expresses his "true love" for Lady with a kiss and a promise to wait for her outside the county. Cynical about easy words like love, she angrily speaks about wages and, grabbing his guitar, his "life's companion," threatens to smash it if he leaves. She says that she can not stay in this house of death.

When the nurse comes down stairs to inquire about the argument, Lady suggests to her that there must be ways of relieving suffering, merciful ways to death. The nurse, who refuses to have anything to do with "killing," looks toward the alcove and says, "There's something burning in there." She also tells Lady that, when she first saw her, she knew that she was pregnant. Lady, ecstatic over the news, repeats the legend about the barren fig tree that once bore fruit and died; as if in delirium, she cries out that she has won over death.

The end is sudden and violent, for the forces of brutality win over the life-loving people. Jabe shoots Lady; and the mob, led by the sheriff, pursues Val with a blowtorch. The conjure Man lifts the snakeskin jacket; and Carol Cutrere, that other spirit of freedom, declaims, "Wild things ... leave clean skins and teeth and white bones behind them ... so that the fugitive kind" can follow their own. The cry of the tortured Val is repeated more terribly as the curtain falls.

Like several of his near contemporaries, Williams attempted to restate an ancient myth in modern terms; however, he tried to combine several myths with a few of his own making. To John Gassner, who called this play "one of the most chaotic contemporary works of genius," its plot was made up of a "multiplication of griefs, evils, and horrors" and of several layers of meaning; but "the snarled symbolism of the play" obscured both character and environment. The two legends about Orpheus, his descent into the underworld and his being torn to pieces by the Bacchantes, are entangled with symbols inherited from D. H. Lawrence and the Romantic tradition. In attempting to portray "Val the poet, Val the idealized male pursued to his destruction by sex-hungry women, and Val the noble savage of Rousseauist romanticism," Williams attempts too much. The work is additionally complicated by Williams' combined presentation of two of his major themes: "The tragic isolation of the artist in the hell of modern society, and the crucifixion of the pure male on the cross of sexuality."[20]

Henry Popkin, after noting the changes from *Battle of Angels,* described the confused pretensions and the garbled symbolism in terms of the Christian references. The last act has shifted from Good Friday to Holy Saturday; Myra, or Mary, has become Lady, or "Our Lady" — a characteristic Williams' habit of imposing his own fantasy upon a universal religious figure and making a sex-starved, mercenary store keeper the Mother of God. (Other critics have likened Lady to Mary Magdalene.) Val becomes Orpheus and is associated with Christ, both of whom descend to hell; but Val-Orpheus is destroyed; Val's guitar, Orpheus' lyre, has been given a phallic significance, for the jealous, sexually thwarted townsmen approach with knives as if to castrate him; Jabe, described as "like the Prince of Darkness," destroys the lovers. A kind of symbolic resurrection seems to be implied by the shafts of light that play upon the scene. The final note of the play combines two familiar Williams' themes — sexuality and religion — for the tribute to the snakeskin jacket is accompanied by a "religious chant."[21] Walter Kerr wrote, apropos Williams' "drift toward Olympian detachment" — one so evident in *Battle of Angels* and *Orpheus Descending* — that there lurks behind his arbitrary juxtaposition of innocence and depravity "an echo of emptiness that will not be quieted."[22]

Battle of Angels so shocked the Boston audience of 1940 that the producers made a public apology. When *Oprheus* was produced in 1957 in Boston, the public was only bored. Williams, not realizing that the play was a parody of himself, was deeply shocked over the failure of a work on which he had labored with so much difficulty and affection for sixteen years. The death of his grandfather in 1955 and of his father in 1957 had added to his gloom. He wrote to his mother: "I knew I must find help or crack up, so I went to an analyst and poured out all my troubles."[23]

And so, late in 1957 and into 1958, he went into "one of the most widely heralded analyses ever held," one that ranks with baseball as a popular sport.[24] Dr. Lawrence Kubie apparently tried to change Williams' sexual orientation. The sessions made Williams understand his father and recognize that his mother's influence may have contributed to his becoming a homosexual. Then the analyst hit a sore spot when he stated to Williams, "You've written nothing but violent melodramas, which only succeed because of the violence of the time we live in." That ended the treatments; and Williams thinks of psychiatry as an antiromantic, antiemotional form of mental therapy. Characteristically identifying personal problems as universal, he has observed that "infantile omnipotence" is common and the root of many dangers in the world.[25]

Among the "black plays" of the 1950s are *Camino Real* (1953),

Orpheus Descending (1957), *Suddenly Last Summer* (1958), and
Sweet Bird of Youth (1959). Williams has repeatedly said that he
has only his work, and he has implied that his work and his life are
one. Whenever his work is criticized, he is deeply hurt, and he
grows belligerent and vocal. Though he has admitted that he writes
to purge an illness of one kind or another, he has not answered
those friendly critics who wonder what has made his world become
so ugly. Perhaps he cannot say; perhaps his experience in psychiatry
in the late 1950s made Williams conclude that "the whole world's a
big hospital." As early as *Battle of Angels,* he was urged not to
wear his heart on his sleeve; but the reception of *Camino Real* and
Orpheus Descending apparently had devastating effects. The play
after the analysis takes a very different turn, but it is unfortunately
not in Williams' best vein, work out of personal experience,
observation, and deep feeling.

III   Period of Adjustment *(1960)*[26]

Subtitled "A Serious Comedy," *Period of Adjustment* portrays
the lives of two couples, and each of the four neurotics has his own
sexual problem. The play opens on Christmas Eve, a time for love;
and the setting, the living room of a "cute" little Spanish-type suburban bungalo, is part of a real estate development called High
Point. Only the owners and dealers in the area are aware that the
house is built over a cavern and that it sinks one or two inches every
year. The standards, business and personal, symbolized by this
peculiar place may or may not have a bearing on the four immature
youngish Americans; but all of them are sick in the same way.
Harold Clurman, among others, found the play not particularly
funny. "In fact, what one finds is something disturbingly ambiguous, not 'quite straight'."[27] Stanley Edgar Hyman, writing on the
disguises of the love theme, calls the writing of homosexual love in
heterosexual imagery the "Albertine strategy," a reference to Marcel Proust who metamorphosed a boy, with whom the male protagonist was involved, into a girl. Hyman cited the Williams' story
"Rubio y Morena" as an example; for in it the mannish girl Amada
is the disguised figure.[28]

In *Period of Adjustment,* Ralph Bates, boyish but thirty-seven
(Williams' heroes grow older with their creator), belongs to the
poet-vagabond-philosopher type who was first portrayed as the
hitchhiker in Williams' juvenilia. Described as having a gentle grav-

ity and a heart capable of love, these traits are hardly noticeable in his acerbic comments about his wife and father-in-law. Bates is married to the "ugly" daughter of a diabetic old millionaire who suffers from gallstones, lacks one kidney (the overloaded biography again), and has been cheating the undertaker. This middle-aged Bates, a Kilroy, worried about his passing youth and weary of his routine job, sends a rude telegram to this same father-in-law with the boast that he has rescued a buck-toothed woman from a psychiatrist and has made her think she was attractive. Her father paid fifty dollars a session for what Ralph, the great lover, cured in one night — a boast that could belong to all the Tennessee Williams boys of the oversized hearts. He received a pay raise when she bore a son, but he has since then been brooding over his wasted talent. His wife, buck-toothed Dorothy, leaves her middle-aged, adolescent husband and takes the boy with her, a sissy according to his father.

A wartime buddy, George Haverstick, and his wife Isabel, who are twenty-four hour honeymooners, unexpectedly drop in on Ralph, George strangely disaappears, and the host and wife exchange marriage complaints. Isabel, with a figure that Ralph ogles continually, is another version of a querulous Southern belle who talks like "an outraged spinster." Daughter of an overprotective father, and born twelve years after his marriage, she quotes her philosophy professor in lines reminiscent of the Proprietor in *Ten Blocks on Camino Real* (1948): "We are all of us born, live and die in the shadow of a giant question mark that refers to three questions: *Where do we come from? Why? And where, oh, where are we going!*"[29] She interrupts her long complaint by repeatedly asking for her blue zipper bag, and she tries in the inevitable telephone scene to tell her daddy all about her marital problems. According to Williams, this little girl, in a sweet and sentimental mood that dissolves in tears, meets life's problems for the first time.

Her new husband, George, though famous during the war years for his yarns about women, is really terrified when before them. He had met Isabel in a veteran's hospital where he had been under observation for a strange tremor; no physical cause had been discovered; he had been dismissed as ineligible for disability payments. The tremor is later explained as "the shakes," a condition he suffers whenever he tries to make love to a girl. The day before his marriage, he quit his job because its monotony affected his nerves. In an antiquated Cadillac funeral limousine, he takes his new bride on a circuit of visits to his wartime buddies.

The play is almost entirely a series of extended two-character scenes that center on recollections of the past. Isabel's hysterical account of her wedding night to her host, Ralph Bates, and her husband's absence, which is slyly explained as a trip to the drugstore, may be an intended script for comedy. She talks at length about her virginity and about her inhibitions, ones complicated by postmarital circumstances: a long ride in a snowstorm in a funeral hack; a silent husband and a heater that did not work; the new husband's revelation that he had quit his job.

During the second act, the wartime buddies talk at length about their camp women and their dreams of agrarian life. George builds fantasies about Texas where they might breed a herd of cattle as a noble breed not destined for the slaughterhouse but for use on television commercials, and as a way of turning their backs on mendacious America. Ralph, who has never had trouble "making out" with the girls, dreams of being the first Adam to land on Mars and Venus where he could fertilize a new colony. George interrupts these Romantic plans with references to the "awful implications" of his own affliction. To prove his point, he holds up his shaking hand that, like "dice in a crap shooter's fist," ruins his business career and his sex life: "I could start shaking so hard when I started to make out with a girl that I couldn't do it." When Ralph states that George is "scared of impotence," the war buddies begin checking experiences.

The dialogue that opens the third act is the kind that prompted George Jean Nathan to call Williams the "genital-man" of the contemporary theater. Ralph's sage lecture on the art of love is interrupted by the arrivals of his in-laws, the McGillicuddys, who are grotesque symbols of commercial success. They have come for daughter Dorothy's belongings; but, before they succeed, she relents and returns to her husband — with love. The play closes with no surprises whatsoever; for each couple, correctly paired, solves the problems of the marriage bed, and apparently of life as well.

For all the talk of sexual fulfillment, there is an overtone in the relationship between the war buddies that recalls that of Brick Pollitt and his friend Skipper. In such seemingly close-knit compatibility, no place exists for women, as Maggie the Cat discovered. In contrast to the caricature of the usual successful American are husbands Ralph and George; each has a dependent wife, and each resigns from his job and talks like an inexperienced adolescent. Comedy, perhaps.

In the misunderstandings surrounding both Elia Kazan's conflict of commitments that prevented his directing the play and the dramatist's reaction to the rewriting asked for by this director, Williams publicly admitted that Kazan had helped put over his "cornpóne melodrama."[30] The playwright vaguely touched on a homosexual theme, which at the time was not acceptable in the popular theater. Apparently unable to judge the quality of his own work, he had to learn from the critics that his play was a diluted repetition of earlier work, and that its preoccupation with sex was funny only to himself. Howard Taubman observed that the characters are thin and one-sided, and that their "temporary sexual incompatibilities" are repetitious "shadows of old portraits in the Williams' gallery."[31] The critic in *Time,* calling Williams "Broadway's laureate of sex writing," found the play to be more theater than truth, or too much "of Freud pinch-hitting for flesh and blood, of amusing little leitmotifs in place of incisive motivations."[32]

According to Harold Clurman, *Period of Adjustment* was Williams' first box-office success in England. This breakthrough of a play on a sex theme, he thought, may have been due to the British recognition that they are as affected as Americans by the Puritan attitude toward sex, the butt of Williams' jest.[33] Robert Hatch wrote that both Tennessee Williams and John Osborne have "a bird dog's instinct for the presently relevant theme" and that both are preoccupied with general symptoms. To Hatch, Williams' play was again concerned "with the guilt of impotence, the horror of castration, and the danger of the devouring female"; but the characters, each one a compilation from all the forms of the popular media, are not people but statistics — and each one is burdened with a characteristic Williams' "tic."[34]

CHAPTER 6

The Deteriorating Artist

W ILLIAMS' four artists of minor or insignificant talent, all of them grotesque figures, illustrate the ugly side of sexual indulgence and the brutal use of other people, a practice that is somewhat concealed by elegance and wealth. The former actress in *The Roman Spring of Mrs. Stone* (1950) disintegrates when the discipline of her profession no longer keeps her mind alert and controls her behavior. Sebastian in *Suddenly Last Summer* (1958) keeps his homosexual nature more or less a secret as long as he and his mother build a stern regimen each day. The Princess in *Sweet Bird of Youth* (1959) tardily recognizes what the camera records: she is becoming an old woman. Flora in *The Milk Train Doesn't Stop Here Anymore* (1963) is surrounded by her garish display as she, in the face of death, grimly holds on to petty forms of power.

Each one of the central figures, his minimal talent made into a commercial asset by factors that have little to do with art, madly clings to the last remnants of youth, fills out the days of his hollow existence with recollections of his past that are often not worth the memory, and tyrannizes those who serve him. Three of the four are domineering women, possessive mother figures or insatiable mistresses. Other ruthless figures, often caricatures of commercial and political corruption, sell themselves for money and power. The most vivid contrast to these human fiends are the occasional truth tellers whose honesty discloses the fraudulent even when such disclosures may bring about their own destruction.

Williams may be interested in exposing the mendacity of our time; but his preoccupation with the sexual theme, his fascination with "rainbow tinted refuse," and his savage portrayal of women (roles he seems to have written for particular actresses) raise questions about the use he has been making of his own talent.

I   The Roman Spring of Mrs. Stone *(1950)*[1]

The short novel *The Roman Spring of Mrs. Stone* was inspired by Williams' first sojourn in Italy, and it reflects an increasing tendency toward precious writing and an interest in vulgarity and decadence. The narrative is about the disintegration of a once prominent actress who retired at fifty because she could no longer play Juliet. A ruthless, self-centered woman whose beauty obscured her lack of talent, she succeeded as a stage personality; and she built by astute politics an image of devotion and kindness. Her twenty-five year marriage to a wealthy business man had been a companionship that was subordinated to her career. At the beginning, because of her frigidity and his awkwardness, they settled into an arrangement satisfactory to both: she had a grown-up child she could mother, and he had a beautiful mother he could adore. She became aware, however, of the loneliness and the barrenness of their life together after his death, her own retirement, and the collapse of her intellectual processes.

During the early days of her return to Rome, Mrs. Stone contacts the Contessa, a "stately witch" whom she knew previously. She realized too late that the Italian woman was a female pimp who provides handsome young men for rich and lonely American widows. Even so, Mrs. Stone accepted three youths, escorts whom she treated well but without profit for the Contessa. As the story opens, the witch has assigned a fourth hungry youth, Paolo, in the hope that the companionship will develop into intimacy with the rich widow and advantage for herself as well as for the youth.

In the early scene, Meg Bishop, Mrs. Stone's classmate turned successful woman journalist, whose ten-year association with prominent figures in the world of business and politics has destroyed all traces of femininity, bluntly compares her actress friend to an imperial eagle who would tear a Romeo to pieces. Later the reader learns how Mrs. Stone obliterated those whose talent might overshadow hers, and how in a blind rage she attacked an actor playing Orlando. Meg Bishop says that Mrs. Stone married a fat little man who looked like "an Easter bunny" to avoid sexual intercourse; that now, because of her filthy millions, she is collecting about herself procuresses, effeminate dandies, and other shady characters; that she is unaware that she is the topic of sniggering gossip in New York, London, and Paris.

The journalist, comparing the decay of the once proud city of

Rome to the deterioration of the woman before her, sees in the aging actress a symbol of all that is corrupt in the world. These two women, who are standing on a high balcony and who are like "two exotic giant birds ... commanding the precipice," are unaware of the waiting youth below whose exceptional beauty is distinguished by "the dreadful poverty of his clothes and his stealth of manner."[2] Throughout the novel, this parasitic figure pursues Mrs. Stone; he taps against the wall or glass, he often urinates, or he merely exposes himself. When she first sees this "young man of remarkable beauty," she turns her back in disgust.

The journalist's truth telling does not waken Mrs. Stone; it only increases her sense of drift and mindlessness. She accepts without reservation the attention of her fourth handsome escort, Paolo. His happiest hour of the day comes in the late afternoon when, in the barber's chair, he luxuriates in talk about his women, a confession that lends meaning to his "butterfly existence." He speaks of his three former "protectors" from whom he profited, and of the present Mrs. Stone who is not so great a lady but that she would "take a turn at the pump if the house was on fire." His three-month association with the actress has not satisfied the Contessa, who accuses him of lying and cheating. He does not report to his barber, in this voluptuous session, the ugly argument over his feathering his own nest, her suggestion that he is only a "common *marchetta,*" or his sneering answer that, born in an evil world, she will die there. He does not mention how in revenge she drove a doubled fist into his groin, hoping to put him "out of business" for that night. Playing the role of concerned friend, the Contessa later visits Mrs. Stone and warns her that Paolo, of good but impoverished family, is a *marchetta,* a boy who lives very well without money; and she urges that she increase her expectations from her young man. The witch then tells a story about a friend desperately in need of money.

Paolo later tells Mrs. Stone the same story and adds a request for ten million lire. When Mrs. Stone comments on the size of his request, he counters with an argument on the value of friendship. Although she realizes that his boy has revealed himself to be what the Contessa warned, she suddenly experiences an awakened desire, one "quite divorced from reason and will." Even though the "extravagant myth" of his innocence has been exposed, for the first time "she felt incontinent longings" that gave her "a sharply immediate sense of being." No longer fearful of the fertility tide, she gives in to the gratification of her desire.

As time passes, her indulgence in sensuality is reflected in expensive, garish clothes and jewelry, and by heavy makeup. She takes Paolo to the tailor, who makes for him a suit of the same grey flannel that he had used for her late husband. On the afternoon when she is trying on a recent purchase, Paolo, dressed in his new dove-grey flannel, bursts into the bedroom, rushes to the mirror, pushes her aside, preens before the glass, and admires "his firm young behind." When her burst of laughter throws him into a fury, he tells her about rich women murdered in bed and about the ugly gossip focused on her — an argument that is terminated when he gives her his mouth to kiss and allows "her hands to indulge their restless cravings to hold him."

This beginning of a sordid evening culminates when she sacrifices a last shred of dignity and loses her young lover to a brash young Hollywood actress who is "between husbands." At the restaurant she is humiliated by Paolo's unabashed attention to this girl and by the violinist who celebrates the voluptuous "sweet play of youth." She leaves the table abruptly, overcome by that same "suffocating weight" she had felt on the opening night of Juliet. Not far from her on the street she hears the familiar tapping sound and running water, recognizes the youthful pursuer, and, her eyes averted, thrusts her aging face toward his and tells him to look. Paolo's angry arrival interrupts the scene. Later in the evening, entering her apartment by an unexpected door, Mrs. Stone recognizes the Contessa's voice, hears "the brutal clarification of phrase" applied to herself, and all of her recent life is made visible to her. Paolo with "outrageous ease" breaks into the scene and focuses attention on the young film star, the Contessa's latest assignment.

The evening erupts when Mrs. Stone exposes the Contessa and Paolo, and Paolo urges her, a fifty-year old rich American, to leave Rome. As if her voice did not belong to her, as so often happened on the stage during scenes of violent emotion, she screams words unconsciously. She bites the hand that Paolo claps over her mouth; he curses her and strikes her face. Soon left alone, she wanders into the bedroom, the bed "a stretch of pure desolation," saying to herself that she is drifting, drifting. The one fixed thing is "the solitary watcher beneath the Egyptian obelisk." When she wraps her keys in a white handkerchief and throws them down to him, her arty, symbolic statement closes the book, "Look, I've stopped the drift!"

The harsh satiric portrait of Mrs. Stone is offset by the voluptuous handling of Paolo and by the curious fiddling with the obscene in the portrayal of the waiting youth. Williams may have created this portrait of Mrs. Stone from his considerable experience in the theater or from the attitude toward women that is a part of his personal problem. She, like Brick Pollitt, for whom he had so much sympathy, seems to be another victim of "moral paralysis." Williams seems to have inserted the unpleasant Meg Bishop into the novel to speak for him, to say that the deterioration of Mrs. Stone is comparable to that of the once admirable city of Rome. But, when Williams' story is placed besides two studies in corruption by Thomas Mann, "Mario and the Magician" and "Death in Venice," *The Roman Spring of Mrs. Stone* is pitifully sick. A bright student, introduced to Tennessee Williams during a visit on a campus, unfortunately told the writer that he did not like the novel. Williams exploded viciously.[3]

Williams is supposed to have created the character of Mrs. Stone for Greta Garbo (who thought it not for her), an idea that would seem to be more than usually out of touch with reality.[4] In his *Memoirs* he comments on prostitution in Rome, male and female; on the impoverished young fawns that he encountered; and about the ones he accepted on his own *letto matrimoniale*. The film which was made from this novel is a favorite of the playwright.[5]

II Suddenly Last Summer *(1958)*[6]

Suddenly Last Summer, a curious modern fable, is set in a wealthy old woman's living room which looks out on an exotic jungle in the Garden District of New Orleans. The flowers, which are compared to human entrails dripping with blood, and the destructive sounds of primitive creatures — hissing serpents, shrieking birds, snarling beasts — suggest an Henri Rousseau painting distorted into a Surrealistic impression of hell. Against this backdrop, *Suddenly Last Summer* lays bare not only the relationship of a Southern aristocrat and her forty-year old son but also their vicious threats against the girl who tells the truth. The recital is heavily orchestrated with sounds — harsh bird cries for the brutal phases and sweet bird songs for honest and tender sentiments.

The "well-groomed jungle"–plants carefully tagged with Latin names and the Venus flytrap kept alive with fruit flies airmailed from Florida — was as much a part of Sebastian Venable's well-designed life as his life work, poetry, which became a ritual. After a nine-month gestation, he delivered a poem, one poem annually for twenty-five summers, each exquisitely hand printed on an eighteenth century press.[7] Mrs. Venable, as if speaking for Williams, says that the life of the poet cannot be separated from his work as can the life and work of a salesman. In reverent memory of her son, as if to suggest a religious rite, she lifts the elegant gilt-edged volume, *Poems of Summer*. Explaining that all good poets have to look harder for God than do priests, she reports that Sebastian's search for a clear image of the Almighty led the two of them to charter a boat for the Encantades, the Enchanted Isles, to watch the hatching of the Galapagos sea turtles and their desperate flight from the flesh-eating birds. Mrs. Venable says, "They were diving down on the hatched sea-turtles, turning them over to expose their soft undersides, tearing the undersides open and rending and eating their flesh."[8] In another attempt to find God, the son almost became a Buddhist monk; but the mother, neglecting her dying husband, saved her boy for Shepheard's in Cairo and the Ritz at Paris.

Mrs. Venable describes herself and her son as a famous couple who were distinguished by the grandeur of their appearance. To keep from growing old, they developed a discipline and constructed each day as a work of sculpture. A slight aneurism, she says as she sits in a wheel chair, not a stroke, had prevented her from joining her son, who she believes was still chaste at forty. Since the stroke made her useless for his purposes, Sebastian took with him on his travels this past summer Catharine Holly, his cousin; and it is her story that the mother wants to block. She hysterically charges that her niece is trying to destroy the legend of their own beautiful relationship and her son's reputation. The rich widow promises the psychiatrist, Dr. Cukrowicz, whom she calls Dr. Sugar, to establish a Sebastian Venable Memorial Foundation for his special use if he will stop the girl's babbling with a brain operation and with a lifetime incarceration in Lion's View, an asylum for the mentally incompetent. Catharine's mother and brother, Mrs. Holly and George, pose a second threat: they want the girl's compliance lest the old woman contest Sebastian's will, which leaves each of them fifty thousand.

Catharine Holly has a passion for truth telling even about herself. When an escort to the Mardi Gras ball got so drunk that he could not stand, a stranger offered to take her home; but he drove her instead to a lover's rendezvous. When he left her at home, he told her to forget their intimacy because his wife was expecting. She became angry, returned to the ballroom; struck her abductor, an act that ostracized her from "society"; and began thinking of herself in the third person. The travels with Sebastian were like a return from dying, but even in the very plush hotels she was running away from the "hot ravenous mouth." When the doctor gives her an injection, supposedly a kind of truth serum, to enable her to give the complete story about Sebastian, her first reaction is to crush her mouth violently to his; clutching his body against hers, she says that she has been lonelier than death. After the big hard kiss, Catharine tells what happened at Cabezo de Lobo; her account, which is given to the company of human birds assembled, is orchestrated by raucous jungle cries and sweet bird calls; a white light focused on her increases in intensity as she reaches the climax of the narrative.

Because she believes that hatred is compatible only with insanity,[9] Catharine does not hate her Aunt Violet, who has confined her to a mental hospital. She, like Marguerite Gautier of *Camino Real,* defines love as a mutual dependence. She and Sebastian needed each other, but she was forced into a motherly role, the only kind of love he would accept. She wanted to save him from himself, from sacrificing himself to a terrible image of.... When she cannot finish the sentence, she nods in agreement when the young doctor adds the word, God. Sebastian's problem was obscured as long as his mother served as a shield, but Catharine soon discovered his sickness. Separated from the dominant Mrs. Venable, he went to pieces: he no longer wrote; he substituted the apparently elegant youths who followed him with ragged urchins; then he forced the girl to wear a white, lisle, one-piece bathing suit, transparent when wet, to serve him as a procuress.

On this last day, as so often with Williams' degenerates, Sebastian was expensively dressed in white. With Catharine he nervously ate a five o'clock lunch at a sea restaurant. The starved, naked children, some of the older ones familiar from his sorties on the beach, watched them eat, made noises with their mouths, and stuffed fists into their faces. Sebastian sneeringly called these beggars the social disease of the country. Some of the children began their serenade with tin cans strung together, tins flattened for cymbals, and stuffed paper bags. Sebastian, like the Judge in *The Purification* and like Brick in *Cat,* or like Mrs. Stone, suffered from a "moral paralysis." Catharine says that her cousin felt that no one had a right to interfere in any situation no matter how awful, even if he recognized the wrong. She adds that Sebastian was never sure "that anything was wrong"; that he considered it "unfitting" to take any positive action unless "something in him directed."

Curiously, Sebastian at the height of the insulting serenade asserted himself; he ordered the waiters to beat away the little monsters; he threw a handful of paper money on the table; he stalked out in a daze — he had been swallowing pills all afternoon — and was soon pursued in the blazing white heat by the naked children. He screamed when they overcame him. When the waiters, police, and others arrived, they found a multilated corpse. Catharine describes the scene: "...tore or cut parts of him away with their hands or knives or maybe those jagged tin cans and stuffed them into those gobbling fierce little empty mouths of theirs." The close resemblance between this scene and the flesh-eating birds attacking the sea turtles perhaps implies that Sebastian found the God he was looking for. The final precious description of what is left — something "that looked like a big white-paper-wrapped bunch of red roses had been *torn, thrown, crushed!* against the blazing white wall" — recalls the detached and rhetorical description of the execution of the one-armed Apollo. The angry widow, trying to strike the girl with her cane, orders the doctor to cut this hideous story out of her brain. The doctor quietly reacts to Mrs. Venable's hysteria by saying, "I think we ought at least to consider the possibility that the girl's story could be true...."

According to Mrs. Williams, her son wrote this play "while in analysis"; and, though possibly shocking even to himself, he felt "it was a catharsis, a final fling of violence."[10] Among personal elements in this play are the tragedy of his sister, Rose, who was institutionalized for life, and the characterization of the mother who had twisted her son's life. The image of the homosexual poet may be a reflection of Hart Crane, whose limited number of poems and whose decadent life led to his suicide. The preoccupation with guilt and subsequent retribution is another Williams' illustration of perverted Puritanism.

Williams has paced the recollection of the Sebastian story to excite emotion and to create theatrical shock; and he builds tension by piecemeal recollections and angry interruptions, the competition sharp between the widow and the girl who threatens to leave but is under compulsion to tell the truth. He would give this grotesque piece of Southern Gothic a universal significance, for he has Catharine say, "I know it's a hideous story but it's a true story of our time and the world we live in.'' He later told an interviewer that people out of greed or ambition are always "eating at someone" for their own gain, and that using one another is what they mean by love.[11]

Perhaps the play can be understood only as a reflection of the playwright's personal problem at the time, and his cynical view of the human race. Brooks Atkinson observed that the frequency of the line, "A poet's life is his work and his work is his life," suggests that this story may express "his sense of reality." The same "joyless, nihilistic point of view" appears in *Camino Real, Cat,* and *Orpheus.* This cleverly written play, which evokes "the central mood of evil, decadent luxury, voracity, tropical degeneracy," reveals how Williams "has made an art out of malignance and maleficence."[12]

The play was a box office success, and it was not as badly reviewed as the playwright expected. He thought that he would be "critically tarred and feathered and ridden on a fence rail" out of New York with no future "except in translation for theaters abroad."[13] At a revival in Key West, Florida, in 1976, Williams laughed over the world he had created.

III   Sweet Bird of Youth *(1959)*[14]

In *Sweet Bird of Youth,* a rather involved relationship between an aging actress and an unsuccessful, not quite so young Southern actor is combined with the machinations of a corrupt politician who is seeking reelection as well as revenge. Princess Kosmonopolis, from her name apparently a universal figure, has achieved commercial success in films, but is shocked by the camera's brutal truth; she clings desperately to the vestiges of youth with her last gigolo, Chance Wayne (another obvious symbolic name), a youngish would-be actor who for years has tried to crash the theatrical world. During this time he has made surreptitious visits to St. Cloud, his home town on the Gulf Coast, to see his boyhood sweetheart, Heavenly, Boss Finley's daughter; to her he bequeathed the venereal disease that necessitated an ovariotomy, a "whore's operation." Boss Finley, a Bible-quoting segregationist, threatens the young man with payment in kind if he ever returns. The kind of Williams excitement that often culminates in the big double bed is here turned to the impending revenge on Chance Wayne.[15]

The play opens in a hotel bedroom on an Easter Sunday morning with the sound of church bells and with a choir that is singing the Hallelujah chorus.[16] The Princess, Alexandra del Lago, emerges from a nightmare; calls for her oxygen bag, a pill, and vodka; and demands to know the identity of her bedmate and what had happened during the night. Her memory block enables her paramour to talk about their mutual careers, both of them dependent on "an appearance of youth"; about her need to put the tiger to sleep with hashish, possession of which is a federal offense; and about her promise to launch him in films, a promise that has not been confirmed. Chance has placed a tape recorder under her bed to test her assurances that the film contract signed in his behalf is genuine. Less sure about his talent, he recalls that he has had many opportunities to make the grade but was blocked by fear.[17] When he replays their conversation, she asks for her mink stole and her jewels; and he counters with the blackmail threats about reporting her to the Federal Bureau of Investigation (FBI). She is not intimidated, but finds endearing the "boy" who was born into a good Southern family but suffers the disadvantage of a "laurel wreath ... given too early," before he had earned it.[18] When she sarcastically asks for his scrapbook of notices, he hands her a book of traveler's checks and orders her to start signing. The Princess, a heart case, meets his demands with her own, the "only dependable distraction" she knows about, lovemaking. Desperate for the illusion that they are young lovers, she orders him to draw the curtains, turn on the radio, and prove himself. After this between-the-acts interlude that is apparently successful, the Princess madly signs the checks and talks about Hollywood contracts.

Chance, speaking directly to the audience, tells about his youth in St. Cloud as a poor boy with more beauty than talent. Somewhat like Kilroy, he was a normal, twelve-pound baby "with some kind of quantity 'X' in his blood, a wish or need to be different." His other profession, making love to celebrities in the social register, gave middle-aged matrons and lonely girls "a feeling of youth" and of really being loved. He tells of his repeated returns to Heavenly, his hysterical fear of losing his own youth, and his desperate need at this time to make a flashy return so that he can claim his dream girl. He believes, along with Williams, that the real differences are not between the rich and the poor but between those who have had "pleasure in love" and those who have had to watch it with "sick envy." Heavenly has warned him not to return, but he holds a naive faith in appearances: the actress's Cadillac, the beautiful clothes that the Princess bought for him, and the movie contracts with her signature.

A complete change of subject occurs in the second act. The first scene belongs to Boss Finley; to his son Tom; to his daughter Heavenly; incidentally to Scudder, her fiancé, who is a conventional and decent young man; and to Heavenly's Aunt Nonnie. A pious-mouthed segregationist, Boss Finley is a caricature of a Southern politician; he is currently promoting the career of his son, whose clubs are only blinds for juvenile delinquents.[19] A grotesque figure of degeneracy, Tom is the eager agent of his father's plan, the castration of Chance Wayne. In a curious but super-charged scene that is reminiscent of the Brick–Big Daddy clash, father and son face each other like two beasts after Tom has sarcastically referred to Boss Finley's expensive mistress, Miss Lucy, and to her lipstick declaration on a public mirror that his father is too old to make love.

This aging politician watches his beautiful daughter with the same lust he had felt for her mother, at the same age when he had desired her so intensely. The aristocratic and refined overtones of the scene, accompanied by formal eighteenth-century music, do not conceal either the girl's contempt for a father who drove away the poor boy she loved and who also tried to force other men on her or her bitter reaction to the operation that had made her a childless old woman. She recalls how her father had married for love but had then broken her mother's heart with Miss Lucy. When she talks of entering a convent, the enraged father orders her to appear on the speaker's platform dressed in white in order to dissipate the ugly rumors of her corruption and to save his political fortunes. He tries to bribe her with a lavish offer of clothes and jewels, just as he had given his wife on her deathbed a $15,000 diamond clip (but had returned it to the jeweler immediately after her death). When Heavenly refuses to appear with him, Boss renews his threat against Chance Wayne.

The second scene of the second act finds Chance Wayne trying to impress some of his contemporaries, the conventional local people he meets in the cocktail lounge of the hotel. Aunt Nonnie repeatedly urges him to leave and avoid danger. Throughout the scene, he swallows "goof balls" and vodka,[20] cries over the brevity of youth, and tells her about his first night with Heavenly. She tells him that he cannot return to his "clean, unashamed youth." High on dope, his talk loud and incoherent, he brags about his exploits, his present companion, and his plans for the future. Miss Lucy, also aware of the plot against him, tries to get him out of the way. Having ignored the calls circulated for him, he is confronted by the Princess, who recognizes in him the failure she knows in herself, "that terrible stiff-necked pride of the defeated." In symbolic language unusual for her, she says he is "lost in the beanstalk country ... the country of the flesh-hungry, blood-thirsty ogre."

The dialogue is interrupted by highly charged pantomime as Boss Finley and entourage enter the hotel lobby. Loud-speakers soon carry this politician's speech in support of white men's actions against a "nigger," one picked at random and castrated to prove that "they" mean business about protecting white women. As he continues to talk in pious tones about saving white man's blood from pollution and about being the Negro's best friend, he is interrupted by the Heckler, an El Greco figure, who objects to these "Voice of God" lies; who raises questions about Heavenly, and who scorns his political trick — making his not so pure daughter symbolize the virtue that must be protected by a racist society: "the fair white virgin exposed to black lust in the South." Earlier he had said to Miss Lucy that he thought the world was lost because of the awful, "absolute speechlessness" of God. The scene closes with the sounds of the Heckler's being brutally beaten, but Chance stands there, frozen. At the height of the beating, there is a burst of applause. Then Heavenly, sobbing, escorted from the platform, collapses.

The brief third act returns to the aging actress and her lover, who is now "past the border of reason." Momentarily excited about her own return to Hollywood, she brutally tells Chance that his time is past; that his youth, the only talent he had, is gone; that the enemy time has eaten away his chances.[21] In a curious telephone scene, supposedly made to promote the youngish gigolo who repeatedly begs her to talk about him, she listens to nonsense about her own triumph. Princess is not deluded about her own future, for she sees both herself and her lover as monsters. As the scene closes, Chance is surrounded by Tom and his deputies who are determined to carry out the long-delayed revenge. The final lines are spoken directly to the audience: "I don't ask for your pity, but just for your understanding — not even that — no. Just for your recognition of me in you, and the enemy, time, in us all."

Marya Mannes, probably expressing the majority opinion of the audience, felt "blank amazement" in the final line when Chance asks the audience "not to judge him but to understand him, for he is in each of us, and our innocence is lost with his. To which I was tempted to shout, as Liza did in *Pygmalion,* if not in *My Fair Lady,* 'Not bloody likely!'"[22] Harold Clurman asked, "What is it we are asked to recognize in ourselves? That we are corrupted by our appetite for the flesh and clamor of success? That we are driven to live debased existences by the constrictions and brutality which surround us? That the sound instincts of our youth are thus frustrated and turned to gall? And that we have inordinate fear of age, for the passing of time makes us old before we mature?"[23]

Henry Popkin commented on the inextricably involved Christian and mythological symbolism in the play (the action is placed on Easter Sunday, and each of the main characters hopes for a rebirth). The racist Boss Finley talks of being inspired by the Voice of God and of being burned in effigy on a university campus on Good Friday.[24] Robert Brustein called the play "a private neurotic fantasy" about time and castration: Heavenly, by a hysterectomy; a Negro, emasculated; Boss Finley declared impotent; Princess, by her advancing age; and Chance about to be. Brustein saw in the confused play about childhood innocence a "nebulous nightmare" in which the playwright confuses frankly sexual images with Calvinist notions of guilt.[25]

Like *Suddenly Last Summer, Sweet Bird* was written during a period of analysis; and it is thought to have come from Williams' own life, ideas, and experiences.[26] The playwright's own longing for "the sweet bird of youth" is associated with Clarksdale, Mississippi, where he was protected from the world by his loving grandparents. There is an autobiographical touch in the lines from Hart Crane that are an epigraph to the play:

Relentless caper for all those who step
The legend of their youth into the noon

In the Foreword, Williams speaks of the terror that gave "a certain tendency toward an atmosphere of hysterics and violence," a quality that was in most of his work from the beginning: the Nicrotis story, the first four plays written in St. Louis, and *Battle of Angels,* "about as violent as you can get on the stage."[27] He admitted that every human weakness he had exposed he recognized in himself. He rejected the idea of hating Boss Finley because hatred was akin to insanity, but he found him difficult to understand. Williams also admitted that he had worked through eight different versions of the play; it had presented problems.[28]

When the play opened in New York, all seven of the metropolitan newspaper critics praised it highly; a few murmured grudging reservations. "Whatever its shortcomings, *Bird* opened with the sweet smell of commercial success in its beak." The advanced ticket sale reached $390,000, and the screen rights were sold to Metro Goldwyn Mayer (MGM) for a tidy sum.[29] The play was appropriately termed, "affluent *Bird*."

IV   The Milk Train Doesn't Stop Here Any More *(1963)*[30]

The Milk Train, the play that follows the basic elements of the earlier short story, "Man Bring This Up Road," a phrase used to introduce an intruding guest, is both an allegory and a "sophisticated fairy tale." The dramatist, experimenting with a device common to the Kabuki theater — the stagehands deliver property as needed and at times participate in the action — employs two stage assistants to move screens and properties and to serve as chorus. As the play opens at daybreak, they raise the banner of the golden griffin, a mythical monster that is "half lion and half eagle ... and completely human" — and an insignia that is appropriate for Mrs. Flora Goforth.[31] This wealthy widow has outlived six husbands and has fortified herself on a high point on Italy's *Divina Costiera* against freeloaders, beatniks, and former acquaintances who would gloat over her vanished youth. She is guarded by a brute named Rudy whose two dogs, lupos, waylay the interlopers who come up the goat path. Her only companion, a Vassar girl known as Blackie, must be available at any lucid moment between pills and liquor to take down scraps of her memoirs, most of which refer either to her sensual awareness of her own body or to her vicious suspicions about strangers who might cheat her. She claims to be working against a publisher's deadline; and, though she ignores pain and heavy sedation, she is fighting for the last two days of her life.

Mrs. Goforth, endowed with a handsome and most durable figure, knows that she is a legend in her own time. Born a "Georgia swamp bitch," at fifteen she joined a carnival show in which she moved her anatomy and her tongue; she rose to the Follies while still in her teens; she entered the social register when she married

Harlon Goforth; and she inherited his entire estate as a widow barely twenty. A bit weary at the time of the play, she is "like a race horse that's been entered in just one race too many." Though within hours of her death, she directs her New York brokers to sell stock; she threatens to cut off her crepe-hanging "bitch" of a daughter with one dollar (the rest is to go to a cultural foundation);[32] she fires the kitchen help for stealing, forgetting that she has safely hidden her valuable china; she spies with a binocular on her most recent caller, Chris Flanders, and decides that she needs a lover.

To check on this young man, she summons a contemporary, the Witch of Capri, alias the Marchesa Constance Ridgeway-Condotti, who appears costumed and bejeweled as if she were the Fata Morgana; and their pseudoaffection and their gossip suggest that they are two of a kind. The Witch reports that Christopher Flanders has been christened the Angel of Death because of his appearance in the home or company of a wealthy person, usually a female who is about to die. She relates that he had been at a Nevada ski lodge with Sally Ferguson who had tried to pretend that she was of a younger generation; he had stayed with her through her last fatal illness; but he had gained little for his services because her children had protested the will.

Christopher Flanders, who is in the tradition of Val Xavier and who is also an itinerant poet and sometimes Christlike figure, is not a lover in this incarnation but a kind of mystical companion for the moribund. Thirty-five years old, he appears on this mountain-top villa in lederhosen and with a knapsack heavy with tools for making mobiles. He has the lean and tough appearance common to many El Greco figures and to one who has faced opposition but has emerged fighting and still undefeated. Chris has discovered that it is possible to offer dying old ladies the kind of love that they do not realize they need most. When Goforth snoops through his sack, she finds the heavy tools, no traveler's checks, but a book of poems entitled *Meanings Known and Unknown* and an address book of women, many whom she has known and all of them dead. His approach is kindly and sympathetic to his latest client; but, not having eaten for five days and having recently been hounded out of Naples for being a vagrant, he only wants a little nourishment. His efforts to find something to eat rouse Goforth's suspicions and afford some comic touches.

With considerable theatrical pretense, the play works toward a philosophical discussion between the aging actress and the visitor. Dictating her memoirs, she begins a chapter she calls "Meaning of Life!" which, she suspects, means "going from one goddam frantic distraction to another" until one too many "leads to disaster." The tension increases between the self-pitying vagrant without a home and the widow who calls him a trespasser and a Trojan horse. Explaining that she enjoys writing her memoirs because doing so makes her "absolutely frank and honest with people," she proposes a truth game, a dangerous suggestion, according to Chris, because someone is always hurt. He advises that he needs to have someone to care for because "caring for somebody gives me the sense of being — sheltered, protected." He likens human beings to kittens without a mother; frightened, they live in houses full of strange noises and are dependent upon one another.

When the Witch reenters, she identifies Chris and tries to lure him away from his "vocation" back into the world of living people; but, when he refuses, he calls her "the heart of a world that has no heart." The widow speaks of "the Oubliette" on the beach below where she transfers the undesirables, those pretending to be Truman Capote or Mary McCarthy, because she can not endure being made "a Patsy."[33] After she orders a breakfast for him, and he casually takes a cigarette, she demands a kiss in payment, but he refuses. When Chris wonders how she could be so unaffected by this beautiful place, she suspects him of exploiting the "desperate loneliness" of rich old women who pretend to be younger than they are, and loved. After she has asked if he hasn't written tender lyrics for these susceptible old ladies, she queries him about how many books he has written, and whether he is not already "burnt out as a poet."[34] When Chris bluntly tells her that she lives a mindless, useless existence, he identifies her problem as the "worst of all human maladies." When he calls the publisher's extravagant praise of her memoirs "a snow job," she explodes in fury. He answers quietly by telling her that she needs companionship.

News of a contemporary's death, accompanied by church bells, puts the widow in a state of shock; but she continues her battle against death. When she answers Chris's question about how places she has visited around the Mediterranean and the Nile have affected her, she avers that none left any "message" for her. She peremptorily orders him to light her cigarette; and, when he does not immediately put down her diamond-studded lighter, she implies that he is a thief. This semiserious dialogue is interrupted by

Blackie's frantic question about the kitchen staff's being fired. The girl is answered by news of her own immediate dismissal.

The soft, gentle, almost effeminate Chris remains firm against the dying old woman, whose accusations are spaced with increased helplessness, coughing, and dizziness. Chris evidently somewhat resembles her fourth husband, Alex, a young poet of Romanov blood who was "clothed in God's perfection" and the only one of several husbands who had satisfied her sexual demands. In the final scene, in which she *"resumes her fierce contest with death,"* the griffin banner is lowered. Chris finds a bottle of milk hidden in his sack; he sips it with reverence, and catches drops, as if "sacrificial wine," from his chin. He tells Mrs. Goforth that all people are trapped on the second floor of a house on fire and that they are forced to remain there until they are nothing but a "vision." When Mrs. Goforth, disrobed, stands naked by her bed, Chris observes that she has a body as beautiful as the fountain figures in Scandinavia; but he rejects her invitation to a long siesta. Forgetting that she has fired the cook, she tells him to order whatever food he desires.

Chris tells her that she is a fool not to realize that he is her friend, someone that she will finally need.[35] He tells of the old Hindu from whom he learned the meaning of silence, of accepting without knowing the moment of existence. In her customary fury, she answers that he miscalculated her: "The Milk Train Doesn't Stop Here Any More." As her strength fades, Chris helps her into her bed, which resembles a "catafalque of an Emperor." She gasps as he draws each ring from her fingers and places them under her pillow. To Blackie he wonders shortly afterwards where "all that fierce life" has gone. Shortly after the widow's death, the servants complain that they had not been paid.

The playwright has returned to a plot about mismatched lovers first exploited in *Battle of Angels.* In this play he is even more preoccupied with death but he again overloads the slender theme with so many symbols from several myths that his meanings are unclear. To Robert Brustein, *Milk Train* was Williams' "434th version of the encounter between a pure-corrupt young man and an aging corrupting older woman in a lush and fruity setting."[36] Richard Gilman deplored that Williams continued to have the spoiled-child antics demand attention, for the playwright was making use of the stage "not to solve his dilemmas aesthetically but to exhibit them in their inchoate form."[37]

The critic in *Time* amused himself by trying to figure out the complicated symbolism. Is Chris, who climbs "the goat's path," to represent both St. Christopher (who carried a child across the river only to discover it was Jesus with his load of the world's sins) and Christ? Is the scene of Chris's lapping of the milk on his chin a "metaphorical baptism"? Is Chris, who has not eaten for four days, like Christ who fasted forty? Is Chris, tempted by the Witch of Capri, like Christ tempted by the devil? Is Goforth's tinkling the dinner bell three times like the triple ringing at the celebration of the sacrament of the Eucharist? Chris at thirty-four suggests action after the crucifixion. For this reviewer, Chris was too much an Apollo and other narcissistic Williams' heroes to make him a credible Christ figure.[38]

When Williams called his *Milk Train* "a tragi-comedy," he admitted that Christopher might be a "purveyor" of his philosophy; that, "deeply impressed" during his sojourn in the Southeast, Williams-Christopher brings to Flora Goforth a message that is "vaguely Oriental with Occidental variations."[39] The playright seems to combine the Oriental idea of resignation, of accepting death, with the myth of Christ wrestling with the problem of good and evil, and finally, in behalf of mankind, carrying his burden of sins.

Although these four studies of dominant women — Mrs. Stone, Mrs. Venable, the Princess Kosmonopolis, and Flora Goforth — may have afforded Williams an opportunity to vent his antagonism toward females, the last two characters are presented with a curious blend of satire and sympathy. The "vocation" of the male protagonist in *Sweet Bird* belongs to all the itinerant poets since *Battle of Angels,* but the "vocation" of Chris Flanders places him in the company of Hannah Jelkes. Flora's preoccupation against time, her memoirs about her fleshly adventures, and her suspicion of those who would seem to be her friends anticipate some of the writing that was to appear in the 1970s; moreover, her indulgence in pills and liquor reflects her creator's own tortured self-destruction.

A Streetcar Named Desire broke theatrical records in 1947–48, but the 1964 revision of *Milk Train* lasted only four performances, a failure more devastating than that of either *Camino Real* or *Orpheus Descending.* In spite of this rejection, Williams continued to offer scripts to audiences and critics who were becoming less and less tolerant about his exposure of his own personal, private problems on the public stage.

CHAPTER 7

Unabashed Confessions

I N his *Memoirs* Williams refers to his total collapse in the 1960s as "The Stoned Age" since he had driven himself for about seven years on pills and liquor. During this decade he not only felt totally alone but found it difficult to talk to people and to keep from falling down. Most of the stories discussed in this chapter belong to Williams' earlier decades and range from very closely fictionized biography to situations that are obviously a combination of experience and fiction. Very frequently and straightforwardly, the author presents descriptions of homosexuals and their "loves" and sometimes portrays desperate cases. Studies in sexual indulgence and corruption, and earthy and at times satiric comedy with the emphasis, as usual, on sex are also characteristic. Some of the best stories may be distasteful to the general reader, and for that same reader some are pornography.

In the earlier plays, when Williams dramatized what he had seen, heard, and felt, he successfully fused experience into an art form. In the later plays, he overloaded this experience with abstract forms and complicated symbols, and he at times contrived a situation that scattered in several directions. Although he lost a good part of his audience, friendly critics recognized and commended Williams for the old magic when they found it no matter how luckless a script. Because his personal life has been so extensively publicized, every play tends to be read in terms of his own history. In fact, the despair of Chance Wayne seems to echo the plight of an artist who could not repeat the successes of his youth, and the rebellion of Reverend Shannon and the courageous resignation of Hannah Jelkes suggest the writer's own suffering.

Plays like *Gnädiges Fräulein, In the Bar of the Tokyo Hotel,* and *Out Cry* reveal an even greater tortured state of mind and a dogged determination to continue in the face of despair. Plays like *Seven Descents of Myrtle* and *Small Craft Warnings,* padded extensions of the past, were perhaps written to make money. If "undisguised self-revelations" gave Williams pleasure in the writing of *Memoirs,* the same spirit is apparent in *Moise,* the first "thing" by his own confession, written for the market. He seems to be attempting, in some of the later works, which may be subject to many revisions, the "outrageous comedy" that has been recommended by some of his critics. The appealing humor of the early works has turned to harshness in the plays of the 1970s. What motivates this extended self-exposure, this laying open to the public of so much bitterness and suffering and his own individual lifestyle, is a question to challenge the most sympathetic doctor for tortured spirits.

I   Slapstick Tragedy *(1966)*[1]

Tennessee Williams supported the cause of the Actor's Studio with two plays, *Mutilated* and *The Gnädiges Fräulein,* that were produced under the title *Slapstick Tragedy.* He called these two short plays kin "to vaudeville, burlesque, and slapstick, with a dash of pop art thrown in."[2] *Mutilated,* set in the old quarter of New Orleans on Christmas Eve and Christmas Day, asks sympathy for "the strange, the crazed, the queer ... the mutilated," and particularly for the fifty-year old Celeste and her near contemporary, Trinket. Much of the sparring between these two "winos" hinges on breasts or the lack of them; for Celeste is well endowed, and Trinket, the victim of a surgeon's knife, is hypersensitive over her loss. Celeste, an active "hooker" and shoplifter, tries to return to her old room in the Silver Dollar Hotel; Trinket, talking about a Texas oil well, drowns her brooding over her mutilated figure with California Tokay. Maxie and his Bird-Girl; Bernie, the night clerk; the shore police; and two sailors who are on leave fill in the background. Carolers at the beginning and end of the scenes plead for the miracle of understanding. The religious experience of the two tramps who kiss the imaginary robe of Our Lady appears to be the called for miracle.[3]

Williams calls the two women in *Mutilated* "bohemian habitués of the old French Quarter in New Orleans during the period I spent there, with the action taking place around 1938."[4] Echoes of Blanche Du Bois are obvious, but the Christmas imagery and the "miracle" are soft and sentimental.

II   The Gnädiges Fräulein

Set on Cocaloony Key, *The Gnädiges Fräulein* presents the rocking-chair gossip between Molly, a hard-boiled landlady with social pretensions, and Polly, the society editor of the local gazette. Molly's rooming house restricts tenants to porch, yard, and kitchen privileges. The area is molested by huge marauding birds, cocaloonies, who swoop down to seize whatever is edible. One of the tenants, the Gnädiges Fräulein, "a personage" but also a "social derelict" (a one-time performer with a blood-stained bandage over one eye), appears in a costume reminiscent of the demimondes of Toulouse-Lautrec at the Moulin Rouge. Molly says that she needs to reestablish her kitchen credit by bringing back fish, a difficult job because she competes with the savage birds for castaways that the fishermen consider not good enough for the market.

When the fish boat sounds the third whistle, the Gnädiges Fräulein charges out, flaps her thin arms, utters harsh cries, and is ready to fight for her share. When a commotion and human cries are heard off-stage, Molly recognizes that her tenant is on her way back. When she soon comes stumbling in with a large fish in her bucket, she is pursued by the angry cocaloonies. Unable to find the gate, she crashes through the fence, she runs to the back of the cottage, but a bird soon returns with a fish in its beak. When the Fräulein appears, a large bloody bandage covers the upper part of her face; and she begins to sing "All Alone" in a clear, sweet voice. Molly orders her to repair the fence, despite the fact that Fräulein's second eye is gone, plucked out by a cocaloony.

When the blinded girl picks up her scrapbook, "her album of press clippings," she recites its contents as long as memory lasts; she then picks up her lorgnon, rubs the lens on her skirt, and tries to read. Molly wonders indifferently what she will do with the scrapbook when she discovers that no one wants it. When the fish boat again gives a third whistle, the girl takes off, *"waddling very rapidly like a cocaloony."* Indian Joe, with blond hair and blue eyes, dressed like a Hollywood Indian in breech-clout and wampum, a curious figure that has been in and out of the scene, kicks the door open and beats his chest, "I feel like a bull!" Polly answers with a "MOOO!" but she follows him into the big dormitory.

At the opening in starlight of the second scene, Polly staggers out in complete disarray and hardly able to keep her balance. To prevent her writing an article exposing the moral condition of the establishment and the corruption permitted by the landlady, Molly takes a flash picture for future blackmail. She also gives her a vicious jab with a safety pin that elicits a cry of pain, and adjusts her skirt. When both women return to their rocking chairs, the journalist wonders if she will have "a little more topicality" if the lady never returns from the docks.

As a result of such a possibility, Molly presents the story of the once successful Gnädiges Fräulein who had shared an act with a Viennese dandy who was a seal trainer but who was also a young nobleman with waxed mustache, perfect teeth, false smile, and a ring with the Hapsburg crest. Molly likens him to Indian Joe because the dandy had evinced contempt for the socially inferior and adoring Fräulein.

One day at the Royal Haymarket in London before an aristocratic audience, Fräulein had "overextended herself." The seal, which had just balanced two medicine balls on two batons on his nose and who had applauded himself with his flippers, was as usual hurled a big fish by the dandy, but this time Fräulein caught it in her mouth. Because the public bought the sensational change, the revised conclusion remained in the act for two seasons in spite of the wrangling of the performers' agents. Then, during a memorable performance in Copenhagen, the seal had turned at the moment of climax on the lady, had clouted her with his flippers, and had knocked out her teeth. The show had disbanded, the girl had "lost her sense of reality" and had drifted into one mean job after another. She is now "running up a big tab at the big dormitory," and Molly does not mix sentiment with business.

There is commotion as Fräulein returns with a large fish in her bucket and is pursued by the cocaloonies. Polly, picking up some orange-colored hair, observes that the birds have scalped her. When they hear the sizzle of fat, Molly says that she has not paid for kitchen privileges, that she must "pick up where she left off in show biz," or drift somewhere else. Fräulein, asking permission to speak to the women, comes out to the porch, the skillet with the fish in her hand, and begins to cry "Toivo! Toivo!" — the name of the Viennese dandy; but she is now calling for Indian Joe. After Polly spears the fish, the two gossips go into the house to enjoy it with a bottle of wine. Unaware of her loss, the girl tells Indian Joe that the fish landed in her mouth as if God had placed it there. Indian Joe shouts, "NO FISH IN SKILLET." Shortly after, when the boat whistles for the third time, the gentle, kind girl makes a mad dash for the docks.

Harold Clurman thought that Williams projected himself into the situation of Fräulein the chanteuse who was applauded and glamorized in success but derided in failure. He proposed the following symbolic explanations: the difficulty of bringing in the fish (prestige, status, success); the Cocaloony (birds of prey, possibly the critics); the Public Transient (the public); the society reporter Polly (the press); Molly (managerial powers such as producers, editors, and publishers): the blond Indian (possibly a director). "Too conscious that the author was in pain," and aware of the odd mixture of "gallows humor and Rabelaisian jest," Clurman could not laugh.[5]

III   Kingdom of Earth, *or* The Seven Descents of Myrtle *(1968)*[6]

In *The Kingdom of Earth,* Williams dramatizes the short story but changes the illegitimate brother from a Cherokee to a Negro. Since scenes of sexual intercourse had not yet become a commonplace on the American stage, Williams resorts to his usual teasing suggestions and makes the sexual act a between-scenes happening. In this tobacco-road episode that occurs in a Mississippi Delta farmhouse at flood time, the older brother, Lot, weak and moribund, brings home a buxom, loud-voiced, somewhat hysterical vaudeville actress whom he had married on television, having won with her a supply of electrical appliances. He tells her, a bit tardily, about his father's stinginess and his mother's indulgence in crystal chandelier and in gold chairs (suggested traits of Williams' own parents); he lies about a Negro "unmarried couple" who care for the place; he describes his half-brother, Chicken, who is "not accepted here" because of his black blood; and he demands that she, now mistress in the house, proclaim how much he satisfies her. When the brothers meet, Chicken reminds Lot that they had signed an agreement about the ownership of the property after Lot dies.[7]

The scenes alternate between the kitchen and the upstairs bedroom, but one scene occurs in the parlor, which has become a kind of mausoleum for the elegant dead mother. The seven descents, according to one critic, may refer to the occasions in which Myrtle abandons Lot's upstairs room to join Chicken in his territory, the kitchen. Lot orders his new bride to steal the signed paper that would give the property to Chicken. As the relationship between bride and farm hand grows warmer, he asks that she steal from Lot the marriage license. The contrast between the two men increases to near caricature. Myrtle is offended by the carving that Chicken digs into the kitchen table as indecent and "insulting to a clean-livin' woman." Lot, seated in his mother's satin-decorated bedroom and dressed in his mother's silk wrapper, smokes a cigarette in an ivory holder, wears a Mona Lisa smile on his face, and orders Myrtle to hit Chicken on the head to get the signed property agreement. Instead, Myrtle, assuring Chicken that she does not want the farm, exchanges confessions with this younger brother. When Lot calls her a whore, a prostitute that he brought home to Chicken, she is so infuriated that she takes the marriage license.

On Myrtle's next trip downstairs, Chicken orders her to write a letter giving up all claim to the property; and, to control her nervousness, holds her hand to guide the writing. The magic touch, in the Williams' tradition, naturally wilts the lady; the man, who must be as hard as a rock to survive, asks if she can kiss a man said to have black blood; she, who admits that she is so passionate that a Memphis doctor gave her pills, quickly responds. Chicken hoists himself on the table, his legs wide apart, saying, "My face ain't all they is to me," and blows out the light. Like a choral comment, Lot's voice from above indicates that, as a gift from the dying, he had brought home a whore for his brother.

At the opening of the new scene Myrtle, who is close to Chicken, is as radiant as if she had been through an exceptional experience; and she tells her lover that never before has she gone "that far with a man." Later, she refers to several children given out for adoption. After Chicken tells her to return the pills and demand a refund, he pushes her away saying that after five or ten minutes of having had such intimate relationships with her, he does not want her too close. When he tells her to stop whimpering, he asserts that she is in a state of shock, because of his black blood and not because of sexual indulgences.

Just as Lot appears in an upstairs lighted area in a gauzy white dress and wig, Myrtle admires Chicken's strong figure and admits that they have reached a "perfeck understandin'." He confesses that he was temporarily saved by the preacher Gypsy Smith, but that "spiritual gates" are not for him. Nothing, he says, "in this whole kingdom of earth" is to be compared with what can "happen between a man and a woman." All the rest is "crap." Neither property nor success is greater than having a woman who desires cohabitation, for that alone means that a man "got a square deal out of life."

This relationship has excluded Lot, and his demise is portrayed with a precious theatrical flair. Bedecked in a picture hat, *"bizarre and beautiful,"* and *"transfigured by a sexless passion of a transvestite,"* Lot descends to the parlor and dies in his mother's mausoleum, a scene accompanied by a muted blues song. Chicken, now come into his own, tells Myrtle that he has always wanted a child by a white woman. He opens the door; looks out at his land; and, as the booming sound of the flood increases, calls out to the frogs and crickets to help him celebrate: "Chicken is king!"

To Wilfred Sheed, *Seven Descents* was "in the tradition of neo-homosexual theater, the steady, fly-wing pulling humiliation of a woman, whipsawed and put upon by a fag and a stud."[8] Brendon Gill found incredible the change of Chicken from a gross beast to a philosopher, of Lot from a desperately weak man to an "incarnation of evil," and of Myrtle, under Chicken's "malicious guidance," emerging from "a fool with feelings" to a sexually fulfilled woman.[9] To John Simon, the play was both self-parroting and self-parody, but coarsened. He cited examples of dialogue that indicate a far cry from that in *Menagerie:* "There's two ways to treat a hysterical woman: one is to slap her face, the other is to lay her. Sometimes you've got to do both." He felt that Williams' description of Myrtle's kind of theater is in the same vein.[10] These and other reviewers, who value the distinctive earlier work of this playwright, deplore the descent he willfully took when he allowed his shabby piece to be produced.

Williams wrote many versions of this play: the short story; the one act; the long version staged in Florida; another version, presented at Spoleto; one printed in *Esquire;* the revision for Broadway, where it failed; and another revision for later presentation. He calls the play a three-character "rabelaisian comedy" that concerns "a lonesome, illegitimate half breed [who] finding the solace of religion inadequate, succumbs happily to the wisdom of the flesh."[11] He told Estelle Parsons, who played Myrtle, that, in killing Lot, he "was killing off all the wispy, willowy women he has written about."[12]

Because Estelle Parsons won a Motion Pictures Arts and Sciences Academy Award, the performances of *Seven Descents* were extended from twenty-two to twenty-nine. This play, another "slapstick tragedy," whose title is the only obscure thing about it, a title that became a source of friction between director and play-wright, seems to be the playwright's attempt to work in a different style.[13] Whatever its merits, there is a smell of commercialism about it. Seemingly depressed over the unfavorable reviews of the play and of *Boom!,* the movie based on *Milk Train,* Williams on June 22, 1968, apparently left a message for his brother to the effect that, if anything violent happened to him, he hadn't com-mitted suicide; however, he admitted that he was not happy "in a net of con men" but that he was working hard, "which is my love, you know." His following disappearance led to wild rumors and to considerable publicity, but both stopped when he "surfaced" to call his brother. His mother laughed: "My son has done such things before."[14] On January 11, 1969, recovering from a severe case of flu, he became a Roman Catholic without accepting the idea of immortality.

IV   In the Bar of a Tokyo Hotel *(1969)*[15]

In the Bar of a Tokyo Hotel presents the main characters who recall those in *I Rise in Flame, Cried the Phoenix;* but they are sketched as a result of Williams' sickness and disgust. Mark, the painter, speaks of the complete unity between the artist's life and his work; but he fears that this new style may lead to his crossing the frontier to an area he is not permitted to enter. Sensing that he has made a great discovery about color, he becomes obsessed with his worry that the images that flash in his brain may be lost before they are recorded on canvas. He has visions of entering a jungle country where primitives, hidden in bushes and trees, are ready to shoot him with poisoned arrows. He believes that only color and light will be left after "the gigantic insects" have taken over. When he first appears in the bar in Tokyo, he is ravaged looking; his face, hair, and clothes are splotched with paint; he stumbles and nearly falls; he spills his drink and has to be fed by his wife; and, as if he were struggling to keep control of himself, he speaks in broken and intensely emotional phrases.

His wife, Mirium, a well-dressed and somewhat mannish woman, ridicules his spray painting and his "circus-colored mud pies" as forms of delirium; and she reports that she saw him "crawling naked over a huge nailed-down canvas." She wants to return him to the states, to his Aunt Grace, and to Leonard Frisbie, the gallery director; for both persons have greater sympathy with his antics than she. Mirium had aggressively married this "shy, gifted man" in the hope that he would lift her out of the "trivialities" of her life; but, when he had failed, she had placed him in an institution and continued her infidelities. She now refuses to allow him to join her and her friend Elaine at lunch, though he pleads like a frightened child not to be left alone. He accuses her of surreptitious night adventures, questions the identity of her present companion, and with surprising vigor flings her out of the bar.

Previous to Mark's entrance, Mirium's brazen sexual pursuit of the Japanese barman who considers himself "engaged and not faithless" and his faltering use of the English language afford a few comic moments. She bribes him to send a cable to Leonard asking that he take her mad husband away so that she can continue her trip. When Leonard appears in the second scene, he is deeply disturbed by Mark's physical condition and by the suffering revealed in his painting. Leonard recognizes that an artist with his kind of talent lives in his own private jungle; he does not paint for money.

Mirium repeatedly answers Leonard's sympathetic concerns with the word "crock" or with a sneer about his "pseudo-philosophical cornball remarks." She confesses that she hopes for momentary love from some casual stranger in order to arrest her onrushing age; and, if this fails, she keeps in reserve "the mortal pill box." She has placed in storage under her own name about two hundred of Mark's paintings "before he discovered color with spray guns" and also many of his drawings. Leonard, appalled by her cynical description of her husband's several styles — "drip, fling, sopped, stained" — speaks with understanding of the torments an artist endures, particularly when working in a new form; and he relates how he has protected Mark and other painters from the public exposure of their lesser work.

Mark reappears, breathing hard and tormented by blurred vision; but surprisingly articulate, he continually refers to Mirium's aggressively sexual advances at widely variable prices. Complaining of being tired, he says, wistfully, "Nobody ever gave me a magnum or a quart or a baby's bottle of confidence." Shortly after, he staggers and falls to the floor, dead. Mirium, who is at first glad to be released, insists that she will remain within "the circle of light," her defense against death and oblivion. She, who had earlier referred to inner serenity as "hogwash," now finds that she has no place to go; and she wonders if she does care deeply for this painter husband who created his own "circle of light."

The description of the painter's style lends credence to the report that the death of Jackson Pollock suggested the play. *Tokyo Bar* is made up of a series of arguments between the wife, a "reptilian carnivore," and barman, "a model of stoic restraint"; or the wife and the helpless moribund artist; or the wife and the homosexual art dealer who understands the artist's hell. The static quality of the play may reflect the playwright's fascination with the ritual form of the Noh play, the classical drama of Japan. An intensely personal note permeates the panic of the artist who is insecure about working in a new form, who seeks the warmth of human kindness, and who dreads to be left alone, as if teetering on the edge of insanity. A curious ambivalence pervades the characterization of the two main figures; but, as for the separate identities or two sides of the artist, the spiritual and the carnal, each betrays the other.

Williams in *Tokyo Bar,* as in *The Gnädiges Fräulein,* exposes his own deep suffering. The public may have been indifferent, but the more perceptive critics were not. Walter Kerr quotes a letter from Williams saying that he "was writing about the Artist who makes in the beginning of his vocation an almost total commitment of himself to his work." The playwright adds that the "artist as a rule strongly sexed, seeks another, Wife, Lover, who is for a time willing to serve in second place. In time, though, the Wife/Lover resents the subsidiary role, and resentment grows strongest just when the Artist can tolerate it least, when he is losing his powers, dying. The resentment helps kill him. Only when he is dead does the Wife/Lover realize what has been lost." Kerr considered this letter to be more persuasive than "its ghostly echo on stage," for he thought that Williams had depersonalized the protagonists into The and The, "two articulate blanks."[17]

Harold Clurman, who viewed this play as most subjective, explained that "an artist at the nadir of his career" is destroyed by a "double awareness": he is caught in uncertainty about whether he is about to reach "a never before attained profundity of insight" or is facing "the prelude to the total disintegration of his talent." This "unabashed confession," which may have provided therapy for the playwright, is a statement that calls for knowledge and perceptiveness about the Williams' "case."[18] And Clive Barnes found the play too personal, too painful for the "cold light of public scrutiny."[19]

Life magazine bought a full-page advertisement printed in the New York *Times* on June 10, 1969: "Tennessee Williams has suf-

fered an infantile regression from which there seems to be no exit
... nothing about *In the Bar of a Tokyo Hotel* deserves its production.'' The advertisement boasts about the theater review ''that pre-
dicts the demise of one of America's major playwrights'' as typical
of the ''strong stuff'' that *Life* offers its 36.5 million readers every
week. Frank D. Kilray, president of the Dramatist's Guild,
demanded a public apology from all those concerned — from those
who would embalm ''one of the most distinguished names in the
American Theater'' for no other purpose than to boost the circula-
tion of a magazine in financial trouble. [20]

Williams recalled that the critics tore apart *Tokyo Bar* with such
''demonic pleasure'' that he contracted an assortment of illnesses. [21]
After a series of tragicomic situations, his brother Dakin maneu-
vered his older brother into the psychiatric division of Barnes Hospital, St. Louis, where Williams was enabled to break in two
months his dependence on pills and liquor; but the convulsions at
one time brought him near death. He apparently thought he had
had repeated heart attacks; he exaggerated his experiences in the
''loony bin'' and vented his anger on nurses, doctors, and the
brother who cared for him. [22]

V   Small Craft Warnings *(1972)* [23]

The title *Small Craft Warnings* alludes to the signals given to
small boats during a heavy incoming fog. The play, a revision of
Confessional, assembles several derelicts in a sleazy bar on the
Southern California coast. The dominant figure is Leona, an itinerant beautician who is generous in spirit and bitter over ingrati-
tude and who accents her intense feelings by striking at anything or
anyone with her sailor cap. She scolds young Bill, her trailer companion for the last six months, who depends on his ''tool'' to provide him a living, and who ''thinks the sun rises and sets between
his legs.'' She spends most of her vitriolic anger on Violet, the
recipient of her motherly care, who is a gentle soul with very large
eyes and with hands always groping for the genitals of the man sitting beside her. Steve, a forty-seven year old short-order cook,
gives Violet a few beers and an occasional hamburger in return for
her favors. Doc, deprived of his license for operating when drunk,
is something of a philosopher. Monk, the bar proprietor, who
insists he is not running ''a pad for vagrants,'' patiently tries to
quiet the frequent outbreaks of violence to keep the police away

from his tavern. Two newcomers, a Boy with "Iowa to Mexico" on his sweat shirt, and Quentin, an effetely dressed youth with a ravaged face, complete the roster of social outcasts. Each one of these characters has his moment of confession as he is spotlighted while on the forestage.

As the scene opens, Leona enters to find Bill luxuriating in Violet's attentions; and she explodes over his leaving the fine dinner she had prepared as a memorial to her late brother. Sobbing, Violet flees into the ladies' room. The contempt of the virile male for the homosexual erupts when Bill says that Leona, when drunk, creates a storm over her brother, a "faggot" who was arrested for loitering in a Greyhound men's restroom. Although Bill identifies the Hollywood scriptwriter as one of the brother's party, he would not beat him up because "they can't help the way they are."[24]

Steve complains that he "has to be satisfied with the goddam scraps in this world" such as Violet, who gave him "clap." Emerging from the ladies room weeping, "like a travesty of a female saint under torture," she complains of being sick to her stomach. Leona scoffs, hits Violet with her cap, says that being sick at heart is much worse, and then grows maudlin over her beautiful brother's playing the violin in a church. When Bill says that he was a "fruit," she crashes a chair to the floor and bursts into hysterical laughter.

A phone call to Doc asking him to deliver a baby elicits his musings in clinical and harsh detail about the holy miracles of birth and death. He describes God as a black man Who moves like a Negro in a "lightless coal mine" and Who is made even more obscure by irrelevant forms of public worship. Leona, outraged that this criminal, this drunken quack, can accept a call, rushes out to phone a warning; but Monk, seeking to avoid a disturbance in the tavern, phones to counteract her message.

When Leona returns, she recognizes the tension between the newcomers, Boy from Iowa and Quentin, and asks what has happened. Calling herself a "faggot's moll," she says that she learned about the sickness and sadness of the gay scene from her brother "who came out early" and that she recognizes in Quentin what her brother might have been. Boy is less enthusiastic about "love" than about seeing the Pacific Ocean. Quentin, who long since has lost the capacity for being surprised, and who is too literate for his first Hollywood assignment, now only adds touches of erotica or "bitchy" dialogue for women. He candidly admits that "there's a coarseness, a deadening coarseness, in the experience of most homosexuals" that formulates an unchanging pattern. "Their act of love is like the jabbing of a hyperdermic needle to which they're addicted but which is more and more empty of real interest and surprise." The realization that this blankness spreads to other areas of sensibility, that he was once "a single, separate intensely conscious being," leaves him with a feeling of panic. He no longer has Boy's wonderful capacity of being surprised by what he sees and hears.

The Boy from Iowa tells about a man in his home town who enticed adolescent males into his flower shop and how public outrage forced him to leave so quickly that he could not cover his tracks. When the boys broke into his shop, they found a few pathetic mementoes — wind chimes, dried flowers, pathetic naked pictures, and a few prints. The Boy also speaks about a night on the Nebraska plains when lying under a blanket between a boy and a girl, each offered him love; but his most distinct memory of that event is of a clear, beautiful night. Rejecting Leona's invitation to live in her trailer, he bids her a courteous good night. His departure draws out several comments. Bill observes that "he'll roll the faggot" just like her sweet, innocent-looking brother. Steve says the coast is overrun with them. Monk, caught between police crackdowns and gangster "protection," voices no moral objections to homosexuality but does not want to operate a gay bar. This tavern is his home, and takes the place of family life.

As the second act opens, Leona again speaks about leaving, even in the fog, to find a new place and a new defense against loneliness. She asks only respect from the person she loves and cares for; and, when she does not receive that, she goes. She leaves the blubbering Violet to Bill since her "form of religion" seems to be in her fingers. Doc returns to report that the baby was born dead; that it was placed in a shoe box and put to sea; that the woman died of hemorrhage; that he gave the father a fifty-dollar bill to forget his name; and that he could not make out a death certificate. Monk urges him to leave immediately because of Leona's call about his illicit practice.

When Leona finds Violet, who fails to make it with Bill or Steve, seated beside Monk with her hand under the table, Leona knows that Violet is "worshipping her idea of God Almighty." Though scared of being alone, she leaves. Monk, resigned to having Violet move in with him, urges her to take a shower; opens the door to clear out the "human odors" in the tavern; closes shop; and, ascending the stairs, his smile grows warmer, even when he remembers that she gave Steve the "clap."

Several American barroom plays, most notably O'Neill's *The Iceman Cometh,* portray derelicts who unravel their miserable lives and achieve a kind of dignity. The Williams play is dominated by homosexual and occasionally by heterosexual themes. With the exception of Leona, who, like Hannah, resolutely faces a grim future, the play is a series of static dialogues. The playwright said the play, based on recollections of a bar on the West Coast known in his youth, was "about communication and how we see people and how they show themselves to be what they really are." He began writing it in the late 1960s, at the time he was working on *Kingdom of Earth, Slapstick Tragedy, Tokyo Bar, Knightly Quest,* and *Out Cry.* To Williams both *Small Craft Warning* and *Out Cry* "are part of the catharsis of that period — which came close to disaster." Borrowing a line from the homosexual Quentin, the playwright said that he had almost lost "the quality of surprise" at the time of writing this play, that he had recaptured it, and that he was "capable of involving with life again."[25]

The play is a wearied repetition of old characters in familiar situations, the work of a man who has forced himself on a treadmill. Harold Clurman wrote that the expansion into *Small Craft Warnings* compounded the faults of the one act, *Confessional.* He felt that the play continues the ambiguity of the writer's "compassionate depiction of damaged souls" and his complicity with them.[26] Walter Kerr thought too much time was given to the "defeated homosexual dude" and that the second half of the play was little more than "frantic padding."[27] Gerald Weales recognized the derelicts at Monk's Bar as refugees from earlier plays: Bill, an inelegant Chance Wayne; Violet, queen of "temporary arrangement," an imbecilic parody of Blanche, Alma, and Hannah; Quentin, the mock-artist, Sebastian; Leona's dead brother, Blanche's dead husband.[28]

VI Out Cry *(1973)*[29]

The play *Out Cry* is a much revised version of *The Two-Character Play,* which was offered in London in 1967. At one point during *The Night of the Iguana,* Williams compares the Reverend Shannon and Hannah Jelkes to actors who have come to the end of the road, to possibly their last performance; and that image is

dramatized in this short play.[30] Brother and sister, Felice and Clare,
perform on a strange stage, dark and cold as if underground and
without set or props; the rest of the company has disbanded. They
talk about their own state of mind — a telegram called them insane
— and conditions: her hysteria, his fears, the inability of either to
carry through a simple action, their last season's disaster. Their
mutual confusion seems to merge into the play itself, as if there
were no line between life and art. Sometimes one and sometimes
the other speaks directly to the audience that neither can see. Mock-
ing laughter off stage at one point answers the sister. Clare talks on
the phone to a Reverend Wiley about the rumor which says that
their father killed their mother and then committed suicide;
instead, the crimes were committed by a housebreaker. Clare
defends their father as "a man who had true psychic, mystical
powers"; and she explains that the two of them continue to live in
the family home but that the neighbor's children throw rocks
through the windows. When Felice takes over the phone to contra-
dict her story and says that she is not well, she bridles over the
word, confused; he stifles her objections by placing a pillow over
her mouth.

At the opening of the second scene, Clare is discovered blowing
soap bubbles — a childhood activity, says Felice, that is not appropriate in public performance; but he bursts into laughter: "Mad-
ness has a funny side to it." When brother and sister continue their
argument over their parents, he accuses the mother of emasculating
her husband. They need provisions at Grossman's market, only one
and a half blocks away, where their credit has apparently been cut
off; but the question of whether they will go alone or together and
of how they will appeal to the man in his office leads to another
argument. They come out of the play long enough to realize that
the audience has walked out; that the man, Fox, has left and taken
the box-office cash; that they have no money; that their personal
belongings have disappeared.

The sister believes that the worst condition is awareness of what
is happening to them, something they dare not talk about. Clare
wonders if "The Two Character Play" hasn't been "a little too personal, too special," but neither of them can remember how the play
ends. She recalls nights of "triumph, ovations — times of public
honor"; but presently they have met "another disaster." When
Felice reports that both the front and back doors of the theater
have been locked, Clare panics, then determines, though bone tired

and cold, to find a way out. She says that they must believe they can survive through whatever barricade. The play closes with the brother's line, "Magic is the habit of our existence."

Each character is obsessed by something in his surroundings — his is over cockroaches and over locked doors since his period in State Haven, an asylum, apparently; hers is over a revolver lying around in the house. Despite their disagreement, he expresses admiration for the sister, who has "the face of an angel"; both feel that the house is like a person breathing; and their mutual understanding throws them together. At one point, they have a "convulsive embrace," as if they were lovers reunited after a long separation. Then, very gently, he pushes her away; and each avoids the other's eyes. The illustration on the cover of the printed edition — the head of a man and of a woman who face each other, each bound with cords that are particularly heavy around the mouth and eyes, and both bound together with a small space between them — suggests the subtle and painful relationship between the two. A huge statue, a "monstrous aberration" that can not be moved, dominates the center of the stage. Clare, on first seeing it, observes that not even *Medea* or *Oedipus Rex* could be performed under such a domination. The question arises whether this is the playwright's attempt to give universal meaning to this short and very private play.

Williams observed, "If you must say what it is about, say it is a tragedy with laughter. It affirms nothing but gallantry in the face of defeat — but that, I think, is no small thing to affirm in the Pentagon's shadow."[31] He told another reporter that he had been working on *Out Cry* for five years and that it was probably his last major play.[32]

Critics seemed to agree that *Out Cry* is Williams' most personal play and that it resembles Pirandello in its treatment of the tenuous margins between sanity and insanity. Many called attention to the form, a play within a play, and to the movement from fantasy to reality to memory, a shift that added to the obfuscation. Most writers felt that this very personal statement had lines of great lyric beauty but also clichés that fall flat and literary affectations that lack the quality of poetry.

Hume Cronyn said that Williams' *Out Cry* represents "something monumental" in the theater of the twentieth century; but, having written two good plays early in his career and having failed to succeed in the latest works, Williams desperately seeks new ways of speaking to his audiences, particularly to the young.[33] Gussow wrote that the play has "been rewritten to the point of metamorphoses," each time for a younger actor. He felt that there was insufficient contrast in the two halves of the hermaphrodite characters, so that the effect was that of a person talking to himself.[34] Clive Barnes, placing himself among the minority, thought that *Out Cry* had "a chance of ultimate survival" even though it is "a very brave and very difficult play" about "the deranged children of a false mystic," a brother and sister caught "in the desolate never-never-land of despair."[35]

VII   Vieux Carré[36]

Vieux Carré, like *The Glass Menagerie,* is a memory play that goes back to the 1930s; but, unlike *Menagerie,* this play lacks the powerful urgencies that make for great drama. It is a static play in two scenes, both of them set in the murky upstairs quarters of a run-down rooming house in old New Orleans. The first scene is about homosexual and the second about heterosexual love. The first scene dramatizes the short story "The Angel in the Alcove," in which an aging tubercular Painter introduces a young Writer to homosexuality. The Angel is the memory of the grandmother that befriended, with both money and love, the young Williams who resisted conventional and boring employment as a shoe clerk so that he could write. In *Vieux Carré,* she appears in a picture that is occasionally spotlighted, as was that of the absent father in *The Glass Menagerie.*

The youthful narrator, like Tom Wingfield after he has left the depressing St. Louis flat in *The Glass Menagerie,* again "plays scenes with ghosts of the past."[37] As in the earlier play, this stand-in for Williams participates as the young Writer and also directly addresses the audience about the role he is playing.

The second scene portrays a delicate girl who is dying of leukemia and her heavily masculine lover who is a drug addict and a petty thief. The woman echoes a long line of refined young women — moth figures like Alma Winemiller and Blanche Du Bois — and the virile lover is a Stanley Kowalski character; but in this play both persons have reached the end of the line. Another major figure is the slatternly landlady, a type that has appeared in a number of Williams' short stories; and two gossiping crones, who are lesser figures intent upon finding something to eat, recall the landlady and the reporter in *The Gnädiges Fräulein*.

Walter Kerr found echoes of the genuine Williams' magic in this latest play — those "characteristically tantalizing inflections" which are the hallmark of his best work. But there are also weary echoes — old themes, old characters, old situations — of earlier work that have been resurrected but not restored to life. Mr. Kerr, who regretted that "the nuances of language and portraiture" were "so ruthlessly masked by an irresponsible production," expressed hope for a more successful revival.[38]

VIII   *Later Fiction*

The stories in *One Arm* (1948, 1954), written before the success of *The Glass Menagerie* changed Williams' life, have been recognized as some of his best, and many of them provided the basis for later and longer works. Subsequent collections represent stories based on experiences of the author's early years as well as his later ones; some reflect a change in the writer's own view of his world and a compulsion toward more explicit confession. *Hard Candy* presents fiction of the late 1940s and 1950s; and *Three Players of a Summer Game,* published in England (1960), includes stories from *One Arm* and *Hard Candy. The Knightly Quest* (1966) and *Eight Mortal Ladies Possessed* (1974) range in subject and technique. *Moise and the World of Reason,* the short novel, and *Memoirs,* both published 1975, seem to be parallel confessions. Some of the stories are like fictionized biography; several focus on homosexuality, on lesbianism, sexual indulgence, or corruption; some turn a sexual theme into earthy comedy and satire.

"Grand" (*The Knightly Quest*) is a beautiful tribute to the grandmother who supported with money and sympathy a grandson determined to write.[39] She married a teacher, taught piano and violin, and together they made a good living. After her husband turned to the ministry, they were always moving, always worrying about money, and always dreading dependence during their final years. He dressed well, traveled to New York and Europe; she remade her wedding clothes and saved for the annual trip to St. Louis to see her daughter. For fifty-five years as a minister's wife, she endured the endless "Southern Episcopalian ladies' guff and gossip"; taught violin and piano; took in roomers; sewed for her daughter and her granddaughter, Rose; and kept house without a servant. When the two retired to Memphis on $85 a month, she had saved $7,500 to purchase government bonds; but her minister husband gave $5,000 to two swindlers. He burned all his sermons the next day. On the eve of her excruciating death, she washed dishes, played Chopin, and then two or three hours later went through her final agony. Her last words, interpreted later, were about money sewn into her corset. A companion portrait of this remarkable woman appears in "Oriflamme" (July 1944), dated "the month of my grandmother's death in St. Louis" (*Eight Mortal Ladies Possessed*); it is an Impressionistic study of a dedicated and self-sacrificing woman who feels that life has passed her by.[40]

In "The Resemblance between a Violin Case and a Coffin" (*Hard Candy*), which is closely autobiographical, Williams recounts his childhood compatibility with his sister, Rose; the tensions between the mother and father; the pestering ridicule of boys who thought him a sissy; his sister's falling in love; and his own awakening sensuality as he is attracted to the boy violinist.[41] His exquisitely beautiful sister at fourteen fell in love; but, wrenched between a morbid shyness and an unexpected voluptuous nature, she bungled the children's recital. The door to childhood closed; the brother, about twelve, begins to write. Another story, "Completed," (December 1973; *Eight Ladies*) tells about the extremely shy girl who, when asked to dance by the very young boy, screams and breaks up the party. Alarmed by her first menstrual experience when she is about twenty, she is cared for by an ultrareligious aunt and feels trapped.

Details in "The Vine" (*Hard Candy*) leave the impression that the writer might be talking about his certainty that he is about to die and also about the critical rejection of his early work. He may also have adapted from his own life the sexual experience described. The main character, an unemployed, forty-year old actor, is told by his doctor that there is no "pathological lesion" in his heart; but the patient develops a "psychic trauma" when he learns that he is sterile. References are made to the man's fairly good acting role, but he is obliterated in Chicago by Claudia Cassidy and her "incorruptible justice"; to his acting a young miner killed in the collapse of a shaft; to a playwright whose play is called a "turkey"; to an innocent man who "blunders trustfully" into the brilliant canyons of Broadway. In their youth, the actor and wife went out to eat after the final curtain and then home to bed; and, after their nightlong lovemaking, they ate a hearty breakfast, returned to bed, but never talked. An attempted infidelity left him shattered when the girl hit him on the head and ordered him out: "You make me sick!" He returns home, finds his wife gone, curls into a ball, and cries into the pillow. The wife returns; like a counseling mother, listens; and says, "I know, I know."

The homosexual theme of these stories is variously treated. "Three Players of a Summer Game" (*Hard Candy*) is told by a growing boy who watches with partial understanding the increasing managerial manner of Margaret, the wealthy wife of a Southern plantation owner, Brick Pollitt, who submerges some mysterious personal problem in liquor. Earlier in the summer, Brick turns to the widow of the young doctor, victim of brain cancer, who with her daughter figures briefly and then disappears. The neighbors commiserate with the wife, criticize the widow, and generally misunderstand the situation. Brick, whose zest for life has been mysteriously squashed, considers the mundane affairs that have hardened his wife no more seriously than a croquet game; and he becomes, in the end, a figure of "senseless amiability."

"Mama's Old Stucco House" (*Knightly Quest*) describes the deterioration of an artist-homosexual who is dominated by a mother now a helpless stroke victim; only her eyes can express horror about her son's indiscriminate lovemaking, the heavy all-night drinking bouts of several men, and the obnoxious male nurse hired for night duty. The quiet dignity and responsibility of the black servant and of her mother stand as a comment on the house.

In the title story, "Hard Candy," a gross seventy-year old shop-owner carries sweets in one pocket and eight quarters in the other; and he climbs three times a week to the gallery of a decrepit theater. His last companion is a youthful vagrant; although the old man had cancer, he may have been a victim of foul play; his body, despite its ugly condition, looked as if he had been praying. In a later version of the same story, "The Mysteries of Joy Rio" (*Hard Candy*), Williams introduces Padro Gonzales, a young protégé who becomes the old man's confessor: "It was his theory, the theory of most immoralists, that the soul becomes intolerably burdened with lies that have to be told to the world in order to be permitted to live in the world, and that unless this burden is relieved by entire honesty with *some one* person, who is trusted and adored, the soul will finally collapse beneath the weight of falsity." Pablo, who became an habitué of the upper balcony with its scene of rape and murder, grew old and fat as did his benefactor; and, like him, he was a victim of cancer. On the last day of his life, Pablo recalled the old man's words to the effect that whether men "have it" or do not, they have to be able to go home, alone, "without it."

Two stories, both about writers, may be disguised homosexual pieces. "Rubio y Morena" (1948; *Hard Candy*) tells about a writer, Kamrowski, who is lonely in spite of his famous name. When he is visited in his Laredo hotelroom by the large-rumped Mexican girl Amada, he rejects her at first and then takes her as blindly and as ruthlessly as he wrote; for he is fearful that he could not complete the act. For about a year, they live and travel together; but she remains silent on her side of the room; he, on the other, engrossed in his work. She becomes ill, begins to steal, threatens to leave, and finally does. So deeply involved in his writing that he was unaware of her acute suffering, he tardily misses her. When he locates the girl, very ill, in a shack outside Laredo, he is embarrassed by her display of affection and leaves abruptly. When he returns the next day and finds her dead, women with telegram forms demand the money belonging to Amada, money she had evidently taken. The writer snatches a doll, an effigy of Amada, and escapes.

"Sabbatha and Solitude" (July 1973; *Eight Ladies*), tells about an aging female poet whose work is rejected for being repetitious and about Giovanni, her gigolo for ten years. She enters a restaurant to find her place taken by a new poet, for her own work has gone out of style. Sabbatha had built Eyrie on the coast for her lover, famed for his beautiful body and his successful "trade." After an exchange of insults, he abandons her; and she prepares to die alone. Giovanni, known to have forged checks to keep going, returns emaciated from the hospital with his clinical report about a *fistula*. Asked about their notorious life together, she answers, "All truth is scandal." The old poet is last seen with the tools of her trade, notebooks and pencils.

Two stories from the volume *Eight Mortal Ladies Possessed* are about sexual deviants. In "Happy August Tenth" (August 1970), Williams describes two older women, possibly lesbians, attracted to and repelled by each other. In "The Inventory of Fontana Bella" (July 1972), Williams reviews the life and death of the Principessa Lizabetta, aged 102, and her memory of her lover Sebastiano, still vivid in her groin, who fifty years before had been stabbed by her five greedy brothers. She once thrust the beak of a stork into her vagina; and, as she thrusts her own fist into her groin, she calls softly *"Amore."* The story is embellished with the accounts of her lawyer's rape of a chambermaid and of an artist who wants a naked youth to parade before him with a peacock feather in his anus. A third story, "Two on a Party" (*Hard Candy*), details the adventures of "a female lush and a fairy who travel together"; and sometimes a stranger sleeps between the two queens. Rebelling against "the squares" of the world, they attract their trade to a motel or to a sleezy hotel; and they are always alert to threats of the law. The author sides with the deviants.

Williams' comic sense sometimes appears in strange guises, as it does in "The Mattress by the Tomato Patch" (*Hard Candy*), which portrays the landlady, Olga Kedrova, an apt model for a "massive primitive sculpture," and her sickly little husband, one of those destined to butt their heads against the wall in frustration. Olga, a Marxist, is capable of expressing her fury against the beast that "tells mean lies," but not against the careless lovers who come to her hotel. The writer describes Olga's taking the mattress pad between her breasts and thighs as if it were a lover — and then heaving it by the tomato patch. In minimum sarong, she luxuriates in the afternoon; at night, she often shares a room with a client, and one of them is Tiger, the wrestler. The writer recalls one night when the very heavy noises from their room sounded to him like "the dying confessions of a walrus." In "The Coming of Something to the Widow Holly" (*Hard Candy*), a trio of eccentrics bedevil the landlady until she is finally "wakened" by an attractive male. "The Kingdom of Earth" (*The Knightly Quest*) contrasts the effeminate and weak husband who brings home a bride, with the powerful sex-starved farmhand, part Cherokee, whose prayers are answered when he seduces his sister-in-law, a buxom and not too bright girl. Heavily erotic, the story develops an old Williams' theme: pleasurable lovemaking solves all problems.

"Miss Coynte of Greene" (November 1972; *Eight Ladies*), which is in a spirit like that of "The Yellow Bird," has the quality of an elaborated dummer's story. A thirty-year old spinster, after the death of a tyrannical and incontinent grandmother, establishes an antique business called "The Better Mousetrap." She seduces Jack Jones, night clerk at the local hotel, a beautiful male and stud for both sexes; and she keeps him as her lover until his untimely death. She next takes on black Sonny Bowles, until her house mysteriously burns down and he disappears. She then takes two blacks, Mike and Moon, who squire her with a charcoaled face to the black dances. In twenty years the antique business has grown into four branches, all the lovers are dead, her illegitimate pregnant daughter cohabits with a black guard, and she is pleased that her mission is being left in her daughter's good hands. The writer raises some interesting questions about business acumen, the sexual drive, and race relations.

In the title story of *The Knightly Quest,* world-traveler Gewinner Pearce returns home to confirm his usual allowance, and finds his quiet home town turned prosperous and gross by a government project in explosives, with his brother Braden as the inhuman and authoritative manager of this classified operation, and with Mother Pearce eager to replace her daughter-in-law, Violet, with any wench who has the right government connections. Across the road from the family estate and on land that was once part of it stands the garish Laughing-Boy Drive-in, run by Billy Spangler, a rising young opportunist who hopes for better things. The sexual theme varies: Billy rapes one of his girls, Big Edna, in the men's room and fires her the next day; Braden's grossly noisy and nightly sex is followed by the usual night snack, always delivered by Billy himself; Gewinner, after long baths, perfumed and dressed in exquisite clothes, "cruises" the city streets late at night.[42] Tension in town and on the government project is intense, and there is talk of those who are uncooperative being torn to pieces by dogs.

In a curious counterplot Gewinner, on the side of the good forces, joins his sister-in-law, Violet, and Gladys, a new waitress at the Laughing-Boy, to wipe out the evil represented by brother Braden and his nefarious venture. The three conspirators drive Billy to The Project with his sandwiches and coffee; but someone has secretly hidden a time bomb beneath the food and drink. They watch the inevitable explosion. The melodramatic plot, which might have been lifted from a comic strip, includes among its "characters" message-carrying pigeons who work only for the good people. This comic version of a thriller carries a number of Williams' caricature types: a dominating mother, a businessman-brother like Gooper, an attractively portrayed homosexual, and a big dumb girl who is raped. The most original and genuinely comic figure is the overeager and ambitious Billy Spangler, who is the willing stooge for the boss.

IX   Moise and the World of Reason

The Narrator of *Moise and the World of Reason* supposedly takes down in two Blue Jay notebooks the observations of the title character who is about to retire from "the world of reason," but he speaks mostly about his own experiences and about his own thoughts on life and art. The "I," a Southerner and a sensualist, had at fifteen committed his life to Lance, "the living nigger on ice," and after his death to less satisfactory lovers. He calls himself *"a distinguished failed writer at thirty"* and admits that he has devoted half his life to "shocking revelations and confessions."[43] He is deeply attracted to Moise, (pronounced "Mo-eeze") a "child of God" and one of the purest painters, who introduced him to Lance and to the advantages of homosexual love. Feeling that God gave him Lance, the narrator finds it difficult to distinguish between a truthful report of their love life and "what they call prurience." Describing himself as one who comes from a heritage of "disappearing ladies," he speaks of boys on street corners who offer their eyes "like startled flowers." He recalls his own near initiation in Thelma, Alabama, when, as a boy of thirteen, he was picked up by four strange men in a limousine, driven out of town, but returned home without "instruction." Sixteen years later, still longing for one of them, he remembers "an atmosphere of death on the invisible road map of existence."

Narrator-Williams remembers the defective heart he inherited or acquired because of a childhood illness at eight or nine that turned him into a bedridden reader and fantasizer. He recalls his education in the public library, his preference for *Titus Andronicus* and other literary extravagances, and his observation is that writers are probably "disposed to laugh at all excesses but their own." He expresses his opinion on Edgar Allan Poe, Walt Whitman, and Sidney Lanier's (Williams' ancestor) rejection of Whitman; but he seems to identify himself particularly with Rimbaud and his drunken boat. He also recalls a hardshell Baptist mother who commented on his "inflamed libido"; a frightened spinster teacher with a caged canary that did not sing; a wretched old woman who scrounged for food and whose mother had turned into a crone. The narrator recognizes his own situation: he is drawn tightly to his mother.

He repeatedly refers to rejection slips and wonders about the future of one "with a chronically inflamed libido when the bird of youth has flown." He prefers the company of hustlers over that of writers, calls writing "the loneliest occupation this side of death," calls companionship the most delightful, but admits that work is more satisfying than lovemaking.

In a particularly adept piece of storytelling, the narrator, in an

interview with a student psychiatrist who knew him as a sexual
deviant, confesses an early experience with a sexually aggressive
girl. The student is excited by the report; and this reaction is significant: "Imagined or not, the consequential thing is that I
thought, or imagined, that I now had the ability to excite with
words, good and bad, that I was now truly committed to writing
which might be, and probably is, despised for its visceral (organic)
content."

A number of characters or caricatures briefly represent the world
outside: Miriam Skates, who belongs to the reasonable world in
contrast to that of the artist's vision, is compared to the spectator
who cheers in the Roman Colosseum when a fallen gladiator is
impaled; a man taking the chain off his dog beats it mercilessly; an
aging queen, a transvestite whose libidinous advances to a truck
driver are first brutally rejected and then accepted grotesquely; a
homosexual, victim of a policeman's brutalities, is freed by Moise
who slaps the lecherous cop.

An aging character who has poor eyesight like the author and
who also belongs to the same warehouse world reappears several
times. He speaks about writing a play that made producers wealthy
though he ended in a Bowery gutter. Shy as a youth, he became a
garrulous old man with the help of wine. After he left home in his
teens, he lived a "nomadic sort of existence" as if in search of
"something of vital importance" which he had lost; he did have a
fellow of his own "gender and inclinations" until four packs of
cigarettes a day destroyed him. The elder feels that his "Collected
Works" make him sound as if he were dead; he must cross out
names in his address book as "victims of time"; he seeks a traveling companion in a younger man. Surprised at the indifference of
the narrator to the older man, Moise identifies him with this derelict playwright; and she urges her friend to rid himself of this companion since there is nothing worse than living with an image of
one's future self.

Moise, the visionary who works compulsively toward the com-
pletion of a painting, speaks to the narrator during one of these
creative seizures. She rebukes him for his self-centered work and
life, accuses him of substituting words and shibboleths "for the
simplicities of true feeling," and criticizes him for his failure to
show anything but himself and his cleverness. Moise works in a
trance, a state of reflection; for she is certain that "reflecting" is a
way of knowing things without attempting to find solutions that do

not exist. The final scene pictures Moise bathing the narrator's feet in warm water and drying them with her hair. The younger of the two men come to photograph these paintings with their box cameras, looks at the narrator with eyes of love.[44]

X   Memoirs *(1975)*

Tennessee Williams approached writing his memoirs as a new art form, "undisguised self-revelation"; and the reader has at times the feeling of eavesdropping on the author's private confession to his analyst. With amazing candor Williams describes his love life, his "cruising" the streets for one-night stands, his always looking for "a good lay," and his remembering on happier occasions how "the nightingales sang and sang." A few pick-ups led to rough action and to considerable danger to the playwright. His long association with Frank Merlo, his paid secretary-companion; his seemingly ruthless dismissal of Frank; this friend's terrible bout with cancer and death; and, afterwards, Williams' bleak loneliness and tardy recognition of the dedication in that friendship afford curious insights into the demands of the playwright. Close friends and casual interviewers have said that these "companions" earn their keep. The sexual excesses described in these *Memoirs* disturb many who recall the impressive number of stage characters Williams has created; they like their voices but not that of their creator. Even more shocking than these sexual rampages is the dependence on drugs and alcohol and what that says about Williams' view of the creative process.

He has known many prominent figures in the world of theater, literature, and public life — so many of them no longer living — and he makes a number of shrewd observations, and some unkind ones. He resents any criticism of his work, even though he has rewritten over and over again to please an actress, an actor, or a director. He is uncharitable to those critics who have spoken most favorably when he is at his best, and who hope for that kind of return, but who have dared to point out his weaknesses. As for his failures in the 1960s and the 1970s, he never recognizes his own problem with a play; he blames the actor, the director, or the audience. There are men and women whose friendship he values and whose talent he admires, but he recognizes that women have been his most devoted audience.

He speaks often of his pride and recalls a number of incidents

when he "put down" someone who offended him; theatrical lines
have become a part of his everyday speech. In one of his hysterical
"mad scenes," he drove away Audrey Wood, his patient and brilliant agent from 1939 until 1971, because he felt that she did not
properly appreciate *Out Cry*. The memoirs, as is to be expected,
provide considerable gossip about who's in and who's out; many
references to parties and having "fun"; spur-of-the-moment overseas phone calls to friends and trips to exotic places, but not many
voyages via Pegasus; references to interviews where he deliberately
would "ham it up" to provide the reporter with "good copy"; sardonic amusement about the television people who got "some foot-
age on the notorious playwright." He says frankly in the introduction that he undertook this "thing" for "mercenary reasons"; and,
though he often makes a case for complete honesty, the question
about the book remains: to what extent truth — or exhibitionism.

CHAPTER 8

The Literary World of
Tennessee Williams

I A New Concept of Theater

TENNESSEE Williams was thirty-four when *The Glass Menagerie* acclaimed him as a new voice, and he was thirty-six when *A Streetcar Named Desire* broke theatrical records. For Williams, theater offered a medium for giving the audience an emotional experience, for exploring the inner mechanisms of human personality and behavior, and for doing so in a way that might be startling or shocking but forceful enough to be remembered. In his determination to reach across the footlights, he has made use of the old theatrical devices that have been effective in popular drama over the centuries; but he has also exploited the endless possibility of technology to add new ones. As a result, he has returned excitement to the theater.

He is said to have "changed the theater and the taste of the theater" and to have opened the way in America for dramatists who, like Pinter, have explored the complex and hidden psychological drives that motivate people. In Williams' continuing presentation of themes previously considered untouchable; of derelicts and misfits, outcasts from a materialistic society; and of the thin line between sanity and insanity, he has revealed a broken world not often portrayed. Because of his bent toward sensationalism, he might seem to have escaped from the realistic tradition dominated by Ibsen and Shaw that continued with the Group Theater, a tradition that viewed the stage as a kind of lecture hall or pulpit. However, because of Williams' preoccupation with the ugly world in which monsters and hypocrites destroy the defeated, frustrated little people, he has given much of his work the quality of morality plays.

II   *Writing as Autobiography*

From the beginning, whatever Tennessee Williams wrote was a record of his own experience that is sometimes directly, sometimes obliquely stated. Williams himself is a highly complex person who has admitted that he has not written anything that he has not known firsthand, that what he finds in himself at the time of writing he assumes to be universal experience, and that he believes in the "absolute one-ness" of the artist and his work.

As has been observed earlier about Williams, his childhood bout with diphtheria restricted his activities and his acquaintance with normal children, drove him to books and his own fantasies, lengthened his dependence on his mother and led to his early estrangement from his father, and developed a lifelong hypochondria over his health in spite of his doctor's assurances. The intense personal commitment to his sister, Rose, the alter ego of his childhood whose mental crisis was so tragically mishandled and without his knowledge, has continued throughout his life; for years he has supported her in a sanitarium at Ossining, New York. It has been said "that the curtain came down with the loss of Rose."[1] She, who never should have been subjected to the rigors of a Southern debut, and whose sexual fantasies shocked the mother, was subjected to one of the earliest and least expensive experiments in prefrontal lobotomy.

As Williams grew older, he understood the incompatibility between his strict and at times unworldly mother and his father, who was a boisterous Cavalier but at heart "a totally honest man." He understood why his father found his relaxation in drinking and poker, and why he was distressed by the growing effeminacy of his son. When Williams could do so financially, he enabled his mother to secure a divorce, but he felt sympathy in the later years for this man of difficult temper who was relegated to a lonely hotel room where he died alone. To Williams' friends, he is in a way his father's own son: he is boastful of his masculinity, unafraid of a confrontation, and for years was a notable drinker and poker player.

Though devoted to his mother, he later referred to his "infantile impotence" as a writer as a consequence of his pampered childhood; and his changing attitudes may be reflected in his increasingly bitter characterizations of mothers. This figure in his writing represents the strictures and morality inherited from the Puritans that have been hardened into a few simplistic rules. Garrulous Amanda, for all her set ideas of goodness, is sympathetically presented; but Mrs. Buchanan in *Eccentricities* is a dominating mother and a fool; Big Mama is silly and coarse. The later works also seem to imply that the mother prevented the normal development of her son: the mother in "Mama's Old Stucco House," the mother described by the Reverend Shannon, and most despicable, Mrs. Venable of *Suddenly Last Summer*. Williams has referred to his own mother as "that slightly cracked southern belle," and he has implied that her "sum total influence" led him into homosexuality. About her verbal compulsion, he observed recently that his mother will "be talking a half hour after she's laid to rest."[2]

Camden or Clarksdale, Mississippi, towns where he lived happily with his grandparents, came to represent the "vanished Eden" and Southern gentility at its best. In contrast to these idyllic scenes of his childhood, he discovered as a young adult the French Quarter of New Orleans where he became a "confirmed Bohemian." The conflict between these two meaningful experiences — the proprieties of his early training and the unlimited freedom discovered in New Orleans — perhaps help to account for the extremes of his own reaction and for the subsequent direction of his own life. This conflict is reflected in the sense of guilt that hounds the "immoralists" in his stories and plays, for they are tormented by having indulged in their deviations. The shock of the bohemian freedom and his pleasure in it may also have supported his early conviction that no subjects are taboo for a writer.

III *Preoccupation with Sex*

There has always been in Williams a quaint absorption in the old-time Puritan preoccupation with sex, the sin that Dante placed at the rim of hell since it is far above and less despicable than fraud and deceit. In the earliest plays, he portrays sexual freedom as a kind of "redemption" that is available only to women and in comic situations. It becomes a panacea for the women in "The Crushed Petunias" and in *You Touched Me!;* it is a glorious indulgence in "Yellow Bird" and "Miss Coynte of Greene"; and it apparently "resurrects" Serafina delle Rose in *The Rose Tattoo,* the raped girl in *27 Wagons,* Myrtle in *Seven Descents,* and Dorothy in *Period of Adjustment*. In other cases, sex takes the form of perversion: Blanche and Alma represent "corrupted innocence," as do Val

Xavier and Chance Wayne and, to a worse degree, Mrs. Stone. Williams paean to male sexual vigor is to Stanley Kowalski, but he also praises Latin lovers like Vacarro and Alvaro. The young doctor in *Summer and Smoke* seems like a parody of Stan.

In the early writing of Williams, disguised references are made to homosexuality or to a contrast between the attractive homosexual and an obnoxious "normal" character. When the subject became commonplace, Williams described the relationship with increased particularity. The poem "San Sebastiano de Sodoma" is a glowing tribute to the saint-homosexual in ambiguous terms. "Night of the Iguana" and "Two on a Party" take a defensive attitude to the theme, and Blanche's husband is a victim of social rejection. "Rubio y Morena" cloaks the theme in the seemingly transvestite character of the large Mexican girl. Baron de Charlus, in *Camino Real,* justifies himself as escaping from the sordid world; Brick Pollitt is also an escapist. Apollo of "One Arm" is favorably contrasted to the host and his guests at the stud party, and the writer-narrator-Williams in *Moise and the World of Reason* elaborates upon his pleasure with Lance, the black ice skater. Sebastian in *Suddenly Last Summer* is a degraded figure. The dude, Quentin, of *Small Craft Warnings,* complains about the dreary monotony and loss of sensibility in the homosexual. The old men, gallery habitués in "Hard Candy" and "The Mysteries of Joy Rio," and the ancient who pursues the writer in *Moise,* are pitifully depraved figures. Williams' sympathy with sexual abnormality in later years has given way to a compulsion to tell all about himself and his world. He knew that his *Memoirs* would bring "considerable embarrassment" to his publishers, but he refused "to dissimulate" the facts of his life.[3]

IV   *The Sensitive and the Predatory*

Williams has always placed his protagonist, a sensitive and lonely individual of either sex, in an unfriendly world. The poet-itinerant-outsider — the male who is often closely identified with his creator — seeks to avoid the full responsibilities of a job and of family life. The protagonist can be recognized as Williams throughout his work: he appears in the early poems; he is the young lumberman in *Moony's Kid Don't Cry;* he is Tom Wingfield, who ran away from home and the shoe factory but could not forget Laura; he is Val writing a book on life; he is Chance Wayne, a failed artist who like

Val is aware of the enemy time, fleeting youth, and imminent death; he is the son in "Mama's Old Stucco House"; he is Christopher Flanders, who eases rich old women into death. The outsider thinks of the creative force as a kind of vision: Val Xavier, Vee Talbott, Mark in *Tokyo Bar,* and Moise. The outsider may be a former athlete, like Kilroy or Brick; he may be an idealist or an innocent; he may be the one-armed Apollo — but all are marked by the "charm of the defeated." Williams first achieved recognition for his delineation of the feminine outsiders, Southern gentlewomen, moth figures destroyed by predators, who appear in the stories "Portrait of a Girl in Glass," "Portrait of a Madonna," "Three Players of a Summer Game," and "The Night of the Iguana." These gentlewomen, "trapped by circumstance," later appear as Amanda Wingfield and her daughter Laura, as Blanche Du Bois, as Alma Winemiller, as Isabel Haverstick, and as Hannah Jelkes.

The predators, the destructive mammoth figures, take several forms: Stanley, the primitive sexual force; the symbols of power and seedy corruption in *Camino Real;* The Gooper clan in *Cat;* the rednecks in *Battle of Angels* and *Orpheus;* Boss Finley and his son Tom in *Sweet Bird;* the black therapist in "Desire and the Black Masseur"; the starving children in *Suddenly Last Summer.* The predator may be a dominant woman like the rich and decadent Mrs. Stone; the rich, moribund Flora Goforth; the Princess Kosmonopolis; Mrs. Faulk, the aggressive padrona in *Iguana;* or Mirium in *Tokyo Bar.*[4]

Tennessee Williams has said that he is unable to create normal characters, but a few stand out: Stella Kowalski, happy with her husband; Nellie, the giggling teenager in *Summer and Smoke;* Baby Doll, a bit addlepated but attractive; Maggie the Cat, scrapping for her share in life; Catharine Holly, with her passion for truth telling; Serafina's daughter, with her healthy view of sex. Among the men are Jim O'Connor, who struggles for self-improvement; John Buchanan in *Eccentricities;* Mitch, who is devoted to his mother but is also an acceptable partner at poker; Scudder, a kind of haberdasher's model who courts Heavenly Finley. The salesman of the solid gold watches is the integrity of the old order, and Big Daddy, a full-blooded, self-made man, is a materialist who is as perceptive as he is rich.

V *Williams as Scenewright*

Williams, always concerned with highly charged dramatic scenes rather than with organic development, has been called "a vivid and exciting *scene* wright." Individual scenes often represent Williams at his theatrical best. Among many examples are the following: the delicately renewed acquaintance between Laura and Jim; the violent erotic clash between Blanche and Stanley; the courtship scene between Serafina and the new truck driver; the comedy scene of Baby Doll protecting her virtue; part of the Brick–Big Daddy argument; the confrontation of Lady and David Cutrere; the dramatic truth telling of Catharine Holly; the confessional Hannah-Shannon scene.

The *Glass Menagerie,* which in form is as simple as a short story, is very effective; and the same assessment might be made of *Eccentricities of a Nightingale.* Williams' habit of overloading characterization is paralleled often by multiplying discordant plot elements and by including too much of everything. *Battle of Angels* and *Orpheus Descending* are complicated by extraneous characters and universal meanings; *Summer and Smoke* and *Sweet Bird of Youth* also attempt too much; and, after two good acts, *The Rose Tattoo* and *Cat* are artificially concluded in a weak third.

The *Glass Menagerie* has been called a series of one-act plays, and the same could be said of *Camino Real.* The clash between two people in one scene or act may be repeated in the following one but with different characters, as in the first and second acts of *Cat* or the two scenes of *Suddenly Last Summer.* The episodic construction lends itself to the memory technique: *The Long Goodbye* preceded its full use in *The Glass Menagerie.* The techniques of delayed bit-by-bit confession make up the early one act, *The Dark Room;* a series of self-revelations unfold the story of Blanche; the story of incest in *The Purification* is revealed piecemeal; *Small Craft Warnings* is almost entirely a series of recollections, as is *Period of Adjustment.*

VI *Idiomatic Language*

When at his best, Williams conveys the impression of idiomatic language, no matter how different the mood and subject. Critics from the beginning have noted the clever way he combines clichés and original speech. Through his use of words, he has been able to increase suspense and to enhance the quality of character and emotion. He has added dramatic intensity by delaying revelations during the dialogue, as in *Cat;* he develops the entire situation in *This*

Property Is Condemned in casual dialogue; he substitutes dramatic argument for action in the later plays, as in *In the Bar of a Tokyo Hotel* and in *Out Cry*. He often concludes an explosive argument with a quiet line: Big Daddy's answer to Big Mama, the doctor's quiet comment after the story in *Suddenly Last Summer*. Unfortunately, Williams has not been able to strike from his plays those rhetorical lines that on occasion hold up a scene. Sometimes lines of self-conscious poetry, of pseudophilosophy, or of schoolmaster's exposition intrude upon the attention. At times characters deliver long speeches or arias, as Elia Kazan called them. As noted earlier, Joseph Wood Krutch, reviewing the opening of *The Glass Menagerie,* spotted this weakness and urged the young playwright to strike any line that he particularly liked.

VII　*Experimental Devices*

Because Williams has had a definite idea of what theater should be, he has experimented with many devices and theatrical techniques to enhance the dramatic impact of his plays. He often sets one scene against another. While Blanche sings in her bath, Stan unravels her ugly story; when Blanche appeals to Mitch, the Mexican woman is calling *"Flores para los muertos";* when Blanche at the phone attempts to contact a former suitor, a drunk and a prostitute struggle off stage. When Rosa pleads for love with Jack, noisy off-stage sounds tattle on Serafina and Alvaro. The ugly squabble over the estate in *Cat* is accompanied by Big Daddy's cries of agony; the *pieta* scene with the Madrecita and Kilroy and the post mortem one occur simultaneously in *Camino Real* — unfortunately; the busy second act of *Sweet Bird* contrasts off-stage brutality with Chance Wayne "frozen" on stage.

Williams has resorted to symbols, some effective and some not; he justifies their use as "the purest language of plays" and as a short cut that eliminates tedious exposition. The little glass ornaments belong to Laura; the snakeskin jacket seems to represent Val's freedom; the trunk of faded dresses and letters in the crowded apartment suggests Blanche and her intrusion. The bird imagery in *Orpheus* and *Suddenly Last Summer* seems literary, and the fountain and the anatomy in *Summer and Smoke* seem forced; *The Rose Tattoo* is cluttered with roses, goat cries, and eccentrics. Other symbols are obvious: A. Ratt, and the plane Fugitavo in *Camino;* the big double bed and the television set in *Cat;* the confectionary in *Orpheus.* Many characters are symbols, and for some reason the degenerates — Blanche, Apollo, and Sebastian — appear in white. When Mrs. Stone represents the corruption of our time, poor Kilroy every little struggling man, or the predicament of Chance Wayne a commonplace, the symbolism then belongs to the private world of the playwright.

To intensify the mood, Williams makes full use of light and color as if he himself were a painter. The vivid poker game in *Streetcar* is likened to a Van Gogh picture; the setting for *Summer and Smoke* is to resemble the nonrealistic design of a Chirico; *The Rose Tattoo* calls for blue sky like that in an Italian painting of the Renaissance. Like the mood music of the films, sound enriches many of Williams' scenes: the cheap music across the alley in *Menagerie* suggests Americans unaware of the Spanish Civil War; the community band in the city park in *Summer and Smoke* conveys an age gone by; the jungle noises in the mad scenes in *Streetcar,* and repeatedly throughout *Suddenly Last Summer,* heighten the tensions; the "blue piano" underscores the sexual theme in *Streetcar.*

VIII   *Williams' Comic Sense*

From the beginning, Williams has shown a talent for comic figures and scenes: the outlandish and amusing riffraff in the poems; Archie Lee Meigham, who builds his own humiliation; the silly tourists in *Lord Byron's Love Letter;* the preposterous McGillicuddys in *Period of Adjustment;* the clumsy salesman in *Tattoo;* the gossiping wives in *Battle of Angels;* Billy Spangler, yes man in "The Knightly Quest"; grotesques like the Gooper "no-neck monsters"; the garish Rosa Gonzales in *Summer and Smoke;* the stately witch in *Milk Train;* the impertinent youth in *Gold Watches* and *Portrait of Madonna*; a clutch of ministers — the Lutheran in "One Arm," and the several reverends in the plays.

Williams' comic sense emerges in several scenes in *The Glass Menagerie:* Amanda's trying to sell subscriptions, the lights going out on the dinner party, Jim's trying out his speech lessons on Laura. There are comic scenes in *Streetcar:* Blanche's outlandish pretensions, Stanley's explanation of the Napoleonic Code, his frustrations over her condescension. Williams can spin a humorous yarn: "The Yellow Bird," "Miss Coynte of Greene," most of "27 Wagons Full of Cotton," and the situation revealed in the play *The Dark Room.* He shows his talent for folk comedy in the ribald humor of Alvaro's courtship of the widow; her discovery of Rosario's infidelity and acceptance of the new truck driver. His bent for satire is evident in such scenes as the literary evening in *Summer and Smoke,* or in the character of Braden Gewinner in "The Knightly Quest."

Often, the public may not share Williams' sense of the comic: his own laughter at *Suddenly Last Summer;* the intended humor of *Period of Adjustment;* the rape of the fat girl in *27 Wagons* and "Knightly Quest"; the cruel laughter in *Gnädiges Fräulein.* The quick flash scenes of a naked or near-naked woman — Carol Cutrere, *Battle of Angels;* Eve, *Camino Real;* Mrs. Goforth, *Milk Train* — may be funnier than the playwright intended. Kenneth Tynan has commented on Williams' "mental deafness" that makes him laugh in the wrong places.

IX *Portrayal of Evil*

His contemporary world is often a kind of hell: the small towns in *Battle of Angels* and *Orpheus* destroy the outsider representing the virtues of the Old South; racist Jake in *27 Wagons* burns the Italian's mill and exploits black labor; in the hell of *Camino Real* the individual is expendable; St. Cloud, in *Sweet Bird,* is dominated by a racist brand of gestapo; the town in "The Knightly Quest" is a government-operated police state. As indicated, the death motif is closely allied with the predator theme: the everpresent Street-cleaners in *Camino Real;* the Val Xaviers are persecuted by the sex envious; atonement in *Suddenly Last Summer* takes the form of cannibalism; the death theme permeates every character in *Sweet Bird. Iguana* and *Milk Train,* with an emphasis on acceptance of the inevitable, represent a turning point.

Williams exploited the dramatic possibilities of the Easter story: the devouring of little Anthony Burns culminates on Good Friday; Val Xavier is crucified by a blow torch on Saturday night before Easter; Chance Wayne is castrated on Easter Sunday. Williams has his own interpretation of Christ as the savior of mankind: Apollo of "One Arm" takes the confessions of participating homosexuals, as if he were Christ; Val Xavier becomes the image of Christ for Vee Talbott; Christopher Flanders becomes a Christ figure with an Oriental slant; and, in the incredible final scene of *Moise and The World of Reason,* narrator-Williams, whose feet the artist Moise bathes and wipes with her own hair, seems to personify Christ. The references to God, as if in human form, emerge in even stranger images when the Reverend Shannon blames God for his faulty construction of the universe; Doc in *Small Craft Warnings* speaks of God as a sightless black man; in the same play, Violet's God apparently exists in her lecherous fingers; little, luckless Kilroy pities everybody, the world, and even God Who made it.

X   *Writing as Therapy*

From the time that Williams was twelve years old, so he has repeatedly said, writing has been a therapy for him, a "purification" of sickness. Often the work that appears after an illness or a traumatic experience reflects a jaded view of a world that is full of monsters and of "enormous hypocrisy." Williams has admitted that it is easier for him to identify with those "who verge upon hysteria." As one critic wrote, Williams' view of life is "always abnormal, heightened and spotlighted and slashed with bogy shadows."[5] His affinity with the disenchanted and with the drug cults has raised questions as to whether or not he was a spokesman for the vocal subculture of the 1960s. Though he denies that his work is autobiographical, the many interviews of recent years, the "psychological dissections," and the *Memoirs* indicate the very close parallels between his work and his own life.

XI   *The Price of Early Success*

Fighting to regain the high position he achieved early in his career with a play about every two years, Williams has subjected himself to merciless criticism when he has been unable to reach his audience. His reaction to these rejections and subsequent illnesses have become part of the public record. Claudia Cassidy suggested that Williams, who was able to create "many valorous characters," was perhaps too vulnerable to bring that same valor into his own life; that the violence in his plays came from within him; that he rewrote to meet directors' demands; that he let himself be injured by unfavorable criticism. Sometimes Williams' multiple revisions suggest that he does not trust his own judgment, or that, as he has admitted, the revising delays the separation between him and his work at hand.[6]

His hard and dedicated labor has earned him both prestige and money. In 1962 Williams was reputed to have earned over six million dollars in his playwriting career, though he does not consider himself in the material class with Terrence Rattigan or Noel Coward.[7] His firsthand experience with theatrical business has sharpened his sense of what should come his way; his later plays reflect a bitterness against those who have exploited him, and he has been his own best publicist. For years, a piece always appeared in the *New York Times* preceding the opening of a play. His absent-mindedness about money is legendary, but so is his generous support of writers and artists who need encouragement.[8]

XII *Ambiguity about Honesty*

Williams has always valued honesty above morality. He praised the honesty of his father and of his long-time companion-secretary, Frank Merlo; the honesty of Alma in *Eccentricities,* of Brick and Maggie in *Cat,* of Catharine in *Suddenly Last Summer.* Whether the demands of honesty in *Memoirs* exist to quiet his own soul or to make the book a best seller remain ambiguous. And yet if an interviewer, having made the conditions clear beforehand, writes about the "hermetic atmosphere" and the "Byzantine complexities" of Williams' Key West establishment, the playwright dashes off a mad letter to the editor.[9]

There has crept into the later works a vulgarity and a coarseness that is not to be found in the early stories and one acts but that may be included because it has become necessary to "hit them with something." Although one critic called Williams "a gentleman who seethes with inner violence and something akin to self hatred,"[10] Williams, except for a few pieces, continues to be preoccupied with sex, about which he is not only explicit but also startling in vocabulary. The soft images of early childhood and the tender feelings for the unfortunate are strangely mixed with the kind of expressions that suggest the graffitti of an early teenager who is thumbing his nose.

Success has brought problems. For years an itinerant like his protagonists, but known worldwide in later years, Williams has had to battle for privacy. Quite early he became suspicious of praise: "I'm afraid I often think they are trying to make a fool out of me."[11] A man of volatile temperament and one who is scrappy when his work is attacked, he can be abusive; but, having tasted the bitter-sweet fruits, he is able to be "reasonably objective about himself." He told Mike Wallace that "all reputations in the theater are in-

flated reputations," and that no one is as good as the publicity
suggests. He added wryly that, as the discrepancy between the
actual being and the public image widens, the reputation
increases.[12] He recognizes that the sex theme is no longer startling,
that his "pseudo-literary style" is on the way out, and that his own
bête noir has been his tendency to poeticize.[13] He continues to be
much interested "in the presentational form of theater, where
everything is free and different, where you have total license."[14]

XIII *Williams' Position in the American Theater*

As Brooks Atkinson wrote in 1956 after seeing a revival of *The
Glass Menagerie,* "To see it again is to realize how much he has
changed. There is a streak of savagery in his work now. The humor
is bitter. The ugliness is shocking. He has come a long way since
1945 — growing in mastery of the theater, developing power,
widening in scope. He has also renounced the tenderness that
makes 'The Glass Menagerie' such a delicate and moving play."[15]
Louis Kronenberger, apropos of *Sweet Bird,* commented on the
development of the playwright: "Whether a world of loathing and
disgust, or sex violence and race violence, of lurid and bestial
revenges, constitutes Mr. Williams' personal reaction to life or sim-
ply his philosophic vision of it, it has come to seem compulsive in
him rather than convincing in his people."[16] The often pilloried
Claudia Cassidy has asked what happened to this playwright
"whose talent for lyric theater was streaked with laughter"; to his
"intuitive sense of direction"; and to his plays that have become
"monstrous."[17]

Stanley Kauffmann paid tribute to the playwright whom all
actors want to play: his "superb theatrical talent; his eye for stage
effect, his skill in scene construction, his gift for dialogue that can
cut to the bone, that can use cliché with humor and poignancy, and
that can combine the odd floridness of lower class character with
his own rich rhetoric." Disappointed in Williams' later work in
which Kauffmann finds an increasingly thinner disguise of old
material, he observes that what was shocking in former years is
later only "tame and self-consciously squalid." He also notes that
what formerly was considered "sexual candor" and "poetic evoca-
tion" has now "taken on taints of merchandizing for the Williams
market." Kauffmann recommended, as has been noted earlier, that
Williams exploit his great talent for "outrageous comedy."[18]

Williams continues to write and to rewrite, and producers continue to mount his plays on American and foreign stages. It is obvious that the playwright is trying to work with a variety of dramatic forms and to exploit changing techniques in order to reach his audience, but he has not very successfully done so in his more recent years. *Vieux Carré* (1977), a restatement of old material in a form reminiscent of *The Glass Menagerie* (1945), is, like *Out Cry* (1959), a static play in the Chekhovian tradition. According to reports, *Red Devil Battery Sign* (1975), combines an incredible plot with political implications; another play of the 1970s, *Whore of Babylon,* is said to be "outrageously funny"; and *This is (Entertainment)* (1975) deals with the funny side of social revolution.[19]

Williams, generally recognized as the foremost playwright to have emerged in the American theater, has for over three decades dominated not only the stages of his own country but also of the international theater. Walter Kerr, who has always been ready to recognize the touch of genius in an otherwise poor Williams' play, has repeatedly proclaimed that his contribution has been considerable. In his latest statement, part of his review of *Vieux Carré,* Kerr acknowledges that "our best playwright ... has already given us such a substantial body of successful work that there is really no need to continue demanding that he live up to himself, that he produce more, more, more and all masterpieces." He recommends that Williams' public gratefully tuck into the portfolio "the casuals ... as small dividends."[20] Walter Kerr — and this writer agrees — believes that the stature of Tennessee Williams has become so well established that, as a playwright, he does not need to wait for the judgment of future generations.

Notes and References

Chapter One

Carson McCullers, *Reflections in a Golden Eye* (New York: New Directions, 1950).

Chapter Two

1. Foreword to *Sweet Birth of Youth* (New York: New Directions, 1959).
2. About his early years, see Tennessee Williams, *Memoirs* (New York: Doubleday, 1975); Prefaces to *Five Young American Poets* (New York: New Directions, 1944); Preface to *Sweet Bird of Youth*. Williams confused his early critics because, when he applied for the prize offered by the Group Theater, he apparently gave his birthdate as 1914.
3. "Talk with the Playwright," *Newsweek,* LIII (March 23, 1959), 75.
4. Preface, *Five Young American Poets*.
5. All of the poems discussed in the following paragraphs appear in Tennessee Williams, *In the Winter of Cities* (New York: New Directions, 1964). The table of contents affords easy reference. Some of the poems are dated but many are not.
6. Preface, *Five Young American Poets*.
7. Foreword, *Sweet Bird of Youth*.
8. Dudley Fitts, "Talking in Verse," *New York Times Book Review,* July 8, 1956, p. 10.
9. John Woods, "Tennessee Williams as a Poet," *Poetry.* CL (July 1957), 256–58.
10. Tennessee Williams, *One Arm and Other Stories* (New York: New Directions, 1954). Some of the stories are dated but some are not.
11. On Hazel Kramer, see *Memoirs,* chs. two and three.
12. Tennessee Williams, *American Blues* (New York: Dramatists Play Service, 1948). Dates have not been recorded by the playwright for all the plays in this anthology.
13. On the frequent performances of these short plays and those in *27 Wagons Full of Cotton,* see the annual volumes of *The Burns Mantle Theater Yearbook,* ed. Otis L. Guernsey, Jr. (New York: Dodd, Mead, 1964-1965, and the years following).
14. Tennessee Williams, *27 Wagons Full of Cotton* (New York: New Directions, 1953). Many of these plays were written in the early 1940s.

15. On the *Battle of Angels* disaster in Boston, see Williams' preface to *Orpheus Descending* (New York: New Directions, 1958) and his *Memoirs;* also Edwina Dakin Williams, *Remember Me to Tom* (New York: Putnam, 1963).

16. Tennessee Williams, *Battle of Angels* published with *Orpheus Descending* (New York: New Directions, 1958). See also *The Theatre of Tennessee Williams,* Vol. I, (New York: New Directions, 1972).

The particular text used in this study has been identified for each individual work, though it may not be available to many readers. The popularity of Tennessee Williams can be illustrated by the fact that in many libraries works that are listed in the card catalogue can no longer be located on the shelves. Many of the individual works are now out of print. To enable the reader to turn to the play under discussion, reference is made to the volume of *The Theater of Tennessee Williams* in which it appears. Readers should be warned that since Williams frequently revises his texts, they can expect to find slight variations in different editions.

17. Edwina Dakin Williams, p. 124.

18. Tennessee Williams, *I Rise in Flame, Cried the Phoenix* (New York: Dramatists Play Service, 1951).

19. On Williams' use and distortion of ideas from D. H. Lawrence, see Norman J. Fedder, *The Influence of D. H. Lawrence on Tennessee Williams* (London: Mouton; The Hague Press, 1966), p. 12f.

20. *You Touched Me!* produced December 5, 1943, Cleveland Playhouse, Margo Jones, director; fifth draft opened New York, September 25, 1945; closed, January 15, 1946, after 109 performances.

21. The D. H. Lawrence story, "You Touched Me," *The Complete Short Stories,* (London: Heinemann, 1955), II, 304 f., is an unromantic study about sexual attractions and conventions, and a blunt account of the economic basis for marriage.

22. Tennessee Williams and Donald Windham, *You Touched Me!* (New York: Samuel French, 1947).

23. Captain Rockley may be an early version of Big Daddy, both possibly patterned after Williams' father.

24. Joseph Wood Krutch, "Drama," *The Nation,* CLXI (October 6, 1945), 349–50.

Chapter Three

For each play, the opening and closing dates of the original New York production and the number of performances are given; as well as major awards won; film version and date; a major revival; any unusual data. For more complete record of major repertory, community theater, and college performances, see the reports in *The Burns Mantle Theater Yearbook,* 1964–1965 and the years following.

1. Fedder, p. 13f.

2. *The Glass Menagerie,* Williams' seventh long play, successfully
opened in Chicago, December 26, 1944, with Eddie Dowling director and
actor, Laurette Taylor, Julie Hayden, and Anthony Ross, and with music
by Paul Bowles; opened, New York, March 31, 1945 and closed August 3,
1946, after 561 performances; won the New York Drama Critics Circle
Award on the first ballot, the first first-ballot victory in its ten year
history. Revived, November 21, 1956, New York City Center; March 1961,
one of three plays to tour Europe and the Middle East, sponsored by the
U.S. State Department; August 1961, Latin American tour; 1964, Guthrie
Theater; May, 1965, New York, twenty-fifth year revival; December 8,
1966, CBS-TV; December 16, 1973, ABC-TV (film version).

3. Production Notes, published with the first edition of the play, are
the playwright's introductory comments and definition of his idea about
modern theater. Tennessee Williams, *The Glass Menagerie* (New York:
Random House, 1945). See also *The Theatre of Tennessee Williams,*
Vol. I.

4. See Preface, *Five Young American Poets,* and *Memoirs,* p. 36f., for
an account of the warehouse experience; for resemblances to Amanda,
"an exact picture of my mother," see Edwina Dakin Williams,
pp. 160–86; for a summary of *Stairs to the Roof,* a fantasy by Williams of
his experience at the shoe company, see Benjamin Nelson, *Tennessee Williams: The Man and his Work* (New York: Oblensky, 1961), p. 66f.

5. Harold Clurman, "Theatre," *Nation,* CXCIX (August 10, 1964),
60. Among other tributes to Laurette Taylor and the cast: *Time,* XLV
(April 9, 1945), 86–88; *Life,* XVIII (June 11, 1945), 12–13; *Theater Arts,*
XXIX (May, June, October 1945).

6. Among other Amandas: Pauline Lord, Helen Hayes, Gertrude
Lawrence, Maureen Stapleton, Mildred Dunnock, Shirley Booth, and
Katharine Hepburn. Pat Hingle emerges as one of the best as the Gentle-
man Caller.

7. Stark Young, "The Glass Menagerie," *The New Republic,* CXII
(April 16, 1945), 505. Other positive reviews: Brooks Atkinson, *New York
Times,* November 22, 1956, 50. Joseph Wood Krutch, *The Nation,* CLX
(April 14, 1945), 424; *Time,* XLV (April 9, 1945), 86–88.

8. George Jean Nathan, *The Theater Book of the Year,* 1944–45 (New
York: Fairleigh Dickinson, U.P. 1945) pp. 89–90, noted that screen pictures interrupted the original production thirty-nine times, that revisions
were made by the director, and that lines were rephrased by those playing
Amanda and Tom.

9. *Newsweek,* LXV (May 17, 1965), 92.

10. Harold Clurman, "The Tyron Guthrie Theater," *The Nation,*
CLCIX (August 10, 1964), 60.

11. Walter Kerr, *How Not to Write a Play* (Boston: The Writer, 1955),
p. 80.

12. Tennessee Williams, "On a Streetcar Named Success," *New York*

Times (November 30, 1947), Sec. 2, p. 1.

13. *Ibid.* On the effects of this sudden fame and affluence see *Memoirs;* Francis Donahue, *The Dramatic World of Tennessee Williams* (New York: Ungar, 1964), p. 19f; Nelson, p. 113.

14. *A Streetcar Named Desire* opened, New York, December 3, 1947; closed, December 17, 1949, after 855 performances, with Jessica Tandy, Marlon Brando, Kim Hunter, and Karl Malden; Elia Kazan directed. Won Pulitzer Prize, New York Drama Critics Circle Award (Williams' second), and Donaldson award, all best for 1947–48. Two-and-a-half-year cross-country tour; return to New York City Center, May 1950. Performed, Manchester, England, September 27, 1949; London, October 12, 1949; Paris, October 17, 1949; Stockholm, Rome, Mexico, 1949; banned, Namur, France; refused production rights, Madrid, December 1949; East Berlin, May 1950; Havana, 1965.

Film version, Kazan directed, 1951; reissued, 1958, won three major awards. Ballet of *Streetcar,* set to Alex North film score, New York, December 8, 1958, broke ballet attendance records. A series of twenty-fifth anniversary productions: December 3, 1972, University of Hartford, honorary degree to Williams; March 20, 1973, Ahmanson Theater, Los Angeles; April 26, 1973, Vivian Beaumont Repertory Theater of Lincoln Center; June 1975, Guthrie Theater, Minneapolis.

15. Tennessee Williams, *A Streetcar Named Desire* (New York: New Directions, 1947). See also *The Theatre of Tennessee Williams,* Vol. II.

16. A favorite line of Williams. See "Prelude to a Comedy," *New York Times* (November 6, 1960), Sec. 2, p. 1.

17. Two academic collections: John D. Hurrell, ed., *Two Modern American Tragedies:* "Death of a Salesman" and "A Streetcar Named Desire," A Scribner Research Anthology (New York: Scribners, 1961); Jordan Y. Miller, ed., *Twentieth Century Interpretations of A Streetcar Named Desire* (New York: Prentice-Hall, 1971).

18. Reprinted in Miller, pp. 36–38.

19. For an example of the American controversy, see Mary McCarthy, "Streetcar Called Success," in *Sights and Spectacles,* 1937–1956, (New York: Farrar, Straus and Cudahy, 1956), pp. 133ff.; and answer by Gore Vidal, "Love, Love, Love," *Partisan Review,* XXVI (Fall 1959), 619. On the London controversy, 1949, and British reactions, see T. C. Worsley, "The Arts and Entertainment," *The New Statesman,* XXXVIII (December 17, 1949), 723–24; and J. C. Trewin, "The World of the Theatre," *Illustrated London News,* CCXV (November 5, 1949), 712. An effort was made in Parliament to ban the play as immoral. See Brooks Atkinson, "Overseas Tornado," *New York Times,* December 11, 1949, Sec. 2, p. 3, on difference between British morality and ours.

20. Edwina Dakin Williams, p. 191.

21. Harold Clurman, *Lies Like Truth* (New York, 1958), reprinted in Hurrell, pp. 92–96. Others playing Blanche: Uta Hagen, Vivien Leigh,

Tallulah Bankhead, Faye Dunaway.

22. On the elaborate technical side of the production, see Randolph Goodman, *Drama on Stage* (New York: Holt, Rinehart and Winston, 1961), p. 314f. For pictures of the original production: *Life,* XXIII (December 15, 1947), 101-104; *Theatre Arts,* XXXII (February 1948), 35. Paris production, *Life,* XXVII (December 19, 1949), 66.

23. Elia Kazan, "The Director's Notebook," in Goodman, pp. 295-304.

24. Brooks Atkinson, "Streetcar Tragedy," *New York Times,* December 14, 1947, Sec. 2, p. 3. See also Irwin Shaw, "Theater: Masterpiece," *The New Republic,* CXVII (December 22, 1947), 34-35.

25. Joseph Wood Krutch, "Drama," *The Nation,* CLXV (December 20, 1947), 686.

26. Walter Kerr, "Of Blanche the Victim — and Other 'Women'," *New York Times,* May 6, 1973), Sec. 2, p. 1. See Kerr, *How Not to Write a Play,* p. 63ff., on best aspects of *Streetcar.*

27. Clive Barnes, "Stage: a Rare 'Streetcar'," *New York Times,* April 27, 1973, p. 31.

28. Stephen Farber, "Blanche Wins the Battle," *New York Times,* April 1, 1973, Sec. 2, p. 1.

29. Harold Clurman, "Theater," *The Nation,* CCXVI (May 14, 1973), 635-66.

30. Foster Hirsch, "The World Still Desires 'A Streetcar'," *New York Times,* April 15, 1973), Sec. 2, p. 1. Answered by Howard Siegman letter. *New York Times,* June 10, 1973, Sec. 2, p. 4.

31. Jim Gaines, "A Talk About Life and Style with Tennessee Williams," *Saturday Review,* LV (April 29, 1972), 25-29.

32. *Summer and Smoke* opened, New York, October 6, 1948; closed, January 1, 1949, after 100 performances. Revival April 24, 1952, José Quintero, director; Lee Hoiby created opera, opened, St. Paul Opera, June 1971; New York City Opera, March 19, 1972.

33. See Fedder, p. 89f., on Williams' use of Lawrence.

34. Glorious Hill is said to represent the author's memory of Clarksdale, Mississippi.

35. Tennessee Williams, *Summer and Smoke* (New York: New Directions, 1964). See also *The Theatre of Tennessee Williams,* Vol. II.

36. Moon Lake is the romantic casino name in *Battle of Angels.*

37. Geraldine Page, who played Alma, spoke of the physical stamina required for the arias in Scene II.

38. Harold Clurman, "Theatre: Man with a Problem," *The New Republic,* CXIX (October 25, 1948), 25-26. John Mason Brown, "Seeing Things," *Saturday Review,* XXXI (October 30, 1948), 31, spoke of high moments but also of too many symbols.

39. Joseph Wood Krutch, "Drama," *The Nation,* CLXVII (October 23, 1948), 473-74.

40. Gaines, p. 27.

41. Nancy Tischler, *Tennessee Williams: Rebellious Puritan* (New York: Citadel, 1961), p. 162.

42. *The Eccentricities of a Nightingale* opened, April 20, 1966, Washington (D.C.) Theater Club, for 31 performances; February 5, 1967, Goodman Theater, Chicago, 23 performances; June 16, 1976, Great Performances, PBS-TV.

43. Tennessee Williams, *Eccentricities of a Nightingale* published with *Summer and Smoke* (New York: New Directions, 1964). See also *The Theatre of Tennessee Williams,* Vol. II. Author's note preceding the text explains its tardy recognition.

44. *The Night of the Iguana* opened, New York, December 28, 1961; closed, September 29, 1962, after 316 performances. Produced as a one act at Spoleto, Italy, September 1959; Actor's Studio, winter 1959; three-act version, Chicago; rewritten for New York, Frank Corsaro, director. Won New York Drama Critics Circle Award (Williams' fourth); film version, 1964.

45. Tennessee Williams, *The Night of the Iguana* (New York: New Directions, 1962). See also *The Theatre of Tennessee Williams,* Vol. IV.

46. Fedder, p. 109.

47. Tischler, p. 134.

48. Miss Leighton spoke of new material given the cast at lunch to be incorporated in that night's performance. *Life,* LII (April 13, 1962), 67.

49. Mike Steen, *A Look at Tennessee Williams* (New York: Hawthorn, 1969), p. 186.

50. Seymour Peck, "Interview with Tennessee Wlliams," *New York Times,* December 24, 1961, Sec. 2, p. 5.

51. Lewis Funke and John E. Booth, "Williams on Williams," *Theatre Arts,* XLVI (January 1962), 17-19.

52. Harold Clurman, "Theatre," *The Nation,* CXCIV (January 27, 1962), 86.

53. Howard Taubman, "Theatre: 'Night of the Iguana Opens'," *New York Times,* December 29, 1961, p. 10.

54. Richard Gilman, "Williams as Phoenix," *Commonweal,* CXXV (January 26, 1962), 460.

55. Donahue, p. 148.

Chapter Four

1. *The Rose Tattoo* opened, New York, February 3, 1951; closed, October 27, 1951, after 306 performances; played the 1952-53 season in Paris; canceled in Rhodesia as "suggestive and objectionable," July 1951; film with Anna Magnani, 1955; revival, New York City Center, October 20, 1966, again with Maureen Stapleton.

2. Tennessee Williams, *The Rose Tattoo* (London: Secker and

Warburg, 1956). See also *The Theatre of Tennessee Williams,* Vol. II.

3. *A Perfect Analysis Given by a Parrot,* 1958, written for television, extends the gossip of these two clowns. Included in *Dragon Country* (New York: New Directions, 1970).

4. "The Timeless World of a Play" (Preface to *The Rose Tattoo*), reprinted from *New York Times* of January 14, 1951, Sec. 2, p. 1.

5. George Jean Nathan, *The Theatre Book of the Year,* 1950–51 (New York, 1951), p. 210.

6. Henry Popkin, "The Plays of Tennessee Williams," *The Tulane Drama Review,* IV (Spring 1960), 59.

7. Walter Kerr, *Pieces at Eight* (London: Max Reinhardt, 1958), pp. 136–37.

8. Henry Hewes, "Theater — off the Leash," *Saturday Review,* XLIX (November 26, 1966), 60.

9. *Cat on a Hot Tin Roof* opened, New York, March 24, 1955; closed, November 17, 1956, after 694 performances; won for Williams his second Pulitzer Prize and his third New York Drama Critics Circle Award; film rights sold to Metro Goldwyn Mayer (MGM) for half a million — homosexuality theme shifted to problem of Brick's growing up; revival, American Shakespeare Festival, Connecticut, summer 1974, transferred to American National Theatre and Academy (ANTA) and opened, New York, September, 24, 1974; closed February 8, 1975, for 160 performances.

10. Tennessee Williams, *Cat on a Hot Tin Roof.* New York: New Directions, 1955). See also *The Theatre of Tennessee Williams,* Vol. III.

11. Another favorite line of the playwright.

12. Author says the multiple rewriting of Act III brought on such "deep psychic violation" that he could not write for a long time.

13. Gaines, p. 27. Kenneth Tynan thought that Kazan misdirected the Brick character. *Mademoiselle,* XLII (February 1956), 202.

14. The reader can compare the playwright's version and the Broadway version of Act III in the above mentioned editions.

15. Brooks Atkinson, "Williams' Tin Roof," *New York Times,* April 3, 1955, Sec. 2, p. 1.

16. *Time,* LXV (April 4, 1955), 98.

17. Marya Mannes, "The Morbid World of Tennessee Williams," *The Reporter,* XII (May 19, 1955), 41.

18. Walter Kerr, "Cat on a Hot Tin Roof," *New York Herald Tribune,* March 25, 1955.

19. Arthur B. Waters, "Tennessee Williams: Ten Years Later," *Theatre Arts,* XXXIX (July 1955), 73.

20. Harold Clurman, "Theater," *The Nation,* CCXIX (October 12, 1974), 349–50.

21. Robert Hatch, "Theater," *The Nation,* CLXXX (April 9, 1955), 314.

22. Catharine Hughes, "Plays with a Past," *America,* CXXXI (October 12, 1974), 194.

23. Brendan Gill, "Family Troubles," *The New Yorker,* L (October 7, 1974), 73.

24. Stanley Kauffmann, "Stanley Kauffmann on Theater," *The New Republic,* CLXXI (October 19, 1974), 16.

25. See *Burns Mantle Theater Yearbook,* various years.

26. West Springfield, Mass., November 9, 1973.

27. Steen, p. 211.

28. Gilbert Maxwell, *Tennessee Williams and his Friends* (Cleveland: World, 1965), p. 162.

29. *Ibid.,* p. 165.

30. *Baby Doll,* the film, opened in New York, December 18, 1956.

31. *Baby Doll,* script for the film, with the two one-act plays, *27 Wagons Full of Cotton* and *The Long Stay Cut Short/ or/ The Unsatisfactory Supper* (New York: New Directions, 1956).

32. "New Kazan Movie Put on Blacklist," *New York Times,* November 28, 1956, p. 32.

33. *Ibid.*

34. Tischler, p. 231.

35. Gerald Weales, *American Drama Since World War II* (New York: Harcourt, Brace and World, 1962), pp. 37–38.

Chapter Five

1. *Camino Real* opened, New York, March 19, 1953; closed, May 9, 1953, after 60 performances; directed by Elia Kazan, with Eli Wallach and Jessica Tandy. Performed, West Germany, March 1955; London, April 1957; revival, New York, May 17, 1960, José Quintero, director.

2. Tennessee Williams, *Camino Real* (London: Secker and Warburg, 1958). See also *The Theatre of Tennessee Williams,* Vol. II.

3. Henry Hewes, "The Theater," *Saturday Review,* LIII (January 24, 1970), 24.

4. For Williams' defense of symbols, particularly in this scene, see Foreword, *Camino Real.*

5. Brooks Atkinson, "Camino Real," *New York Times,* March 29, 1953), Sec. 2, p. 1.

6. Harold Clurman, "Theater," *The Nation,* CCX (January 26, 1970), 93–94.

7. Kerr, *How Not to Write a Play,* pp. 186–78.

8. "The Theater," *Time,* LCV (January 19, 1970), 61.

9. Clurman, "Theatre" (January 26, 1970), 93–94.

10. Foreword, *Camino Real,* reprinted from the *New York Times,* March 15, 1953, Sec. 2, p. 1.

11. To add to his gloom, his grandfather died during rehearsals of this play.

12. See *Memoirs,* p. 167; Tischler, p. 194.

13. Particularly sensitive; to attack his work is to attack him.

14. Donahue, p. 58.

15. *Orpheus Descending* opened, New York, March 21, 1957; closed, May 18, 1957, after 68 performances. Fifth rewriting of *Battle of Angels.* Performed, Paris, February 16, 1959; London, May 15, 1959; became a "smash hit," the first for Williams, in Moscow, August 28, 1961. Film, *The Fugitive Kind,* 1960, with Anna Magnani and Marlon Brando.

16. See "The Past, the Present, and the Perhaps," Foreword, *Orpheus Descending,* reprinted from *New York Times,* March 17, 1957, Sec. 2, p. 1.

17. Tennessee Williams, *In the Winter of Cities,* p. 28.

18. Tennessee Williams, *Orpheus Descending* with *Battle of Angels* (New York: New Directions, 1958). See also *The Theatre of Tennessee Williams,* Vol. III.

19. Nelson, p. 225, referred to the "confused sexual repression with religious exaltation" of this character.

20. John Gassner, *Theater at the Crossroads* (New York: Holt, Rinehart and Winston, 1963), pp. 223–25.

21. Popkin, pp. 60–61.

22. Kerr, *Pieces at Eight,* pp. 132–33.

23. Edwina Dakin Williams, p. 241.

24. Brooks Atkinson, "His Bizarre Images Can't be Denied," *New York Times,* November 26, 1961), Sec. 7, p. 1.

25. *Time,* LXXIX (March 9, 1962), 54.

26. *Period of Adjustment* opened, New York, November 10, 1960; closed, March 4, 1961, after 132 performances; produced in England, 1962.

27. Harold Clurman, "Theatre," *The Nation,* CXCI (December 3, 1960), 443–44.

28. Stanley Edgar Hyman, "Some Trends in the Novel," *College English,* XX (October 1958), 2.

29. Tennessee Williams, *Period of Adjustment* (London: Secker and Warburg, 1960). See also *The Theatre of Tennessee Williams,* Vol. IV.

30. On the Williams-Kazan squabble, see Donahue, p. 125; Tischler, p. 287.

31. Howard Taubman, "Hospital Ward," *New York Times,* November 20, 1960), Sec. 2, p. 1.

32. *Time,* LXXVI (November 21, 1960), 75.

33. Harold Clurman, "Theatre," *The Nation,* CLCV (August 11, 1962), 59.

34. Robert Hatch, "Human Beings and Substitutes," *Horizon,* III (March 1961), 102–103.

Chapter Six

1. The novel was made into a film in 1950, directed by José Quintero, with Vivien Leigh and Warren Beatty.

2. Tennessee Williams, *The Roman Spring of Mrs. Stone* (New York: New Directions, 1950).

3. Maxwell, p. 144.

4. W. J. Weatherby, *Manchester Guardian Weekly,* July 3, 1959.

5. *Memoirs,* p. 144ff.

6. *Suddenly Last Summer,* with *Something Unspoken* (relationship between an overbearing Southern aristocrat and delicate, tough-minded companion of fifteen years) as *Garden District,* opened off-Broadway, January 7, 1958; film, 1958.

7. Compare expensive limited editions of *I Rise in Flame, Cried the Phoenix.*

8. Tennessee Williams, *Suddenly Last Summer* (New York: The New American Library, 1958). See also *The Theatre of Tennessee Williams,* Vol. III.

9. See Foreword on hatred, *Sweet Bird of Youth,* reprinted from *New York Times,* (March 8, 1959), Sec. 2, p. 1.

10. Edwina Dakin Williams, p. 241.

11. Donahue, pp. 105–106.

12. Brooks Atkinson, "Garden District," *New York Times,* (January 19, 1958), Sec. 2, p. 1.

13. Donahue, p. 96.

14. *Sweet Bird of Youth,* Williams ninth play since *The Glass Menagerie,* opened, New York, March 10, 1959; closed, January 30, 1960, after 375 performances; Elia Kazan, director. *Boom!,* the film, with Paul Newman and Geraldine Page, 1961.

15. Tennessee Williams, *Sweet Bird of Youth* in *Three Plays of Tennessee Williams* (New York: New Directions, 1964). See also *The Theatre of Tennessee Williams,* Vol. IV.

16. Kenneth Tynan asked what castration had to do with Easter: "Ireland and Points West," *The New Yorker,* XXXV (March 21, 1959), 90.

17. See Foreword, *Sweet Bird,* on Williams' own fear.

18. Williams became an internationally known figure in his thirties.

19. Tom is thought to be an early George Wallace.

20. Williams told Tom Buckley of "seven years behind a veil of pills and whiskey," "Tennessee Williams Survives," *Atlantic,* CCXXVI (November 1970), 100.

21. An unpublished one act, *The Enemy: Time,* is the basis of *Sweet Bird.*

22. Marya Mannes, "Sour Bird, Sweet Raisin," *The Reporter,* XX (April 16, 1959), 34.

23. Harold Clurman, "Theatre," *The Nation,* CLXXXVIII (March 28, 1959), 281.

24. Popkin, pp. 59–61.

25. Robert Brustein, "Williams' Nebulous Nightmare," *The Hudson Review,* XII (Summer 1959), 256–60.

26. Steen, pp. 152–53.

27. Foreword, *Sweet Bird.*

28. On the difficulties of composition, see Henry Hewes, "Tennessee's Easter Message," *Saturday Review,* XLVI (March 28, 1959), 26; and Weatherby.

29. Sam Zolotov, "Williams' Drama Attracts Throng," *New York Times,* March 12, 1959.

30. *The Milk Train Doesn't Stop Here Any More* opened, New York, January 16, 1963; closed, March 16, 1963, after 69 performances; rewritten for Tallulah Bankhead, lasted for four performances, January 1964. Film, *Goforth,* with Elizabeth Taylor and Richard Burton, 1967.

31. Tennessee Williams, *The Milk Train Doesn't Stop Here Anymore* (New York: New Directions, 1964). See also *The Theatre of Tennessee Williams* (1975), Vol. V.

32. Williams has established a Rose Isabelle Williams Foundation for creative writers. Buckley, p. 105.

33. Perhaps part of the truth game.

34. Williams' fear, after failures, was that he was "burnt out."

35. Walter Kerr observed that only slight changes would make this scene a Peter Arno cartoon. *Thirty Days Hath November* (New York: Simon and Schuster, 1969), p. 222.

36. Robert Brustein, "A Buccaneer on Broadway," *The New Republic,* CXLVIII (February 2, 1963), 26.

37. Robert Gilman, "Mistah Williams He Dead," *Commonweal,* LXXVII (February 8, 1963), 515.

38. *Time,* LXXXI (June 25, 1963), 53.

39. "'Milk Train' Gets a Second Chance," *New York Times,* September 18, 1963, p. 32.

Chapter Seven

1. *Slapstick Tragedy* opened, off-Broadway, February 22, 1966; closed, February 26, 1966, after seven performances.

2. Preface to *Slapstick Tragedy, Esquire,* LXIV (August 1965), 95.

3. Tennessee Williams, *Mutilated* and *The Gnädiges Fräulein* appear in the anthology, *Dragon Country* (New York: New Directions, 1970).

4. Sam Zolotov, "Tennessee Williams Gives Play to Actors Studio," *New York Times,* April 12, 1962), p. 43.

5. Harold Clurman, "Theatre," *The Nation,* CCII (March 14, 1966), 309.

6. *The Seven Descents of Myrtle* opened, off-Broadway, March 27, 1968; closed, April 20, 1968, after 29 performances. Film, *Last of the*

Mobile Hot Shots, 1970; Sidney Lumet, director.

7. Tennessee Williams, *The Kingdom of Earth (The Seven Descents of Myrtle)* (New York: New Directions, 1968). See also *The Theatre of Tennessee Williams,* Vol. V.

8. Wilfred Sheed, "Tired Scene Turned into Sad Parody," *Life,* LXIV (April 26, 1968), 18.

9. Brendan Gill, "Before the Flood," *The New Yorker,* XLIV (April 6, 1968), 109.

10. John Simon, "The Self-Tormentor," *Commonweal,* LXXXVIII (May 3, 1968), 208.

11. On dispute between director, producer, and playwright, see *New York Times,* February 28, 1968, p. 39.

12. Steen, pp. 265-66.

13. On controversy over the title, see *New York Times,* February 21, 1968, p. 61.

14. On Williams disappearance and furor, *New York Times,* June 30, 1968, p. 54.

15. *In the Bar of a Tokyo Hotel* opened, off-Broadway, May 11, 1969; closed, June 1, 1969, after 25 performances.

16. Tennessee Williams, *In the Bar of a Tokyo Hotel* appears in the anthology, *Dragon Country.*

17. Walter Kerr, "Keep on Tennessee Williams," *New York Times,* May 25, 1969, Sec. 2, p. 5.

18. Harold Clurman, "Theatre," *The Nation,* CCVIII (June 2, 1969), 709-10.

19. Clive Barnes, "Theater: 'In the Bar of a Tokyo Hotel'," the *New York Times,* May 12, 1969, 54.

20. Score acceptance of the *Life* advertisement by the *Times, New York Times,* June 22, 1969, sec. 2, p. 11.

21. Mel Gussow, "Williams Looking to Play's Opening," *New York Times,* March 31, 1972, Sec. 2, p. 1.

22. Buckley, p. 98.

23. *Small Craft Warnings* opened, off-Broadway, April 2, 1972; closed, September 17, 1972, after 200 performances.

24. Tennessee Williams, *Small Craft Warnings* (New York: New Directions, 1972). See also *The Theatre of Tennessee Williams,* Vol. V.

25. Gussow.

26. Harold Clurman, "Theatre," *The Nation,* CCXIV (April 24, 1972), 541.

27. Walter Kerr, "Talkers, Drinkers, and Losers," *New York Times,* April 16, 1972, Sec. 2, p. 8.

28. Gerald Weales, "The Stage," *Commonweal,* XCVI (May 5, 1972), 214-16.

29. *Out Cry* opened, off-Broadway, March 1, 1973; closed, March 10, 1973, after 12 performances.

30. Tennessee Williams, *Out Cry* (New York: New Directions, 1973). For an earlier version, *The Two-Character Play,* see *The Theatre of Tennessee Williams,* Vol. V.

31. Interview with Lewis Funke, *New York Times,* May 2, 1971, Sec. 2, p. 1.

32. Interview with James F. Clarity, *New York Times,* August 24, 1972, p. 26.

33. Steen, pp. 162–63.

34. Mel Gussow, *New York Times,* March 11, 1973, Sec. 2, p. 1.

35. Clive Barnes, *New York Times,* March 2, 1973, p. 18.

36. *Vieux Carré* opened, New York, May 11, 1977; closed, May 15, for five performances.

37. Walter Kerr, *New York Times,* May 22, 1977, Sec. 2, p. 5.

38. *Ibid.*

39. Tennessee Williams, *The Knightly Quest* (New York: New Directions, 1966).

40. Tennessee Williams, *Eight Mortal Ladies Possessed* (New York: New Directions, 1974). As with earlier poems, stories, and short plays, some of this later fiction is dated, some not.

41. Tennessee Williams, *Hard Candy* (New York: New Directions, 1959).

42. For Williams as a night rider, see Maxwell, p. 131.

43. Tennessee Williams, *Moise and the World of Reason* (New York: Simon and Shuster, 1975).

44. For autobiographical accounts, see prefaces cited above, Chapter 2, and *Memoirs.*

Chapter Eight

1. Maxwell, p. 28.

2. Tennessee Williams, "Let Me Hang it All Out," *New York Times,* March 4, 1973, Sec. 2, p. 1.

3. Robert Berquist, "Broadway Discovers Tennessee Williams," *New York Times,* December 21, 1975, Sec. 2, p. 1.

4. See Weales, *Tennessee Williams,* p. 18 ff. for a discussion of parallel characters.

5. Kenneth Tynan, "Valentine to Tennessee Williams," *Mademoiselle,* XLII (February 1956), 202.

6. Claudia Cassidy, "Cheers and Sighs over Tennessee's 'Menagerie'," *Life,* LVIII (May 28, 1965), p. 16.

7. "Angel of the Odd," *Time,* LXXIX (March 9, 1962), p. 54.

8. Steen, p. 196.

9. Buckley, p. 103.

10. _____, "Angel of the Odd," *Time,"* LXXIX (March 9, 1962), p. 54.

11. Joanne Stang, "Williams: 20 Years after 'Glass Menagerie'," *New York Times* March 28, 1965, Sec. 2, p. 1.

12. Donahue, pp. 96–97.

13. Funke and Booth, p. 18.

14. Gaines, p. 28.

15. Brooks Atkinson, "Theater: Early Williams," *New York Times,* November 22, 1956, p. 56.

16. Louis Kronenberger, "The Season on Broadway," *The Best Plays of 1958–1959* (New York, 1959), p. 14.

17. Cassidy, p. 16.

18. Stanley Kauffmann, "About Williams Gloom and Hope," *New York Times,* March 6, 1966, Sec. 2, p. 1.

19. Berkvist.

20. Walter Kerr, "The Touch of the Poet Isn't Enough to Sustain Williams's Latest Play," *New York Times,* May 22, 1977, Sec. 2, p. 5.

Selected Bibliography

PRIMARY SOURCES

A. Major Works (Plays, Poems, and Prose)

"The Summer Belvedere," *Five Young American Poets*. Third Series. New York: New Directions, 1944.

Battle of Angels, Pharos, nos. 1-2 (Murray, Utah), 1945; New York; New Directions, 1945.

The Glass Menagerie. New York: Random House, 1945; acting edition, New York: Dramatists Play Service, 1948; London: Lehmann, 1948; New York: New Directions, 1949.

27 Wagons Full of Cotton and Other One-Act Plays. New York: New Directions, 1946; London: The Grey Walls Press, 1947; new edition, New York: New Directions, 1949; London: Lehmann, 1949; London: Secker and Warburg, 1949; third edition, New York: New Directions, 1953.

You Touched Me! (with David Windham). New York: Samuel French, 1947.

A Streetcar Named Desire. New York: New Directions, 1947; London: Lehmann, 1949; acting edition, New York: Dramatists Play Service, 1953.

One Arm and Other Stories. Limited edition. New York: New Directions, 1948; trade edition, 1954.

Summer and Smoke. New York: New Directions, 1948; acting edition, New York: Dramatists Play Service, 1950; London: Lehmann, 1952; London: Secker and Warburg, 1952.

American Blues: Five Short Plays. Acting edition, New York: Dramatists Play Service, 1948.

The Roman Spring of Mrs. Stone. Limited autographed edition, New York: New Directions, 1950; London: Lehmann, 1950; new edition, London: Secker and Warburg, 1957.

The Rose Tattoo. New York: New Directions, 1951; London: Secker and Warburg, 1955.

I Rise in Flame, Cried the Phoenix. Two special limited editions, New York: New Directions, 1951; acting edition, New York: Dramatists Play Service, 1951.

Camino Real. New York: New Directions, 1953; London: Secker and Warburg, 1958.

183

Hard Candy. Limited edition, New York: New Directions, 1954; new edition, New York: New Directions, 1959.

Cat on a Hot Tin Roof. New York: New Directions, 1955: London: Secker and Warburg, 1956.

Four Plays (The Glass Menagerie, A Streetcar Named Desire, Summer and Smoke, Camino Real). London: Secker and Warburg, 1956.

In the Winter of Cities. Poems. New York: New Directions, 1956.

Baby Doll. Screenplay. New York: New Directions, 1956; London: Secker and Warburg, 1957.

Orpheus Descending. London: Secker and Warburg, 1958; same, with *Battle of Angels,* New York: New Directions, 1958.

The Fugitive Kind. "A Signet Book." New York: The New American Library, 1958.

Suddenly Last Summer. New York: New Directions, 1958.

Garden District (Something Unspoken and *Suddenly Last Summer).* London: Secker and Warburg, 1959.

Sweet Bird of Youth. New York: New Directions, 1959.

Period of Adjustment. New York: New Directions, 1960.

Three Players of a Summer Game. London: Secker and Warburg, 1960.

The Night of the Iguana. New York: New Directions, 1961.

The Milk Train Doesn't Stop Here Any More. New York: New Directions, 1963.

Grand. New York: House of Books, 1964; limited edition.

Three Plays of Tennessee Williams (The Rose Tattoo, Camino Real, Sweet Bird of Youth). New York: New Directions, 1964.

The Knightly Quest and Other Stories. New York: New Directions, 1966.

Out Cry. New York: New Directions, 1969.

Dragon Country. New York: New Directions, 1970.

Small Craft Warnings. New York: New Directions, 1972.

Eight Mortal Ladies Possessed. New York: New Directions, 1974.

Moise and the World of Reason. New York: Simon and Shuster, 1975.

Memoirs. New York: Doubleday, 1975.

The Theater of Tennessee Williams. New York: New Directions. Vol. I: *Battle of Angels, The Glass Menagerie, A Streetcar Named Desire,* 1972; Vol. II: *The Eccentricities of a Nightingale, Summer and Smoke, The Rose Tattoo, Camino Real,* 1972; Vol. III: *Cat on a Hot Tin Roof, Orpheus Descending, Suddenly Last Summer,* 1972; Vol. IV: *Sweet Bird of Youth, Period of Adjustment, The Night of the Iguana,* 1972; Vol. V: *The Milk Train Doesn't Stop Here Any More, Kingdom of Earth, Small Craft Warnings, The Two-Character Play* (New version of *Out Cry*), 1975.

Tennessee Williams' Letters to Donald Windham, 1940–1965. Ed. D. Windham. Limited edition. New York; S. Campbell, 1976; New York: Holt, Rinehart and Winston, 1977.

Androgyne, Mon Amour. Poems. New York: New Directions, 1977.

B. Articles by Tennessee Williams (listed chronologically)

Two Prefaces, "Frivolous Version" and "Serious Version," to poems. In *Five Young American Poets.* Third Series, New York: New Directions, 1944. Early poems written about itinerant years, with tribute to Hart Crane.

Production notes to *The Glass Menagerie.* 1945. Explains reasons for using screen devices, music, and lighting.

"Something Wild ..." Foreword. *27 Wagons Full of Cotton.* New York: New Directions, 1946. Tribute to Willard Holland, director of Mummers, St. Louis, 1935–40.

"On a Streetcar Named Success." *New York Times,* November 30, 1947, Sec. 2, p. 1. Escape from sudden popularity to Mexico and work on *The Poker Night,* later a part of *Streetcar.*

"Questions without Answers." *New York Times,* October 3, 1948, Sec. 2, p. 1. Observations on pretensions in the theater; difficulties of a popular playwright and his own unintentional obscurity.

Introduction. *Reflections on a Golden Eye,* by Carson McCullers. New York: New Directions, 1950. Southern writers' concern with perversion and horror; the mystery that inspires dread; use of grotesque and violent symbols.

"The Timeless World of a Play." Foreword. *The Rose Tattoo.* Reprinted from *New York Times,* January 14, 1951, Sec. 2, p. 1. Plea for understanding of the little people; art a means of catching the fleeting, significant moments and of communicating hidden feelings.

"A Writer's Quest for a Parnassus." *New York Times Magazine,* August 3, 1950, p. 16. Writer's need for privacy.

Foreword. *Camino Real.* Reprinted from *New York Times,* March 15, 1953, Sec. 2, p. 1. Play makes use of symbols to state writer's idea of his time and world and his own sense of freedom. "Afterward." A reply to negative critics: some broad generalizations on art.

"Critic Says 'Evasion', Writer Says 'Mystery'." *New York Herald Tribune,* April 17, 1955.

"Person-to-Person." Foreword. *Cat on a Hot Tin Roof.* Reprinted from *New York Times,* April 3, 1955, Sec. 2, p. 1. Intense need for communication among all people; the lonely, personal nature of writing.

"Note of Explanation." Foreword to the Broadway version of Act III of *Cat.* New York: New Directions, 1955. Some observations on the changes made at the request of the director, Eliz Kazan.

"The Past, the Present, and the Perhaps." Foreword. *Orpheus Descending* (1959). Reprinted from the *New York Times,* March 17, 1957, Sec. 2, p. 1. Early writing years and itinerant life; reminiscences of Boston production of *Battle of Angels;* revisions leading to *Orpheus Descending.*

Preface to the text of William Inge's *The Dark at the Top of Stairs.* Reprinted from *New York Times,* March 16, 1958, Sec. 2, p. 1.

"Williams' Well of Violence." *New York Times,* March 8, 1959, Sec. 2, p. 1 (foreword to *Sweet Bird of Youth*). Fears and hysteria; violence of first story and surprising public acceptance of his plays; denies feeling of hatred but not guilt sense.

"Reflections on a Revival of a Controversial Fantasy." *New York Times,* May 15, 1960, Sec. 2, p. 1. Thematic idea of *Camino Real* and important lines.

"Tennessee Williams Presents His POV." *New York Times Magazine,* June 12, 1960, p. 19. "No significant area of human experience and behavior reaction to it" should be inaccessible to the creative writer; like an X-ray machine, current artists indicate which are healthy cells and which are not.

"Prelude to a Comedy." *New York Times,* November 6, 1960, Sec. 2, p. 1. Difficulties of writing as a public figure; source of work in his life; tribute to Marcel Proust.

"The Agent as Catalyst." *Esquire,* LVIII (December 1962), 216ff. Williams' ambivalent appreciation of this thirty-year agent, Audrey Wood, suggesting reasons for the break; Audrey Wood replies on Williams' feelings "close to the skin."

"Let Me Hang It All Out." *New York Times,* March 4, 1973, Sec. 2, p. 1. On the twenty-fifth anniversary of *Streetcar,* speaks of *Cat* as expressing his hatred of liars; forthright candor of upcoming *Memoirs;* homosexuality not a theme for a full-length play; humor in all his works, in *Streetcar;* his own capacity to laugh and talk about his work.

"Homage to William Inge." *New York Times,* July 1, 1973, Sec. 2, p. 1.

C. Interviews or reports of interviews with Tennessee Williams (listed chronologically)

LEWIS, R.C. "A Playwright Named Tennessee." *New York Times,* December 7, 1947. Changes made in *The Glass Menagerie* as suggested by Eddie Dowling.

WATERS, ARTHUR B. "Tennessee Williams: Ten Years Later." *Theatre Arts,* XXXIX (July 1955), 72. Williams denies Brick a homosexual; expresses affection for Blanche and Maggie.

————. "The Playwright: Man Named Tennessee." *Newsweek,* XLIX (April 1, 1957), 81. On pessimism and violence in the plays; the strain of creative activity.

SHANLEY, JOHN P. "Tennessee Williams on Television." *New York Times,* April 13, 1958, Sec. 2, p. 13.

RICE, ROBERT. "A Man Named Tennessee." *New York Post,* April 21–May 4, 1958. Review of writer's life and work, source of subsequent studies by critics.

WEATHERBY, W.J. "Lonely in Uptown New York." *Manchester Guardian Weekly* (air edition), July 23, 1959. Candid report on personal life and writing; on writing for actresses.

GELB, ARTHUR. "Williams and Kazan and the Big Walkout." *New York Times,* May 1, 1960, Sec. 2, p. 1. Comments about the end of a fabulously successful partnership.

FUNKE, LEWIS, and JOHN E. BOOTH. "Williams on Williams." *Theatre Arts* XLVI (January 1962), 17ff. Williams compares own writing with that of new playwrights; preference for off-Broadway for production of his own plays; talk about *Iguana;* on the violence in his plays; on work as the best part of his day.

STANG, JOANNE. "Williams: 20 Years After 'Glass Menagerie'." *New York Times,* March 28, 1965, Sec. 2, p. 1. Williams never secure about work; always eager for major awards; mad frenzy after *Orpheus* failure; his transient, homeless life; affinity with "flawed people"; on reactions to praise; on influences on his life and work.

FUNKE, LEWIS. "Williams Revival? Ask the Playwright." *New York Times,* January 8, 1970, p. 45. Williams talks about recovery after seven years on pills and liquor; conversion to Catholicism; reaction to critics and reviewers.

BUCKLEY, TOM. "Tennessee Williams Survives." *Atlantic,* CCXXVI (November 1970), 98ff. Interview at Key West after Williams' recovery from pills and alcohol; recent theatrical fiascos; Williams' theatrical mannerisms, dramatized scenes with friends; summary of early years at Key West; childhood with grandparents; analysis after failure of *Orpheus;* assessment of mother and father; Williams' companion-secretaries; account of "snake pit" experience at Barnes Hospital; digression on his will; need to appeal to youth; his volatile changes of mood. For Williams' furious accusations of an unsympathetic report, see *Atlantic,* CCXXVII (January 1971), 34.

GAINES, JIM. "A Talk about Life and Style with Tennessee Williams." *Saturday Review,* LV (April 29, 1972), 25-29. Interviewed at his Key West home, Williams talks about how plays develop, of characters as living people, of evaluation of own work, of writing and sexual power, and of writing as therapy.

BERKVIST, ROBERT. "Broadway Discovers Tennessee Williams." *New York Times,* December 21, 1975, Sec. 2, p. 1. Williams discusses work of 1975; comments on mother, on sister, on own sexual life; changes in professional theater in the last twenty years.

SECONDARY SOURCES

Selected critical evaluations. Reviews of individual productions recorded in "Notes and References" are not listed here, nor are foreign comments included.

ATKINSON, BROOKS. Review of *Rebellious Puritan* (Tischler) and *Tennessee Williams* (Nelson), *New York Times Book Review,* November 26, 1961, p. 1. Good review of work since *Menagerie.*

BRUSTEIN, ROBERT. "Williams' Nebulous Nightmare." *The Hudson Review,* XII (Summer 1959),255–60. Weaknesses: cartoon characters, involved metaphors and symbols, sexual obsession, nightmarish element in later plays.

———. "Why American Plays are not Literature." In *Writing in America.* New Jersey: Rutgers, 1960. Commercial influences prevent good dramatic writing.

CANBY, VINCENT. "I Never Depended on the Kindness of Strangers." *New York Times,* May 8, 1966, Sec. 2, p. 1. A memory play: comic interview with Audrey Wood in the style of a Tennessee Williams play.

CLURMAN, HAROLD. "Tennessee Williams: Poet and Puritan." *New York Times,* March 29, 1970, Sec. 2, p. 5. Thematic core: "fatal incapacity to integrate the conflict of body and soul"; Williams more perceptive of lost souls in debased civilization than O'Neill; consummate theatrical artist.

DA PONTE, DURANTE. "Tennessee Williams' Gallery of Feminine Characters." *Tennessee Studies in Literature,* (Knoxville: University of Tennessee) X (1965), 7–26. Excellent discussion of the subject.

DONAHUE, FRANCIS. *The Dramatic World of Tennessee Williams.* New York: Ungar, 1964. Biographic data based on the Robert Rice articles; the "troubled personal life" reflected in the works and the basic themes: violence, sex, homosexuality, and neuroticism; his self-doubts.

DONY, NADINE. "Tennessee Williams: A Selected Bibliography." *Modern Drama,* I (December 1958), 181–91.

DOWNER, ALAN. *Recent American Drama.* No. 7. University of Minnesota Pamphlets on American Writers, pp. 28–33. Minneapolis: 1961. A guarded appraisal of this "gothic writer."

FALK, SIGNI. "The Profitable World of Tennessee Williams." *Modern Drama,* I (December 1958), 172–80.

———. *Tennessee Williams.* Twayne's United States Authors Series, No. 10. (New York: Twayne, 1961).

FEDDER, NORMAN J. *The Influence of D. H. Lawrence on Tennessee Williams.* London: Mouton; the Hague Press, 1966. Major themes and symbols from Lawrence but Williams' sympathy for perversion and sexual abnormality, his vulgar admiration for gross vagrants, and his "lament for moth" figures and sentimentality not to be found in the British writer. Williams didactic and given to "nursery school simplifications"; Lawrence better at appropriately described experience.

FITCH, ROBERT E. "La Mystique de la Merde." *The New Republic,* CXXXV (September 3, 1956), 17–18. Sex and obscenity by a skilled literary artist.

GARDINER, HAROLD C. "Is Williams' Vision Myopia?" *America,* CIII (July 30, 1960), 495–96. Reply to Mannes-Williams argument. Attacks Williams' artistic philosophy: portrays man in terms of "shame and fears," mostly sexual.

GASSNER, JOHN. *The Theatre in Our Times: A Survey of Men, Materials, and Movements in the Modern Theatre.* New York: Crown, 1954. Contrast between "poetic realism" and symbolism in earlier plays.

————. *Theatre at the Crossroads.* New York: Holt, Rinehart, and Winston, 1963. Relation between the early one acts and later plays; increasing technical skill but dangerous symbolic involvement; peculiar sense of the comic.

HEWES, HENRY. "Tennessee Williams — Last of Our Solid Gold Bohemians." *Saturday Review,* XXXVI (March 28, 1953), 25-26. Problems of interpreting a play like *Camino Real* to prospective backers.

HIGHET, GILBERT. "A Memorandum." *Horizon,* I (May 1959), 54-55. Witty exposé of increased interest in sex and horror.

ISAAC, DON. "A Streetcar Named Desire — or Death." *New York Times,* February 18, 1968, Sec. 2, p. 1. Williams the one American dramatist concerned with "solving a set of philosophic and religious problems"; intricate and ambiguous thought rather than action in later plays.

JACKSON, ESTHER MERLE. *The Broken World of Tennessee Williams.* Madison: University of Wisconsin, 1965. Learned discussion in esthetic and historical terms; the synthetic myth, the antihero, the plastic theater, with focus on *Camino Real;* sees in Williams the "development of a comprehensive moral structure."

JONES, ROBERT EMMET. "Tennessee Williams' Early Heroines." *Modern Drama,* II (December 1959), 211-19. The Southern gentlewoman in different stages.

KAUFFMANN, STANLEY. "About Williams: Gloom and Hope." *New York Times,* March 6, 1966, Sec. 2, p. 1. Williams' sex, sensation, and "glandular pietism" are dead; suggests that he exploit his great talent for "outrageous comedy."

KERR, WALTER. *How Not to Write a Play.* Boston: The Writer, 1955.

————. *Pieces at Eight.* London: Max Reinhardt, 1958. Lavish in his praise for Williams at his best, patient with his mistakes, constructive in his criticism; always hopeful that Williams will return to what he can do so well.

KRUTCH, JOSEPH WOOD. "Why O'Neill's Star is Rising." *New York Times Magazine,* March 19, 1961, p. 36. Williams' characters involved not in "tragic predicament" but in "unsavory mess."

KUNKEL, FRANCIS L. "Tennessee Williams and the Death of God." *Commonweal,* LXXXVII (February 23, 1968), 614-17. Williams equating the Creator with "the lowest created beings" fits Him into his "literature of decadence."

MAGID, MARION. "The Innocence of Tennessee Williams." *Commentary,* XXXV (January 1963), 34-43. Questions Williams' message behind the theatrical excitement; his adolescent preoccupation with bodily functions; immaturity of his view of the world: child's refusal to face facts.

MANNES, MARYA. "Plea for Fair Ladies." *New York Times Magazine,* May 29, 1960, p. 16. On depravity and violence in current theater. Williams' answer — "Tennessee Williams Presents his POV." *New York Times Magazine,* June 12, 1960, p. 19.

MAXWELL, GILBERT. *Tennessee Williams and his Friends.* Cleveland: World, 1965. Antidote to decades of gossip; a sympathetic account of the complex Williams personality, the tension under which he works, the stress or production, social life, capacity for friendship; wealth of names and stories.

MUELLER, W. R. "Tennessee Williams: a new direction?" *Christian Century,* LXXXI (October 14, 1964), 1271–72. Integrity of two early successes has changed to "author-generated" action in the later plays.

NELSON, BENJAMIN. *Tennessee Williams: The Man and his Work.* New York: Obolensky, 1961. Study of the strengths and weaknesses of the work as "protagonist" of the romantic quest; biographical additions; summary of *Stairs to the Roof.*

POPKIN, HENRY. "The Plays of Tennessee Williams." *The Tulane Drama Review,* IV (Spring 1960), 45–64. On the archetypal patterns, Williams' bohemian doctrine, his sensationalism; on truth and self-deception; on symbolism and taboos in the plays.

PRESLEY, D.E. "Tennessee Williams; 25 years of criticism." *Bulletin of Bibliography,* XXX (January 1973), 21–29.

SIEVERS, W. DAVID. *Freud on Broadway.* New York: Hermitage, 1955. Ch. 13: "Tennessee Williams and Arthur Miller." Williams' scorn for dishonesty that distorts sex; public rejection of his pessimism and cynicism.

STEEN, MIKE. *A Look at Tennessee Williams.* New York: Hawthorn, 1969. Anthology of interviews with friends in theater and the film industry who have "happier memories of Tennessee"; illuminating details about his working habits, relationship with friends, reaction to critics, commercialism of Hollywood; particularly good dialogue between Anäis Nin and Mike Steen.

TAYLOR, HARRY. "The Dilemma of Tennessee Williams." *Masses and Mainstream,* I (April 1948), 51–55. Williams remains the "traumatized youngster."

TISCHLER, NANCY. *Tennessee Williams: Rebellious Puritan.* New York: Citadel, 1961. Careful, detailed biographical account without indication of sources; summary of plays, analysis, and critical evaluation; attention to symbolic meanings.

TYNAN, KENNETH. "Valentine to Tennessee Williams." *Mademoiselle,* XLII (February 1956), 130ff. Close relation between own life and that of characters; his "mental deafness' that makes him laugh at the wrong times; summary of early years; marvel that he can communicate across footlights.

VOWLES, RICHARD B. "Tennessee Williams and Strindberg." *Modern Drama* I (December 1958), 166–71. Affinity with rather than influence of older writer.

WEALES, GERALD. *American Drama Since World War II*. New York: Harcourt, Brace and World, 1962. Ch. 2: "Tennessee Williams' Fugitive Kind." A candid analysis of the printed page without benefit of theatrical production and audience participation; serious questions about the world he created, about characters he admires, values he offers.

WILLIAMS, EDWINA DAKIN (as told to Lucy Freeman). *Remember Me to Tom*. New York: Putnam, 1963. A mother's devoted care for every scrap of writing, news item, reference about her son; candid charges against her husband and inadvertent revelations about herself.

————. "Angel of the Odd." *Time,* LXXIX (March 9, 1962), 53–56. In spite of violence and disease in his plays, Williams, one of the wealthiest playwrights, fills the theaters, American and foreign; his is a dark view of life, but "desperately honest"; compassion for losers; relation between life and work, his only religion; danger of "unhealthy narcissism."

————. *Tennessee Williams: A Tribute.* ed. Jac Tharpe (Jackson, Miss.: University of Mississippi, 1977). An extensive collection of academic essays solicited from over fifty contributors, most of whom hold the playwright in high regard. The involved discussions, most of which view Williams as a thinking playwright and not one who merely feels, afford interesting comparisons to the drama critics who write of Williams as a man of the theater rather than of the library.

Index

192